This book traces the evolution of Vladimir Nabokov's prose fiction from the mid-1920s to the late 1930s. While individual works by Nabokov have attracted extensive commentary, the precise contours of Nabokov's development as a writer of fiction have hitherto received little attention. Julian Connolly traces this development by focusing on a crucial subject: the relationship between self and other in its various forms (including character to character, character to author, author to reader).

Beginning with early sketches which highlight the protagonist's yearning for an absent other, Professor Connolly reveals how concern for an absent other shades into anxiety about the potential of the other to define and delimit the protagonist's own autonomy. This analysis uncovers a powerful structure of bifurcation in Nabokov's work, between the character dimensions of a protagonist's identity and its latent authorial dimensions. As Nabokov's works grow more sophisticated, the author manipulates the relationship between these two dimensions, creating a series of memorable characters who seek to attain the status of authentic author by shedding that aspect of the self which functions as a character. Julian Connolly's investigation into the relationship between self and other in the early fiction provides an original model for approaching all of Nabokov's fictional writing.

CAMBRIDGE STUDIES IN RUSSIAN LITERATURE

Nabokov's early fiction

NABOKOV'S EARLY FICTION

Patterns of self and other

JULIAN W. CONNOLLY

Department of Slavic Languages and Literatures
University of Virginia

CAMBRIDGE
UNIVERSITY PRESS

Published by the Press Syndicate of the University of Cambridge
The Pitt Building, Trumpington Street, Cambridge CB2 1RP
40 West 20th Street, New York, NY 10011-4211, USA
10 Stamford Road, Oakleigh, Victoria 3166, Australia

© Cambridge University Press 1992

First published 1992

Printed in Great Britain at the University Press, Cambridge

A cataloguing in publication record for this book is available from the British Library

Library of Congress cataloguing in publication data

Connolly, Julian W.
Nabokov's early fiction: patterns of self and other/Julian W.
Connolly.
p.   cm. – (Cambridge studies in Russian literature)
Includes bibliographical references.
ISBN 0 521 41135 1 (hardback)
1. Nabokov, Vladimir Vladimirovich, 1899–1977–Criticism and
interpretation.   2. Self in literature.   I. Title.   II. Series.
PG3476.N3Z615   1992
891.73'42 – dc20   91–32773   CIP

ISBN 0 521 41135 1 hardback

UP

To my family

Contents

Contents

Acknowledgments

This study is the result of several years of close reading of Nabokov's work and of numerous conversations with colleagues, students, and friends. I would like to thank the University of Virginia for the support it provided for this project through the Summer Fellowship program and through travel grants to attend scholarly meetings. I would also like to thank Lorraine Aten Ranchod and Patricia Hayward, the research assistants who helped me gather material in various stages of the project. My colleague, Grace Fielder, offered sound counsel and encouragement, as did numerous Nabokovians with whom I met and corresponded. I owe a special debt of gratitude to D. Barton Johnson and Gene Barabtarlo, who read a draft of the manuscript and generously shared their insights with me.

Acknowledgements

Abbreviations

The following abbreviations are used to denote the editions of Nabokov's works cited in this study.

BS   *Bend Sinister* New York: McGraw-Hill, 1974

CE   *Conclusive Evidence* New York: Harper and Brothers, 1951

D   *Despair* New York: G. P. Putnam's Sons, 1966

Df   *The Defense* trans. Michael Scammell in collaboration with the author, New York: G. P. Putnam's Sons, 1964

Dr   *Dar* Ann Arbor: Ardis, 1975

DS   *Details of a Sunset and Other Stories* New York: McGraw-Hill, 1976

E   *The Eye* trans. Dmitri Nabokov in collaboration with the author, New York: Phaedra, 1965

EO   *Eugene Onegin: A Novel in Verse* by Aleksandr Pushkin, trans. Vladimir Nabokov, 2 vols, Bollingen Series 72, Princeton: Princeton University Press, 1981

IB   *Invitation to a Beheading* trans. Dmitri Nabokov in collaboration with the author, New York: G. P. Putnam's Sons, 1959

G   *The Gift* trans. Michael Scammell with the collaboration of the author, New York: G. P. Putnam's Sons, 1963

Gl   *Glory* trans. Dmitri Nabokov in collaboration with the author, New York: McGraw-Hill, 1971

KDV   *Korol', Dama, Valet* 1928 Ann Arbor: Ardis, 1979

KQK   *King, Queen, Knave* trans. Dmitri Nabokov in collaboration with the author, New York: McGraw-Hill, 1968

KO	*Kamera obskura* 1933 Ann Arbor: Ardis, 1978
L	*The Annotated Lolita* New York: McGraw-Hill, 1970
LD	*Laughter in the Dark* New York: New Directions, 1960
Ler	"The Lermontov Mirage" *The Russian Review* 1 (1941): 31–39
LL	*Lectures on Literature* ed. Fredson Bowers, New York: Harcourt Brace Jovanovich, 1980
LRL	*Lectures on Russian Literature* ed. Fredson Bowers, New York: Harcourt Brace Jovanovich, 1981
M	*Mary* trans. Michael Glenny in collaboration with the author, New York: McGraw-Hill, 1970
Mk	*Mashen'ka* 1926 Ann Arbor: Ardis, 1974
ND	*Nabokov's Dozen* Garden City: Doubleday, 1958
NG	*Nikolai Gogol* New York: New Directions, 1961
O	*Otchaianie* 1936 Ann Arbor: Ardis, 1978
P	"Pushkin, or the Real and the Plausible" trans. Dmitri Nabokov, *The New York Review of Books* 31 March 1988: 38–42
PF	*Pale Fire* New York: G. P. Putnam's Sons, 1962
PK	*Priglashenie na kazn'* 1938 Ann Arbor: Ardis, 1979
Pn	*Pnin* Garden City: Doubleday, 1957
Pod	*Podvig* 1932 Ann Arbor: Ardis, 1974
PP	*Poems and Problems* New York: McGraw Hill, 1970
RB	*A Russian Beauty and Other Stories* New York: McGraw-Hill, 1973
S	*Sogliadatai* 1938 Ann Arbor: Ardis 1978
SK	*The Real Life of Sebastian Knight* New York: New Directions, 1959
SM	*Speak, Memory. An Autobiography Revisited* New York: G. P. Putnam's Sons, 1966
SO	*Strong Opinions* New York: McGraw-Hill, 1973
TD	*Tyrants Destroyed and Other Stories* New York: McGraw-Hill, 1975
VCh	*Vozvrashchenie Chorba* 1929 Ann Arbor: Ardis, 1976
VF	*Vesna v Fial'te* 1956 Ann Arbor: Ardis, 1978
ZL	*Zashchita Luzhina* 1930 Ann Arbor: Ardis, 1979

Introduction

Recent years have witnessed a bracing expansion in the critical scope of Nabokov scholarship. Countering the trend which dominated the field in the late 1960s and early 1970s – a quest to decode the author's elaborate verbal puzzles and literary allusions – scholarship in the last decade has delved increasingly into the ethical dimensions of Nabokov's work (see, for example, the studies *Nabokov and the Novel* by Pifer and *The Novels of Vladimir Nabokov* by Clancy). Contemporary commentators have taken to heart David Richter's observation that while "we must certainly heed Nabokov's plea not to read his narratives as social sermons, we need not turn him into a mere manufacturer of crossword puzzles and chess problems" ("Narrative Entrapment" 419–20). Critics such as D. Barton Johnson, Pekka Tammi, Brian Boyd, Leona Toker, and Vladimir Alexandrov have produced excellent studies that display a sensitive appreciation for the peerless fusion of technical virtuosity and philosophical inquiry that makes up Nabokov's best work.

The present study aims to delineate Nabokov's growth as a literary artist during the first phase of his career in fiction (1924–39) by focusing on his changing approach to one of the most significant concerns of his art: the relationship between self and other. Nabokov's fiction is renowned for its intricate allusiveness, linguistic play, and elaborate authorial patterning. It is the assumption of this study that the complexity of Nabokov's work reflects its creator's unique response to the richness of human experience, from the rapturous potential of the human imagination to the stark realities of alienation, loss, and suffering. At the core of this experience lies the crucial relationship between self and other.

This relationship assumes many forms in fiction: the relationship of one character to another; the relationship of one character to some part of his identity that he may view as other; the relationship between a character and the author who stands outside the text and manipulates its designs; the relationship between the narrator and the reader; the relationship between the author and other writers. Such a diverse set of relationships offers abundant opportunities for manipulation and variation, and Nabokov took full advantage of these opportunities. Over the course of his career he explored several dimensions of the self–other relationship, gradually extending the depth and sophistication of his fictional representations. His literary *œuvre* resembles an intricate kaleidoscope: every turn in his career creates new perspectives, dazzling and unexpected.

This study will examine the major stages in the evolution of Nabokov's Russian fiction, focusing on its critical moments of discovery and transformation. The study begins with several of the short stories Nabokov wrote during his first sustained period of prose fiction creation, and it goes on to discuss most of the novels he originally wrote in Russian.[1] Except for passing commentary, the study will not deal with Nabokov's poetry or dramatic works and it will not give close treatment to every piece of fiction which features the self–other relationship. Only those individual works which provide special insight into the changing topography of Nabokov's aesthetics will come under analysis. While *Glory*, for example, introduces a character whose sense of self is shaped in part by his consciousness of an intangible other – the land of Russia itself – its treatment of this subject does not represent a moment of decisive change in the evolution of Nabokov's work. For this reason *Glory* will not be analyzed in this study.

The order of presentation of works to be discussed will be broadly chronological, with some exceptions. Certain short stories and novels will be grouped together because Nabokov's treatment of thematic material in the shorter works often anticipates his handling of similar material in the longer works.

A few of the short stories even seem to serve as preliminary sketches for the more complex constructs of his full-length novels. The study as a whole develops an analytical approach that should provide a conceptual framework for a further examination of Nabokov's English-language fiction.

Although any attempt to divide Nabokov's fiction into discrete segments must be undertaken with caution, one can delineate within his Russian *œuvre* four broad stages or phases in the continuous spectrum of his development. In the first phase he often focuses on protagonists who are absorbed with an absent other – a lost love, a dead child, a missing spouse. This absorption with the other has a pervasive quality, and it can create an emotional or psychological filter through which the entire world is perceived.[2] Several of Nabokov's early works point to the danger stemming from such an obsession: characters absorbed with another may lose touch with everyday reality and become lost in the world of inner fantasy. In fact, in the next phase of Nabokov's evolution, the writer focuses on just this experience of estrangement. Works such as *King, Queen, Knave* (chapter 2) and *The Defense* (chapter 3) depict individuals who have become so consumed with internalized images of others that they are trapped in a world of shimmering illusion.

Gradually, however, Nabokov's protagonists begin to alter the shape of their preoccupation with the other. They become less concerned with the possession or cognition of an external other, and more concerned with the way the other views *them*. The major works of this third phase – *The Eye* (chapter 4) and *Despair* (chapter 5) – depict characters who are eager to register the opinions others have of them but who fear those very opinions. Anxiety-stricken, these protagonists search for creative responses to their vulnerability to the other. One solution involves a full-scale transformation in their approach to the other. Worried about the image they present to the outside world, they try to forestall any negative evaluation by others by defining themselves first. Treating their own self as an other, they attempt to manipulate the image they show to the world.

Ironically, however, the protagonists' attempt at *self*-percep-
tion often involves *mis*perception. Much of the cutting irony in
Nabokov's fiction arises from the contradiction between what
his characters claim about themselves and what the reader
perceives as true.

The characters' shift in perspective unleashes a fundamental
bifurcation in identity in Nabokov's work. His fiction suggests
that each protagonist possesses two distinct components of
identity that are arrayed in a pattern of complementary
contrast. One component of the self functions as the center of
creative consciousness. Apprehending the external world, it
organizes and shapes those perceptions, sometimes creating
new, highly personal constructs. This component may be
termed the "authorial" self: it represents the seat of authorial
potential. The second component of the self is that which
operates in the outside world and may be seen, evaluated, and
defined by an external other. This component may be termed
the "character" aspect of identity, since its susceptibility to
manipulation and definition by others leaves it in much the
same position as a literary character created and manipulated
by an author.[3] Above all, of course, reigns Nabokov, the
human creator of the fictional world and of both aspects of his
protagonists' identities. It is the existence of this extra dimension – that of the human authorial consciousness – that adds
metaphysical depth to Nabokov's work.[4]

The presence of these two basic potentials within Nabokov's
protagonists assumes interesting ramifications when the more
creative individuals begin to evaluate their relationship to the
outside world. Nabokov's most significant fictions in the mid-
1930s concentrate on characters who seek to attain the power
and autonomy of literary creators by freeing their authorial
potential and purging themselves of their character dimensions. Once oriented in this direction, Nabokov's fiction evinces
ever greater degrees of metafictional self-awareness. In the
fourth phase of his literary evolution, represented by such
works as *Invitation to a Beheading* (chapter 6), "Recruiting," and
The Gift (chapter 7), he examines the relationship of the
creative consciousness to the subjects of creative apprehension

and he explores the way creative individuals transform both themselves and others into fictional constructs. In Nabokov's subsequent English-language fiction, from *The Real Life of Sebastian Knight* to *Lolita*, *Pale Fire*, and *Look at the Harlequins!*, the protagonists' struggle to mediate the dichotomy between their authorial and character dimensions serves as a base on which Nabokov's complex imaginative worlds are built.

Although at every stage of Nabokov's career one finds structures of bifurcation, duality, and metamorphosis, the vital evolution in Nabokov's conception of the self–other relationship effects a transformation in narrative technique as well. While Nabokov's works never place primary emphasis on a naturalistic, mimetic representation of material reality, one can observe an evolution from the early sketches, which provide detailed depictions of the external physical world, to the later works, which augment the descriptive dimension with narratives that highlight in their very structure the subjective and self-reflexive elements involved in personal perception. As Nabokov's characters concentrate increasingly on the creations of their own internal visions, the narratives which portray them become more involute and self-reflexive as well.

At the same time, though, Nabokov utilizes the central characters' self-absorption as a mask through which he, the authentic author, can establish his own covert communication with his readers. The idiosyncratic discourses generated by the narrators of *The Eye* and *Despair* stand out as remarkable examples of what may be called a "dual-voiced" discourse in Nabokov's fiction. Nabokov utilizes the intrinsic narrator's own words to convey a message to the reader that is quite different from the one intended by the narrator himself.

In the final phase of Nabokov's Russian fiction, the author creates narrative texts that display a distinctive duality in point of view. Segments of narrative conducted from an intrinsic, first-person perspective alternate with segments conducted from an extrinsic, third-person perspective. The resulting fugue of shifting perspectives foregrounds the issue of creative control and raises such questions as "Who is the narrating subject?" and "Who is the narrated object?" As this study shall demonstrate, Nabokov's unusual narrative strategy is neither inchoate nor confused, but clearly ordered: it is designed to illuminate the inherent problems of fiction-making and their attendant solutions.

An examination of the self–other relationship in Nabokov's fiction points to one of the most compelling concerns raised in his work – the fundamental tension between the impulse to withdraw into a self-contained world of creativity and the need to engage in productive relationships with others in the external world. Nabokov touches upon this tension in his classroom lecture entitled "The Art of Literature and Commonsense." While affirming that it would be a foolish author who shuns the rewards to be derived from close contact with other people, he ultimately recommends that the writer choose "the much abused ivory tower" for his fixed address (*LL* 371).[5]

A similar choice confronts Nabokov's characters. While they seek to gauge the efficacy of their personal visions through contact with another, they also evince a persistent anxiety – the fear that their unique individuality will be lost through expropriation or finalization by an impersonal other. Desperate to assert their worth in the face of others, many of Nabokov's characters either try to subordinate others to their own creative designs or withdraw entirely from meaningful interaction with another.

While Nabokov explored this central tension repeatedly in his work, he shied away from making declarative pronouncements about it. Separating himself from other writers who come across as "rank moralists and didacticists" (*SO* 33), Nabokov jealously guarded his work from readers looking for "great ideas" (*SO* 41; see also *LL* 376). Yet while his fiction avoids the kind of didacticism one finds in the work of the late Tolstoy, it also demonstrates an abiding concern for the relationships established between one person and another. Those readers (including many of Nabokov's contemporaries) who viewed Nabokov as a cool writer, unsympathetic to the human condition (see, for example, Struve, "Notes on Nabokov" 54), failed to understand the nuanced approach he took toward this subject. Nabokov eschewed the "social" or "general" in favor of the personal. His fiction instructs through individual example, not universal prescription. In each of his works, he depicts characters who have made a choice as to how they will live their lives in relation to others, and he depicts the specific pitfalls lurking at each turn of the chosen path.

Taken together, these individual examples combine to create a cohesive and consistent model of ethical interpersonal relationships. As Richard Rorty has pointed out, Nabokov's delineation of the attributes of art in the afterword to *Lolita* – "curiosity, tenderness, kindness, ecstasy" – lists "curiosity" first (*Contingency* 158). Only if one is genuinely curious about the external world, a world in which others serve not merely as reflectors for one's own projections but as autonomous beings with *their* own unique identity, can one gain access to the realm of authentic art. Those who merely develop the intellect, the resources of inner vision, will never attain this access.

Nabokov's enduring concern with the tension between the personal and the public also informs his attitude toward his audience, the world of his readers. Two pronouncements he made on the relationship of the artist to the audience are worth examining. On the one hand he declared: "I don't think that an artist should bother about his audience. His best audience is the person he sees in his shaving mirror every morning. I think that the audience an artist imagines, when he imagines that kind of thing, is a room filled with people wearing his own mask" (*SO* 18). Just two years later, however, he stated: "I am all for the ivory tower, and for writing to please one reader alone – one's own self. But one also needs some reverberation, if not response, and a moderate multiplication of one's self throughout a country or countries; and if there be nothing but a void around one's desk, one would expect it to be at least a sonorous void, and not circumscribed by the walls of a padded cell" (*SO* 37). As we shall see, the images with which Nabokov characterizes the writer's relationship to his readers – the use of masks, mirrors, and multiplication of the self – all figure prominently in his fiction; such recurrence testifies to the centrality of the issue of self and other in his thoughts. Taken together, the two statements suggest that Nabokov may have experienced some ambivalence regarding the potential of others to judge and respond to his work. Nonetheless, a comment Nabokov made in his Cornell lectures indicates his ultimate hopes. Describing the trek made by the master artist to the summit of his creation, Nabokov declares that the writer meets there the "happy reader." The two embrace, and they are connected forever as long as the book has timeless merit (*LL* 2; see also *SO* 40–41).

The subtle tension evident in Nabokov's comments about the artist's relationship to the reader points to a dynamic source of energy in his work. His fiction continually returns to the conflict between the impulse to nurture one's creative potential in private and the need to remain responsive to the sensibilities of others. The writer's inquiry into this complex field has resulted in a body of work that finds few equals in its depth and brilliance. This study hopes to shed new light on the formation and consolidation of Nabokov's unparalleled literary achievement.

A NOTE ON TERMINOLOGY

Nabokov's fiction offers a complex array of entities with narratorial or authorial attributes. For the sake of consistency and clarity, the following terms based on Tammi's and Genette's studies in narratology will be used to denote the major categories of such entities.

Narrator figures

Intrinsic narrators are those narrators who appear as characters within the narrated world (see Tammi *Problems of Nabokov's Poetics* 38–40). An *autobiographic intrinsic* narrator depicts himself as the main hero of the narrated story (for example Hermann in *Despair*), while a *biographic intrinsic* narrator depicts another character as the main hero of the narrated story (for example the narrator in *Pnin*).

Extrinsic narrators "exist only on the level on which the

history is produced" (Tammi 38). Such narrators may make reference to themselves or their backgrounds, but they do not appear as characters within the narrated world. An example of an extrinsic narrator who makes some reference to himself is found in *Mary*; one narrative in which the narrator makes no overt self-reference is *King, Queen, Knave*.

Authorial figures

Here the key distinction must be made between diegetic characters who try to demonstrate authorial power within the created world of the text, and the "authentic" *auctor* – that figure who gives rise to the created world of the text as well as to the discourse which depicts it. This figure is ostensibly responsible for generating the text, but he may not be the same as the real, human author Vladimir Nabokov.[6]

CHAPTER I

The quest for the other

The prose works Nabokov wrote early in his career are structurally and stylistically simpler than his later works, but in them he introduces elements of the self–other relationship that will remain significant throughout his *œuvre*. One of the most dynamic of these is the effect of an individual's obsession with an absent other. Many of Nabokov's early stories center on protagonists who become so preoccupied with the image of an absent other that they lose touch with the everyday world and find their ability to cope in this world threatened.

Nabokov's concern with absence and loss undoubtedly reflects his own recent experience – first his exile from Russia, and then the murder of his father in 1922. During the mid-1920s he wrote a series of works weighing the impact of personal loss on sensitive individuals. In "Christmas" ("Rozhdestvo" 1925), a man suffers such grief over the sudden death of his child that he contemplates committing suicide.[1] In "A Letter that Never Reached Russia" ("Pis'mo v Rossiiu" 1925), a man who has been separated for eight years from the woman he loves creates a text in which he tries to assert his sense of joy in life but which dwells on images of solitude, emptiness, and again, suicide. "Bachmann" ("Bakhman" 1924) presents the tale of a musician who first becomes infuriated when his sick lover fails to attend one of his performances and then becomes deranged when she dies shortly thereafter.

The discussion in the first part of this chapter begins with three stories of extrinsic narration in which romantic infatuation with another is followed by loss or separation – "The Return of Chorb" ("Vozvrashchenie Chorba" 1925), "Details of a Sunset" ("Katastrofa" 1924), and "The Potato Elf" ("Kartofel'nyi El'f" 1924). Attempting to compensate for their loss, the protagonists in these stories retreat into a world of inner fantasy and projection. The next two sketches feature autobiographic intrinsic narrators, and in these works – "Grace" ("Blagost'" 1924) and "A Guide to Berlin" ("Putevo-ditel' po Berlinu" 1925) – the specter of solipsistic isolation is countered by the narrator's sensitivity to the presence of an external other in his environment. In "Grace" this other is a stranger who nonetheless shares the protagonist's space in the narrated world. In "A Guide to Berlin," however, the writer's awareness of the other extends beyond the boundaries of the narrated world to the world of the anonymous reader as well. Taken together, these five works provide five distinct yet intersecting facets of the self–other relationship which become an integral component of Nabokov's later, more complex fictions.

"THE RETURN OF CHORB"

"The Return of Chorb" is one of the most impressive works of Nabokov's early career. Like the brief sketch "Christmas" it provides a poignant picture of the devastation which attends the untimely loss of a loved one. Published just ten months after "Christmas" (in November 1925), it reveals a remarkable increase in sophistication of narrative technique. Through this work Nabokov demonstrates how a character's absorption with an intangible image of an absent other triggers a profound state of alienation from the others who are physically present in the surrounding world, causing pain to all concerned. The emotional center of the piece is the protagonist Chorb's grief-stricken reaction to the accidental electrocution of his new bride. This event immediately severs Chorb's contact with the external world, and that world seems to "retreat" at once (*DS* 60; *VCh* 7).

The main portion of the narrative depicts a seminal Naboko-vian pursuit – the attempt to retrieve and retain that which has been lost through an elaborate process of mental restoration.

Here, Chorb tries to recover an image of his lost love by retracing their honeymoon travels and gathering all the things they had noticed together. He hopes that if he is able to recreate his past in this way, his wife's image will become "immortal" and replace her forever (*DS* 61; *VCh* 8). The story's climax occurs on the night Chorb seeks to attain the culmination of his quest. Returning to the cheap hotel room where the couple had spent their wedding night, Chorb seeks to pass the emotional "test" he had set for himself and thereby render perfect the image of his dead wife. The resulting experience, however, is not what the character anticipates.

Nabokov's narrative evokes both the extent of Chorb's profound love for his dead wife and the palpable cost such a single-minded obsession with her memory entails. Chorb is so fixated on recovering an image of his lost love that he remains insensitive to the effect his actions may have on the living others in his environment. He chooses not to tell his wife's parents about the death of their daughter immediately after the accident, because he does not wish to "taint" his own personal grief with any "foreign" substance. The narrative stresses the insular nature of Chorb's grief when it states that Chorb did not wish to "share" his grief with any other soul (*DS* 60; *VCh* 6).[2] Chorb's desire for privacy is understandable, as is his reluctance to contact his wife's parents. They are shown to be narrow-minded and banal, and the newlyweds had actually run off on their wedding night to avoid staying in the bedroom which had been so cloyingly prepared for them in the parents' house. Nonetheless, even these parents have feelings, and Chorb's desire not to contaminate his own grief by informing the parents of the loss of their child seems overly self-centered and inconsiderate.

Chorb later compounds the gravity of his initial oversight when he finally does arrive at their house to share the news. Surprised to find only their maid at home, he instructs her to tell the parents merely that his bride is ill and that he will call again in the morning. He does not wait for them to return. Once more, he tries to avoid confronting a difficult moment of interpersonal interaction by postponing it. A poor student of human nature, however, he does not anticipate that the distraught parents may seek him out that very evening.

Chorb's absorption in his personal world comes to light in his dealings not only with the Kellers, but also with a prostitute he picks up the same evening. Throughout his quest to restore the image of his dead wife he had felt his wife's presence: the rapid step of her boots and the ceaseless motion of her hands had accompanied him throughout the journey (*DS* 61; *VCh* 7). Night, however, filled this presence with terror for Chorb (*DS* 62; *VCh* 8). Unnerved by the prospect of spending the night alone in the hotel room, Chorb decides to seek the companionship of a prostitute, not for sexual purposes, but simply to keep him company. Even the reclusive Chorb feels an instinctual need for another at this stressful moment.[3]

The climactic episode of the night occurs when Chorb suddenly awakens and begins screaming horribly, for he had just seen his wife lying next to him. This is a significant episode, and it emblemizes Chorb's tendency to view the world exclusively in terms of his own personal concerns. Having awakened in the dark, he fails to recognize the prostitute for who she is; instead, he projects onto her an internalized image of his own making. The projection lasts only a moment, but during that instant Chorb's gaze burns "with a mad flame" (*DS* 69; *VCh* 15). Nabokov's imagery indicates the perilous brink to which Chorb's obsession has led him. Dire madness threatens those Nabokov characters who obscure the physical features of those around them with their own subjective projections.

Nabokov underscores the depth of Chorb's alienation from the surrounding world by engineering a distinctive shift in the center of focalization during the scene in the hotel room. From the moment Chorb returns to his room with the prostitute, the reader views nearly all the subsequent events from *her* perspective. The narrative thus depicts Chorb as she sees him – a strange, eccentric man totally uninvolved with the living individual he has brought into his room.

Nabokov maintains this detached, externalized perspective on Chorb during the narrative's final scene. As Chorb and the prostitute digest the recent shock of his awakening, footsteps are heard in the hallway outside the room, followed by a knock at the door. The prostitute gets up, answers the door, and sees an elderly couple accompanied by the porter; as the latter beckons to her, she slips past the couple, who then enter the room. The door closes, and the reader is left in the hallway with the prostitute and the porter. The narrative concludes with this externalized perspective: "'They don't speak,' whispered the lackey and put his fingers to his lips" (*DS* 70; *VCh* 16).

By focusing on such secondary characters as the prostitute and the porter here, Nabokov hammers together a neat frame for his account of Chorb's experience. He began the story with a depiction of secondary characters, showing the Kellers returning from the opera to learn from the maid that Chorb had returned to town with their daughter, and he concludes with the secondary characters of the prostitute and the lackey. Such a technique effectively highlights the painful, albeit self-imposed, circumscription of Chorb's life. Obsessed with his dream of recovering a living image of his dead wife, Chorb has shut himself off from the outside world. Yet as the frame of the narrative illustrates, the outside world surrounds him always, and at the end of the story, that outside world – in the person of the distraught Kellers – irrupts harshly into the cocoon he has tried to spin around himself.[4]

The intrusion of unwanted others into Chorb's hermetic world creates a denouement of painful irony. The question remains, however, as to how successful Chorb has been in his original quest – to restore the image of his dead wife. Here too, the evidence suggests a mixed outcome. On the one hand, after mistaking the prostitute for his wife and then coming to his senses, Chorb feels immense relief, for he believes that his ordeal is over. Yet the mere fact that he has survived the ordeal does not mean that he has truly resurrected the image of his wife. Indeed, as Chorb lies sleeping on the bed, the reader sees through the eyes of the prostitute a statue of Orpheus on a nearby street, and this image has direct implications for Chorb's mission. Like Chorb, Orpheus had embarked upon a quest to recover his dead wife, but his attempt to lead her back to the world of the living was doomed by his need to see her in the flesh, and not merely be content with her unseen presence on the return journey. In similar fashion Chorb, who had felt the presence of his wife accompanying him throughout his quest, may have erred in trying to find and fix a concrete physical image of his wife, rather than being content with her presence in less tangible forms.[5] As John Kopper has written in reference to Sineusov's attempt to revive the image of his dead wife in "Ultima Thule": "Restoration does not require absolute presence – in fact, the powerful dialectic of nostalgia that runs through Nabokov's canon usually implies the reverse" ("Art of Translation" 264).[6]

In this regard one should recall the ending of the story "Christmas." There the protagonist's solipsistic grieving was countered by the wondrous emergence of a moth from an apparently lifeless cocoon. The moth's emergence need not be taken as evidence of actual reincarnation so much as a sign that something of the son's spirit survives the destruction of the physical body. Significantly, a moth appears in "Chorb" too. As Chorb paces his hotel room upon his return to the city, a moth strikes the lamp and makes a pinging sound (*DS* 64; *VCh* 10). This slight noise grates on Chorb's nerves and he rushes out of the room. Could this moth be an emblem of his wife's spirit? Moths commonly carry such emblematic weight in Nabokov's work, and the proximity of the moth to the lamp makes the connection more plausible. Chorb's wife had died by electrocution, a mode of death that Chorb considers uniquely "pure" since the same electricity, when poured into a glass receptacle, produces the purest *light* (*DS* 60; *VCh* 6). Later in Nabokov's career the connection between electricity and the spirit of the dead surfaces again. In John Shade's poem "The Nature of Electricity," the poet writes that the gentle dead may abide in "tungsten filaments" and that therefore Shelley's "incandescent" soul may attract "the pale moths" of starless nights (*PF* 192).[7] It is possible that the spirit of Chorb's wife was hovering about the character throughout his journey of restoration, and he may have been better served to take note of the small, barely perceptible signs of this presence rather than to try to revive her image through a physical substitute.

Nabokov's work suggests the existence of two realms surrounding human life: the material world of physical phenomena, and an invisible world of intangible presences. Each has its own way of making an impression on the consciousness, and any individual who ignores one or the other realm lives an impoverished life. Chorb's behavior indicates that he is not fully comfortable with either realm, but his attempt to block out all that is uncomfortable in his environment and to absorb only that which he can cling to within his solipsistic cocoon leads to further anguish. The conclusion of "The Return of Chorb" provides a poignant illustration of the emotional dislocation that develops out of a failure to give the external world its due.

"DETAILS OF A SUNSET"

"Details of a Sunset" (published July 1924) offers a different slant on the latent disparity between the world of a character's inner vision and the world of external reality. The protagonist here does not fixate on a figure whose absence he mourns, but rather on one who he mistakenly believes will become his wife. Nonetheless, the process through which the protagonist's mental absorption with another leads to a rupture with the everyday world has a similar shape. Moreover, the story provides an early glimpse into a dynamic that will assume major significance later in Nabokov's career – the potential bifurcation within a character into two distinct components, an internal center of creative consciousness and an external form that can be manipulated and influenced by the outside world. In this work Nabokov lays the foundation for the subsequent evolution of his fictional cosmos.

Structurally, the story divides into two parts. In the first, the reader becomes acquainted with Mark Standfuss, a "lucky fellow" swept up in dreams of wedded bliss with a girl named Klara. Yet while Mark believes that Klara loves him, the reader learns that her interest in Mark was only temporary, a reaction to her abandonment by a man she had loved earlier; when he returns, she is ready to reject Mark. The opening section of the story underscores the degree to which Mark's obsession with his personal image of Klara renders him oblivious to surrounding reality. This disparity emerges, for example, when Mark misinterprets Klara's tearful reaction to his description of their future wedded bliss: "Of course Mark had understood that these were tears of joy (as she herself explained) . . . And her face was pale and bewildered, also from happiness, of course. It was all so natural, after all . . . " (*DS* 20; *VCh* 150). The phrases "of course" and "after all" suggest that this segment represents Mark's own personal perception of the situation, rather than Klara's actual feelings.

Mark insists on providing a positive interpretation for everything that enters his field of vision, and he remains untouched by all warnings that come his way. Thus, when his mother reminds him that Klara had recently been infatuated with another man, he dismisses her with the remark that she doesn't understand anything (*DS* 19; *VCh* 150). Likewise, he remains oblivious to the subtle warnings emanating from the Berlin cityscape itself. While walking home intoxicated with drink and with his fantasies about his future with Klara, Mark sees several moving vans standing in a vacant lot "like enormous coffins." The narrative continues: "Heaven knows what was piled inside them. Oakwood trunks, probably, and chandeliers like iron spiders, and the heavy skeleton of a double bed" (*DS* 18; *VCh* 148). Although these descriptions could originate with the narrator, the personalized, colloquial expressions such as "Heaven knows what" and "probably" may indicate that this portion of text reflects Mark's conjectures. If so, he does not pause over the implication of such an image as the "skeleton of a double bed." Viewed in hindsight, however, the image clearly points to the latent tension between Mark's hope for marital bliss and the actual destiny to which his self-absorbed dreams will lead him – a fatal accident.[8]

The tension peaks in the second half of the story. As he travels to Klara's house by tram, Mark again indulges in solipsistic reveries about his imminent union with Klara. Characteristically, he projects his inner joy onto the world around him: "Oh, how happy I am . . . how *everything around me* celebrates *my* happiness" (*DS* 22, emphasis added; *VCh* 152). Carried away by this fantasy, he misses his stop, and he is forced to jump off the moving tram. At that very instant, he feels something slamming into him from behind. Although he does not realize it, he has been struck by a bus, and this moment marks the onset of an elemental split within the character's perception of experience.

Throughout most of the preceding narrative Mark's perspective on events had served as the primary point of orientation for the reader.[9] During the accident scene, the narrative again adopts Mark's perspective, and the credulous reader may accept Mark's own perception that he has emerged unscathed from a near-accident. The only marker that something out of the ordinary has occurred is Mark's momentary sense of doubling: "He looked around. He saw, at a distance, his own figure, the slender back of Mark Standfuss, who was walking diagonally across the street as if nothing had happened" (*DS* 23; *VCh* 153). Here he sees himself as "Mark Standfuss" – that is, he views himself from the outside, the way a bystander might view him. An instant later, though, he overcomes his sense of dissociation by "catching up" with himself, and Nabokov skillfully manipulates the reader's perspective on this experience by providing Mark's internal view of the event without indicating that this view is, in fact, only the character's *subjective* impression: "Marveling, he caught up with himself in one easy sweep, and now it was he nearing the sidewalk, his entire frame filled with a gradually diminishing vibration" (*DS* 23; *VCh* 153). In the absence of any statement to the contrary from the narrator, the reader is likely to accept Mark's perception that he is able to continue on his journey.

Yet while Mark believes that he has overcome his momentary bifurcation, the semblance of reintegration gradually unravels, and it soon becomes evident that Mark has actually undergone a profound internal schism. In his mind he continues his journey to Klara's house where his fiancée greets him joyfully, but in actuality, his body has been fatally mauled in the collision with the bus.[10] By the end of the story the wracking pain which intermittently irrupts into his fantasy of reunion with Klara becomes insurmountable; the physical experience overwhelms the psychological one.

Nabokov's treatment of this bifurcation experience deserves special attention, for it provides an early model of a structure of paramount significance in his work. While Mark's consciousness creates a fantasy in which he and others act out roles he creates for them, his body remains subject to physical forces beyond his control. This division displays the faint outlines of a seminal duality in Nabokov's work: the split between the authorial and character dimensions of the self. While the authorial aspect of the self generates its own personal narrative, the character aspect of the self continues to be affected by the world in which it has been placed.[11]

That Mark's trauma triggers latent auctorial tendencies within him is suggested in Nabokov's description of the youth's view of the surrounding cityscape after the accident:

Upper stories and roofs were bathed in glorious light. Up there, Mark could discern translucent porticoes, friezes and frescoes... winged statues that lifted skyward golden, unbearably blazing lyres. In bright undulations, ethereally, festively, these architectonic enchantments were receding into the heavenly distance, and Mark could not understand how he had never noticed before those galleries, those temples suspended on high. (*DS* 23; *VCh* 154)

This passage is significant for several reasons. In the first place, the passage suggests that Mark had never before had access to the world of vision now open to him ("he had never noticed those galleries"). In his ordinary life, Mark is a "day-person," one who is so wrapped up in his personal concerns that he fails to observe the resplendent beauty which surrounds him. Once he has been hit by the bus, however, Mark suddenly finds himself catapulted into the realm of heightened vision, the realm of the creative artist. Both the image of "winged" statues and the image of the "lyres" that these statues lift upward are extensively associated with inspiration in Western art and literature.[12]

At the same time, however, one recognizes that Mark's ascension into the realm of creative vision results from a sudden physical trauma. It is not something that he can either control or sustain. As such, it is a fleeting and transient experience, unlike the grandiose creative schemes pursued by subsequent Nabokov heroes. Ultimately, Mark's brief flight into authorial fantasy is cut short by the persistent intrusion of physical reality and its inescapable pain. At the end of the tale the narrator withdraws from Mark's consciousness altogether and once again portrays him from the outside, now as the subject of another's discourse, and this move underscores Mark's status as a literary character: "The doctor frowned and clucked his tongue. Mark no longer breathed ... " (*DS* 26; *VCh* 156).

"Details of a Sunset" again exposes the dangers stemming from an obsessive preoccupation with another. One who ignores external reality in favor of a world of internal fantasy runs the risk of being wounded by that very reality. Mark's ability to create an inner world impervious to external threat is undisciplined; it proves inadequate to render him invulnerable to the shocks of the physical world in which he lives. Later Nabokov heroes, however, will evince more highly developed powers of concentration and creativity, and they will mount more formidable challenges to the reality they seek to transfigure.

"THE POTATO ELF"

"The Potato Elf" (published June–July 1924), is the longest of Nabokov's early stories, and it provides the most nuanced character studies of this phase of his career. Although the two secondary characters, the conjurer Shock and his wife Nora, emerge as complex individuals in their own right, it is the title character, Fred Dobson, who merits special attention in this study of self–other relationships. Through this character, Nabokov works on the theme of projection found in "Details of a Sunset" and develops it to unique ends. Fred's entire sense of self, the narrative suggests, derives from his perception of his relationship to others. In contrast to many of Nabokov's works in this period, the theme of the other in this story not only involves an *absent* other, it also focuses on the potential benefit of interaction with those who are *present* in one's environment. This is a story of growth – psychological, not physical – and

Fred's sense of personal growth, which occurs during two distinct moments in his life, is facilitated almost exclusively by his encounters with another.

From the outset, Fred's sense of self is molded by the perceptions of those around him. A physical dwarf, he is perceived by others as something less than a "grown-up" adult in every sense of the word. Significantly, the narrative itself characterizes his interactions with others with repeated reference to child imagery. For example, when Fred first meets the Russian giant with whom he is later to work, he conquers the man's heart by "stretching up to him . . . and pleading like an infant to be taken up in Nurse's arms" (*RB* 222; *VCh* 166). After telling a story about his father (a tailor of children's clothing), he would spread out his little hands and the conjurer Shock would "bend down, pick up Fred like a baby, and, sighing, place him on the top of a wardrobe" (*RB* 221; *VCh* 165).[13]

Ironically, it is Fred's child-like stature that leads to his first experience of growth. When Shock brings Fred home, Nora initially sees him as a lost child. The next morning, when she sits alone with him, she tries to imagine that "it was not an adult dwarf sitting there, but her non-existing little son in the act of telling her how his schoolmates bullied him" (*RB* 230; *VCh* 174). Her tenderness then becomes transformed into something else as she calls forth "a curious, vindictive vision." She has been angry with Shock for his incessant trickery, and she decides to avenge herself on him by seducing Fred.

Unaware of Nora's true motives, Fred feels transformed by the experience of making love to her. The description of Fred's excursion around London after leaving Nora contains some of Nabokov's most radiantly joyful observations. A central element of this episode is Fred's sensation that the whole city had been created "only for him" (*RB* 232; *VCh* 175). One is reminded here of Mark Standfuss's solipsistic projections about his environment. In both cases, the character's perception of union with another results in the subjective view that the whole world resonates with his joy. In Fred's case, though, this experience has unique implications. For the first time in his life he displays no awareness of his child-like stature. Thus the narrator notes: "a rosy nurse in a starched bonnet offered him *for some reason* a ride in the pram" (*RB* 232–33, emphasis added; *VCh* 176). The phrase "for some reason" is a marker of Fred's own incomprehension of the nurse's gesture. Flushed with joy and pride, he forgets that others see him as child-like. Subsequently, he goes into a shop "where only *men's* handkerchiefs were sold" (*RB* 233, emphasis added; *VCh* 176).

This sensation of maturation lasts only as long as Fred believes that Nora loves him. After receiving a letter from her stating that his involvement with her has all been a misunderstanding and that she is leaving for the United States with her husband, Fred experiences his first attack of angina pectoris and retires to a small country village. Significantly, this retreat into the country is accompanied by a partial return to the child-like demeanor he had displayed earlier. Anxious to avoid public notice in the village of Drowse, Fred appears in public not in his true identity – that of an adult dwarf – but in the telling disguise of a "quiet fair-haired little boy" who sometimes ventures out in the evening. Fred's sense of growth has been suspended following the collapse of his dreams of love with Nora. Consequently, the child-disguise he assumes at night remains static: "the supposed grandson of the supposed paralytic *did not grow* as the years went by" (*RB* 242, emphasis added; *VCh* 185).[14]

All this changes, however, with the return of the other who had stimulated Fred's earlier experience of growth: after eight years, Nora unexpectedly arrives at Fred's home and informs him that she had a child by him. This revelation has the force of an epiphany for him, and triggers his ultimate transition from child to adult. The transition itself involves a two-step mental operation of fundamental significance in Nabokov's work. The first step occurs as Fred tries to form an image of an external entity: "He kept trying to imagine his son, and all he could do was to imagine his own self dressed as a schoolboy wearing a little blond wig" (*RB* 249; *VCh* 192). Even though the imaginary other carries Fred's own features, this very act of mental creation facilitates the completion of the process of psychological growth Fred had begun when he made love to Nora. Having envisioned a complementary other, Fred can divest himself of his undesirable self-image – that of a child-like dwarf – and transfer it onto his creation. The narrative elucidates the effects of this process: "And by the act of transferring his own aspect onto his boy, he ceased to feel that he was a dwarf" (*RB* 249; *VCh* 192).[15]

What has occurred here is a powerful example of projection and transference. Creating the image of a child in the outside world, Fred projects onto this creation his own features.[16] This act of projection is noteworthy. Through it, Fred becomes one of the first characters to manifest, even on an unconscious level, that seminal impulse in Nabokov's fiction – the impulse to actualize one's authorial potential by shedding the aspect of the self which functions as a character, defined and controlled by others. When Fred divests himself of that aspect of his identity which others have defined as child-like, he engages in a creative act that liberates within himself a new identity as an autonomous adult. Although Fred is not aware of this, the very act of imagining an externalized alter ego (his supposed child) is a vital element in the Nabokovian process of self-(re-)creation as an author.

Both this and Fred's earlier experience of growth derive from his perception of his relationship to others. His sexual encounter with Nora initially enabled him to feel that he was a grown man, emotionally if not physically. Now, his belief that he has fathered a son promotes his perception of himself as a full-fledged adult. As is often the case in Nabokov's work, however, both moments of perceived growth rest on illusions. Fred's earlier sense of growth stemmed from his belief that Nora loved him; his current sense of growth stems from his belief that he has a son. At the end of the narrative, after Fred has collapsed while trying to catch Nora to set up a visit with her son, Nora abruptly informs the curious onlookers that her son has died a few days earlier.[17] Fred's fate here recalls that of Mark Standfuss. For both men, death comes as a bittersweet experience. Although it terminates their lives, death spares each man from learning that the vision which has charged his life with such joy is only a fantasy.

The concluding section of "The Potato Elf" depicts the transformation of Fred the child-man into Fred the adult, a transformation born of his interaction with another. Yet the ending also reveals a process of transformation within a second character – Nora – and her metamorphosis also seems to have been shaped by her encounter with Fred. Although she comes to see Fred to tell him about their child and to find in him a living model of the dead boy's features, she leaves without telling him of the child's demise. She is touched by the joy she sees in Fred's features when he learns that he has fathered a son, and she reacts with selfless compassion quite different from the spirit of vindictiveness involved in her earlier seduction of Fred.[18] "The Potato Elf" is a tale of metamorphosis and growth, and it attests to the importance of interaction with others in promoting these core transformations.[19]

"GRACE"

In this brief sketch, published in April 1924, Nabokov extends the premise he suggests at the end of "The Potato Elf" that empathetic contact with another can facilitate a process of growth and creativity. Unlike the last work, however, the character's epiphanic experience is neither accompanied nor terminated by death. On the contrary, the story concludes on a note of affirmation with few equals in Nabokov's early prose.

The sketch begins, however, in quite a different key. The work features an autobiographic intrinsic narrator whose thoughts are permeated with the image of an absent other – in this case a lover who has recently jilted him. Yet although the narrator addresses the other as "you" several times, the actual narrative status of the discourse is unclear. There is no indication that the narrative is delivered to her in either written or oral form. The intimate tone of the work suggests that it is a kind of personal monologue similar to an extended diary entry that may not be intended for actual delivery to the ostensible addressee.[20] Nonetheless, the narrator's awareness of a specific other provides a poignant emotional focus for his mental commentary.

The woman in question is a former lover with whom the narrator has recently quarrelled. The narrative records the narrator's unsuccessful attempt to meet the woman by the Brandenburg Gate; she simply fails to appear. The emotional issues of separation and loneliness engendered by this situation are similar to those informing Nabokov's other works at this time, but the narrator undergoes a major psychological change which distinguishes this sketch in a crucial way. The catalyst for change here is the introduction of a new "other" with whom the narrator experiences a significant element of emotional empathy.

The narrator's initial descriptions teem with foreboding imagery. He recalls finding a "burial mound of ash" and a "coarse, masculine" cigarette butt in a matchbox on the table by his lover's bed. As he remembers the strains in the relationship, one salient trait emerges – a palpable breakdown in their ability to communicate with each other. The images he uses in describing her voice on the telephone are telling. Her voice was "distant and anxious." It kept "slipping and disappearing" (*VCh* 158). He acknowledges the emotional distance between them when he comments: "Paradise seemed to me to be precisely thus: silence and tears, and the warm silk of your knees. *You could not understand this*" (*VCh* 158, emphasis added).

This aura of mutual unintelligibility forms the background against which ensuing events unfold. As the narrator takes up his position on a cold day at the Brandenburg Gate, he notes a woman selling maps and postcards at a nearby stand. Instinctively he identifies with her as a kindred being forced to wait for another, and he wonders which of them will finish waiting first. Locked out of active emotional involvement with the other who has abandoned him, he forges here a link of emotional empathy with an unknown other. The narrator's emotional receptivity opens the door for him to escape the confines of his self-pitying, self-absorbed isolation.

As his vigil continues, his receptivity to the presence of the other pays a rich dividend. He observes an interchange between the saleswoman and a soldier stationed in a nearby guardhouse. The soldier summons the woman to his booth and gives her a cup of hot coffee. Watching her drink the coffee, the narrator becomes engrossed in her rapt enjoyment of the drink. As she forgets about the cold wind and her postcards because of her attention to the beverage, so too does the narrator forget his fruitless vigil because of his focus on the drinking woman. The empathic bond established earlier now becomes complete. Her *physical* nourishment becomes his *spiritual* sustenance as well: "Into my soul poured a dark, sweet warmth. My soul was also drinking, was also warming itself – and the brown old woman gave off the flavor of coffee with milk" (*VCh* 162).

The woman's acceptance of the gift of the coffee from the soldier – her receptivity to the generosity of another – finds a parallel in the narrator's receptivity to *her* experience. Significantly, this generosity is not unidirectional. As the woman starts towards the guardhouse to return the cup, she turns back to the booth to select two postcards, which she hands to the soldier along with the cup. This spontaneous display of simple gratitude has a profound effect on the narrator, and triggers for him a moment of epiphanic revelation in which he perceives clearly the "tenderness" of the world, the deep "grace" in everything around him, and the "sweet bond" that exists between himself and everything else. He now realizes that that joy which he had sought in his lover lies not only within her, but breathes all around him. In what is surely one of the most exuberant passages in Nabokov's work, the narrator expresses his understanding that life is not rapacious struggle, but "a shimmering joy" and a "gift" that people do not appreciate (*VCh* 162–63).

The significance of this moment of insight must not be underestimated. Not only does it help mitigate his feelings of personal sorrow and isolation, but his heightened receptivity to the flow of life around him stimulates in turn an impulse toward artistic creation. As he watches the ever-changing expressions and gestures of those around him during his homeward journey, he feels the soft "tickling" of a creative thought (*VCh* 164). What is noteworthy here is the suggestion that creativity for a Nabokovian artist is fostered by receptivity to the outside world and an ability to establish empathic connections with others. As it turns out, however, this principle is more often honored in the breach than in the observance in Nabokov's early fiction. Numerous characters who possess creative potential but who are unable to feel emotional links to others experience failure on both the personal and the artistic level. An inability to bridge the gap separating creative individuals from those around them looms as a fatal flaw in the aspiration to attain emotional and artistic maturity.

"A GUIDE TO BERLIN"

Nabokov's most comprehensive statement about the value of remaining receptive to the everyday flow of life and of establishing channels of communication with external others arises in the unusual sketch entitled "A Guide to Berlin." Published in December 1925, this sketch is the only one of the period to have an overtly programmatic orientation. While most of the early works revolve around a protagonist's preoccupation with the absence of a beloved other, this work has a different focus: the relationship of the writer to the outside world and to his potential audience. Nabokov's treatment of the self–other relationship here establishes principles which remain in force throughout his literary career.

The sketch consists of an untitled introductory paragraph and five separate vignettes bearing the titles "The Pipes," "The Streetcar," "Work," "Eden," and "The Pub." Much of the text presents the narrator's detailed observations of ordinary Berlin street scenes. In the second vignette, however, the narrator articulates the reason why he believes that such a record of observed detail is valuable. Stating that trolley cars will disappear some day, he declares that future writers will have to resort to museums to view the authentic remnants of the past. In those future days, every "trifle" (*meloch'*) from the past will be precious and meaningful (*DS* 94; *VCh* 97). It is up to the writer, then, to take the interests of future generations into account. The narrator now introduces a key image – that of the mirror – to explain his view of the "sense" of literary creation. As he puts it, literary creation is meant to portray "ordinary objects *as they will be reflected in the kindly mirrors* of future times . . . when every trifle of our plain everyday life will become exquisite and festive in its own right" (*DS* 94, emphasis added; *VCh* 97). The implications of this mirror image will be discussed below. For the moment, however, one should recognize that the narrator's awareness of the inevitability of loss in life and of the role that verbal art may play in preserving life's transient experiences points to a basic concern of Nabokov's own art. His fiction is permeated both with a haunting recognition of the fragility of all that is precious in life and with a fervent desire to find a way to preserve treasured moments of experience.[21] The narrator also reveals here his sensitivity to the needs of an unknown "other" – in this case, future generations of curious readers. He underscores this conviction in the last vignette.

Describing a pub in which he sits with a companion, the narrator observes that the pub consists of two rooms. He and his companion sit in one room, while in the other – part of the proprietor's apartment – he sees a couch, a mirror, and a table at which a child sits eating soup. This segment may seem at first glance to be a passage of neutral description, but two elements herald its special import. First, the reference to the mirror echoes the theme of the perception by future generations introduced earlier in the sketch. Moreover, as the narrator continues the description, he includes not only *his* view of the scene, but also that of the *child*: "he is now looking our way. From there he can see the inside of the tavern – the green island of the billiard table, the ivory ball he is forbidden to touch . . . a pair of fat truckers at one table and *the two of us* at another" (*DS* 98, emphasis added; *VCh* 101. The last detail is important, and will be discussed below).

This incorporation of the child's perspective draws attention to an important feature of the narrator's approach to the outside world. As in the earlier passage about the writer's responsibility to the future, he expresses an awareness of the perspective of an external other. He even speculates on the child's psychological attitude toward the scene he beholds, stating that the child has long grown accustomed to this scene and therefore is not "dismayed" by its proximity (*DS* 98; *VCh* 101). The narrator's ability to imagine the inner world of another is a vital attribute of the artist in Nabokov's world, so long as this capacity does not cascade into massive personal projection, thereby obliterating the other's autonomy.

The narrator's comprehension of the other's viewpoint has a positive effect on him. Mentally responding to his companion's lack of appreciation for the import of this moment, he expresses his delight at having glimpsed "somebody's future recollection" (*DS* 98; *VCh* 102).[22] Although the narrator's satisfaction in achieving a sense of empathic connection might be rewarding for any artist, this experience may have an additional benefit for him. Focusing on the fact that the child "will always remember" the view he had of the pub scene, and perceiving that an image of the narrator himself is included in the child's view, the narrator may have discovered here a possible means of transcending the personal limits of his own time and space.[23] By envisioning himself as part of the scene that the boy will remember in the future, the narrator perceives that he will remain alive in the boy's memory, and therefore will not be consigned to oblivion as long as the child himself survives. A small emendation that Nabokov made when revising his story for translation supports this premise. In the original version, the items listed by the narrator in his description of the child's perspective included the billiard table, a billiard player, and the child's father. The English version, however, adduces a new item: "my empty right sleeve and scarred face" (*DS* 98). An image of the narrator himself is now explicitly included among those things which the boy will recall in future years and which therefore will survive the passage of time.[24]

At several points in the text, then, Nabokov's narrator indicates the importance of forging a connection to an external other, whether it be making an impression on the memory of a child or conveying the essence of things "as they will be reflected in the kindly mirrors of future times." What makes "A

Guide to Berlin" particularly distinctive, however, is that Nabokov not only articulates the premise within the narrator's discourse, he also illustrates it by manipulating the very building blocks of that discourse – the letters of the text itself. As D. Barton Johnson has pointed out, Nabokov carefully embedded in his text "mirror image" palindromes and anagrams of key words such as "OTTO" ("A Guide to Nabokov's 'A Guide to Berlin'" 358–59); this mirroring technique "prefigures" the central theme of "future memories" (359). At the same time, however, it reaffirms the narrator's fundamental concern – the importance of being aware of the perceptions of anonymous others. That is, while the narrator's discourse speaks *overtly* about a potential audience of future generations, the text of his discourse – composed by the authentic *auctor* – speaks *covertly* to just such an other: the presumed reader of the sketch itself.

It is worth noting that Nabokov's narrator does not find a receptive audience for his observations within his narrated world. Although the narrator shares his collected observations with his drinking companion, the latter remains unresponsive. He calls the narrator's guide "very poor" and suggests that no one cares about the narrator's experiences (*DS* 97; *VCh* 100). Nor does the narrative mention any other addressee in the text. Yet while the other who is physically present within the narrator's world is not receptive to the narrator's vision, there exists a different type of other who is not physically present in that world but who may indeed be more receptive – the presumed reader of the text. Nabokov's works frequently focus on characters who find themselves surrounded by an unresponsive world and who look to an anonymous audience for understanding and acceptance.

The presence of encoded verbal material within the text of "A Guide to Berlin" thus discloses a seminal feature of Nabokov's art: the potential of his narratives to speak on two distinct levels simultaneously. In addition to the surface-level message which his fictional narrators intend their readers to absorb, one may perceive a second message from the implied author to the implied reader which may modify or contradict the first message. In "A Guide to Berlin," the message of the secondary channel of communication opened by the embedded verbal material reinforces that of the surface level: both levels indicate the importance of establishing communicative links to external others. In later Nabokov texts, however, the two messages can diverge radically.

"A Guide to Berlin" offers direct insight into the writer's concerns and convictions during his first years as a prose writer. Foremost among these is his belief in the importance of sensitivity to the potential perceptions of others. Not only does such sensitivity sharpen the observation and the description of life in art, it may provide a way to transcend the narrow spatial and temporal limitations of one's own life. The sensitivity to the perceptions of others which the narrator reveals in "A Guide to Berlin" is, however, not matched by most of the other protagonists in Nabokov's early fiction. While many of his protagonists express concern for the feelings of others, they often submerge that concern under their own needs and projections. In his first novel *Mary*, Nabokov provides his first detailed treatment of this problem.

All together, Nabokov's stories of the 1924–25 period lay down the foundations upon which the complex edifice of his subsequent fiction will be built. They highlight the dangers of obsession with an internal image of another, while signalling the benefits of establishing empathic bonds with others. They also disclose the first traces of the seminal bifurcation between the authorial and character dimensions of the self in Nabokov's fictional world, and they suggest the central role that projection and creation can play in the development of a character's identity. Although the early stories do not explore the implications of these processes in detail, they indicate the direction Nabokov's subsequent fiction will follow.

MARY

Moving from the restricted dimensions of his early sketches to the broader canvas of his first novel *Mary* (*Mashen'ka*, published

1926), Nabokov provides an extended treatment of the central premises found in these short works, while at the same time introducing new facets of the self–other relationship that will assume major importance later in his career. The most salient of these is the writer's exploration of this relationship on two distinct levels: the relationship of the protagonist to other characters, and the relationship of the protagonist to himself.[25]

These two levels do not receive equal attention; the first is the more prominent. *Mary* follows the early sketches in its detailed depiction of a character's obsession with an absent other. The protagonist, Lev Glebovich Ganin, a Russian émigré living in Berlin, becomes so caught up in his remembrance of his first love affair in Russia with a girl named Mary that he becomes estranged from those around him. This alienation from others is also reflected on the second level of the self-other relationship – the relationship of the character to himself. As Ganin's absorption with the internal realm of memory deepens, the narrative depicts the process in terms of a significant split: while one part of Ganin – his consciousness – inhabits a cerebral realm of memory, his physical body continues to inhabit a Berlin *pension*. This split recalls the bifurcation occurring within Mark Standfuss at the end of "Details of a Sunset," and it can be seen as a forerunner to a central pattern in Nabokov's work – the division between that aspect of the self which displays authorial potential and that aspect of the self which functions as a character. Nabokov's treatment of this duality within Ganin, however, provides only a preliminary structure for the future development of the concept.

Before examining Ganin's relationship to the outside world and to himself, a few comments on Ganin's world are in order. Nabokov places Ganin in a milieu in which dreaming, the surrender to personal reverie, is the norm and not the exception. The *pension* in which Ganin lives contains a diverse set of characters that reminds some readers of *Père Goriot*,[26] but Nabokov's portraits of these characters suggest that they owe more to the spirit of Chekhov than to Balzac. Each of the characters dreams wistfully of someone or someplace else. Lamenting the fact that life is passing (*M* 37; *Mk* 60), the 26-

year-old Klara pines away with feelings of love for Ganin, even though she knows he has been involved with her friend Lyudmila. The old poet Podtyagin, the most Chekhovian of the *pension* dwellers, longs to move to Paris, and his exclamation – "I only hope to God I can get to Paris. Life's more free and easy there" (*M* 54; *Mk* 84) – echoes the repeated cry of Irina and her sisters in Chekhov's *Three Sisters*: "Let us go to Moscow! I implore you, let us go! There is nothing in the world better than Moscow!" The banal Alfyorov looks with such eagerness to the arrival of his wife Mary from Russia that he almost hustles Ganin out of his room at the *pension*. Even the two male dancers who live together (and thus might have no reason for longing for another) share this trait: Ganin believes that one of the two is making advances toward him when he asks if he can sit in Ganin's room for a while, adding that he feels "so bored" that day (*M* 65; *Mk* 100).

Augmenting this mood of longing is a complementary dissatisfaction with quotidian "reality." Podtyagin finds it impossible to cope with the German bureaucracy (see *M* 14–15; *Mk* 26), and Klara is so troubled by Lyudmila's fondness for sharing intimate details of her relationship with Ganin that she begins to avoid Lyudmila "for fear that her friend would end by spoiling for her that enormous, always festive sensation that is daintily called 'reverie'" (*M* 12; *Mk* 23). The Russian original for "reverie" is *mechta*, a word that appears prominently in the text either in direct form or in related words such as *mechtatel'nost'* ("dreaminess"). Summing up the degree to which the *pension* dwellers live in their dreams, Iulii Aikhenval'd wrote that they are all "dreaming themselves up" ("Literaturnye zametki" 2). This is a novel about the lure of a life lived in the shadows – static and calm – and about the need to reject that lure.[27]

Lev Ganin enters the novel as a consummate dreamer, one who has difficulty leading a vibrant waking life. At the outset of the novel the narrator utilizes imagery that characterizes Ganin's entire existence as a kind of extended semi-slumber: "It was a dreadful, agonizing state rather like that dull sense of unease when we wake up but at first cannot open our eyelids, as though they were stuck together for good" (*M* 18; *Mk* 31).[28] He is currently involved in a love affair, but this intimate relationship with another leaves him dissatisfied. An important factor in his dissatisfaction may be his preference for dreaming and fantasy over the reality of the physical experience. As the narrator notes: "Only for a very short time had he been genuinely in love – in that state of mind in which Lyudmila had seemed wreathed in a seductive mist, a state of questing, exalted, almost unearthly emotion" (*M* 19; *Mk* 33). (The image of the "mist" introduced here is significant, and further discussion of the image will follow below.) Ganin's infatuation with Lyudmila lasts only until the moment when they make love for the first time and she becomes physically "real" to him. Once he "possesses" her on the floor of a dark taxi, the entire affair instantaneously becomes banal (*M* 19; *Mk* 33). From that moment on, Ganin is not only bored with Lyudmila, he is even "repelled" by her (*M* 11; *Mk* 20). Nonetheless, he lacks the will to end the affair with her until the image of Mary enters his life.[29]

At that juncture, however, Ganin's obsession with the absent other becomes so entrancing that he abruptly cuts off his relationship with Lyudmila. He curtly announces to her that he now loves another, and he offers no further explanation. Ganin's shortness with Lyudmila, which is further manifested when he rips up a letter from her without reading it, is just the first of a series of actions which he now takes that reflect a willingness to sacrifice the feelings of others to pursue his own goals. At one point Klara calls him "heartless" (*M* 77; *Mk* 116). Ganin's absorption with his memories of Mary and his mental scheme for engineering a reunion with her render him indifferent to the emotions of those around him.

What is particularly striking about Ganin's infatuation with Lyudmila, however, is the way it echoes certain aspects of his earlier relationship with Mary. If one were to evaluate the two relationships on the basis of the rhetoric used to describe the two women, one would undoubtedly conclude that Ganin's love for Mary was much deeper than his feelings for Lyudmila. Yet by examining the passages which portray Ganin's initial conception of Mary and his subsequent interaction with her, one discovers that Ganin's preference for fantasy played a role in *that* affair as well. A brief look at Ganin's relationship with Mary will flesh out his essential mode of relating to others.

Even before Ganin had met the real Mary, he had conceived of an idealized image of a love object during a period of recuperation from a bout with typhus: "In that room ... was conceived that happiness, the *image* of that girl he was to meet *in real life* a month later" (*M* 32, emphasis added; *Mk* 53). As he looks back on that experience, Ganin characterizes it with a significant metaphor: "It was after all simply a boyish premonition, a delicious *mist*" (*M* 33, emphasis added; *Mk* 53). Ganin's initial infatuation with Lyudmila was characterized with a similar image – "Lyudmila had seemed wreathed in a seductive mist" (*M* 19; *Mk* 33). The recurrence of this image should alert the reader to a potential link between Ganin's romance with Mary and his affair with Lyudmila.[30]

As Ganin painstakingly reconstructs the initial stages of his romance with Mary, he finds a significant gap in his memory: he cannot recall when he actually saw her for the first time. The explanation for this gap is noteworthy:

The fact was that he had been waiting for her with such longing ... that *he had fashioned her unique image* long before he actually saw her. Now, many years later, he felt that their imaginary meeting and the meeting which took place in reality had blended and merged imperceptibly into one another, since *as a living person she was only an uninterrupted continuation of the image which had foreshadowed her.* (*M* 44, emphasis added; *Mk* 69–70)

This last comment contains the seeds of a psychological phenomenon that assumes tremendous importance in later Nabokov works: the tendency to create an internal image of an idealized "other" which is then superimposed onto an actual living person, often at the expense of that person's autonomy.[31]

The above passage suggests that Ganin's infatuation with Mary may be as much a case of projection as it is of love for a specific individual. It could be significant that Ganin's most passionate memories of their relationship are set in darkness (*M* 67–68; *Mk* 103–4), and that the relationship itself begins to chafe when the couple moves from the country into the city and they have to deal with the reality of everyday life – constraints on privacy, difficulty in arranging meetings, and so on. Ganin finds the entire business so frustrating that Mary's departure from Petersburg is a "relief" to him (M 71; Mk 108).

Although Ganin felt during this Petersburg winter that everything would be well if Mary were to become his mistress (M 70; Mk 108), when he at last has the opportunity to make this a physical reality during a brief rendezvous the following summer, he finds only disillusionment. While their initial conversation during this meeting is "rapturous," he is curiously put off at the actual moment of lovemaking. Nabokov's description emphasizes the physical discomfort involved: "the public park was alive with odd rustling sounds . . . the chill and the hardness of the stone slab hurt his bare knees; and Mary lay there too submissive, too still" (M 73; Mk 111). This moment of awkward contact leads Ganin to conclude that the affair is over and that he is no longer "enamored" of Mary (M 73; Mk 112). The scene thus anticipates Ganin's future interaction with Lyudmila.

Yet if physical intimacy with Mary proves disillusioning to Ganin, physical separation from her rekindles his desire. This dynamic begins after his last meeting with Mary. Unexpectedly running into her on a train, he finds it "terribly sad" to look at her, but as soon as she leaves the train, an interesting shift transpires: "*the further away she went* the clearer it became to him that he could never forget her" (M 75, emphasis added; Mk 114). This episode suggests that Ganin's longing for Mary may grow in direct proportion to the physical distance that exists between them, a conjecture that subsequent events do not dispel. Engaging in a sporadic correspondence with her during the Russian Civil War, Ganin finds himself full of happiness and he wonders how he could have parted from Mary (M 90; Mk 135). Inspired by such emotions, Ganin experiences moments when he feels ready to give everything up and go look for Mary in the Ukraine (M 90; Mk 135–36). It is telling, however, that he never does act on this impulse.

With Mary's imminent arrival in Berlin, Ganin finally has

the opportunity to realize his dream of reunion with her. Characteristically, he chooses not to. Although he has engineered matters in such a way that he, and not Alfyorov, will be able to meet Mary at the train station, he decides at the last moment to forego this opportunity. To the very end, Ganin seems to display a marked preference for the tantalizing world of fantasy over the stark realm of physical reality. His decision not to meet Mary, on the other hand, could also signal a *change* in the character's approach to the outside world, and it thus merits closer inspection.

Before looking at the final scene, however, one should direct some attention to the bifurcation that develops between Ganin's mental absorption with Mary and his external interactions with his fellow lodgers. Nabokov's handling of Ganin's experience provides a suggestive hint of that basic dichotomy noted earlier – the split between a protagonist's authorial and character dimensions. Nabokov does not foreground the author–character implications of the split which occurs within Ganin. These implications can only be discerned shining like a faint watermark through the form the split assumes in *Mary*: the dichotomy between what the protagonist perceives as "real" life and what he perceives as "dream" life. Such an opposition figures prominently in Nabokov's early novels, and Nabokov underscores the contrast here through an image system that he will employ repeatedly in later works – the image of shadows.

Once Ganin glimpses a photograph of Mary and begins to recall his romance with her, he plunges into a state of mental reverie that gradually appears to him to be more real than the physical world in which his body continues to move.[32] Although Michael Glenny's translation somewhat obscures the prominence of the shadow imagery in Ganin's sense of bifurcated existence by translating the word *ten'* ("shadow," "shade") as "ghost," the essential effect remains clear: "Coming to lunch it had not occurred to him that these people, the ghosts of his dream-life in exile, would talk about his real life – about Mary" (*M* 52; *Mk* 81). Later one reads, "His shadow lodged in Frau Dorn's *pension*, while he himself was in Russia, reliving his memories as though they were reality" (*M* 55; *Mk* 85). In the next formulation of this dichotomy, the qualifying phrase "as though" is dropped, cementing the perception that Ganin's cerebral life seems more real than his physical life: "It was not simply reminiscence but a life that was much more real, much more intense than the life lived by his shadow in Berlin" (*M* 55–56; *Mk* 86).

Ganin's immersion in his memories of Mary recalls Mark Standfuss's visions of his happiness with Klara in "Details of a Sunset." In fact, Ganin, like Mark, becomes so preoccupied with his inner visions that a car nearly runs him over (*M* 33; *Mk* 54). Yet Mark was only a "demigod" (*DS* 17; *VCh* 147), and his fantasies of union with Klara were continually interrupted by waves of physical pain. Ganin possesses more highly developed powers of imagination – "He was a *god*, re-creating a world that had perished" (*M* 33, emphasis added; *Mk* 54) – and his rupture with the external world is almost total. What is more, Ganin's ability to recreate a vanished world is not unleashed by an external trauma such as Mark's bus accident. Rather, it arises organically from within the character's consciousness itself.

Indeed, it is this element of conscious mental creation that allows one to view Ganin's endeavor as an exercise in authorial activity, and the split between Ganin's "real" life and his "shadow" life as an embryonic model of the author–character bifurcation. When Ganin painstakingly recreates scenes from his past in his mind, he acts much like an author creating an imaginary world. In formulations Nabokov provided for interviewers years later, the author directly links the processes of memory and of creative imagination (see, for example, *SO* 86: "The act of retention is the act of art, artistic selection, artistic blending, artistic re-combination of actual events" cf. *SO* 78).

The authorial dimensions of Ganin's mental activity will be discussed in more detail below, but for the moment it is worth noting that while Ganin's consciousness is involved in creating its rich internal narrative, his physical body continues to move about in the external world, and remains open to manipulation and definition by others.[33] In other words, his physical self displays the broad properties of a literary character: it is subject to "reading" and interpretation by others. The clearest sign of Ganin's susceptibility to such a reading is the episode in which Klara finds him snooping about Alfyorov's desk. She immediately suspects him of thievery, and he does not disabuse her of her suspicion (*M* 35–37; *Mk* 57–59). In essence, Klara relates to Ganin here much as a reader does when evaluating a literary character – she observes his behavior and then arrives at an interpretation: "He is bad, he deceives women and he is capable of committing a crime" (*M* 84; *Mk* 126). Not only does Ganin acquiesce in such a reading, he himself seems to invite speculation about his identity since he travels under an assumed name and a forged passport. He even tells Podtyagin that he finds it "convenient" and "fun" to have such a passport (*M* 81; *Mk* 122). While he permits his external self to be subject to interpretation by others, he keeps his authentic identity a mystery.[34]

In part, Ganin is content to allow others to read him as they wish because after he discovers the photograph of Mary, he creates an alternate world in which his consciousness prefers to dwell. Ganin's pursuit anticipates a quest undertaken by numerous successors in Nabokov's fiction: frustrated with their everyday status in life, Nabokov's heroes often seek to attain the power and autonomy of a creative artist. Disregarding the way his behavior might be evaluated by the outside world, Ganin creates a vibrant fantasy in which he can manipulate material as he chooses, speeding up and slowing down the pace of events to suit his desire (see, for example, the pacing with which he recreates his initial image of Mary: *M* 33; *Mk* 54).

Although the scenes Ganin re-creates are meant to represent actual experience, the manner in which they are stitched together seems suspiciously polished and refined, more like a calculated work of art than the raw flow of personal memory. In addition, the narrative point of view with which the younger Ganin is depicted adds to the impression that the remembered affair is closer to a fictional artifact than to the remembrance of actual experience. Throughout the main narrative line of the novel Lev Ganin is denoted with a third-person pronoun, the

object of an extrinsic narrator's observations. Significantly, the
same mode of presentation is utilized in the inserted narratives
about Ganin's romance with Mary, even though these passages
are meant to be the personal recollection of Ganin himself, and
therefore the first-person pronoun might be equally suitable to
denote the figure of the younger Ganin as recalled by the older
man. The following passage is representative:

> For a moment Ganin [1] stopped recollecting and wondered how he
> [2] had been able to live for so many years without thinking about
> Mary – and then he [3] caught up with her again: she was running
> along a dark, rustling path ... Suddenly Mary pulled up, gripped
> him [4] by the shoulder, lifted her foot and started to rub her sand-
> dusted shoe against the stocking of her other leg ... (*M* 60; *Mk* 93)

Although it is clear that the experiences of both the adult
Ganin (denoted by the numbers 1 and 2) and the young Ganin
(3 and 4) are presented through the same filter of the intrinsic
narrator's perspective, the use of the identical third-person
pronoun to denote both the adult Ganin and the young Ganin
(who is being recalled by the adult Ganin) promotes the
illusion that when he recalls his younger self, Ganin functions
much like a detached author–narrator. One might even gain
the impression that the adult Ganin views his remembered self
as an "other" – as "he," not as "I." The appearance of such a
figuration is noteworthy, and it underscores a significant
affinity between Ganin's mental re-creation of a younger alter
ego and the work of Nabokov's later authorial aspirants. To
attain the status of autonomous author in Nabokov's world,
one must shed that aspect of the self which functions as
character, and this may be achieved through the conscious
creation of a fictional alter ego. Ganin's activity, however,
exhibits just the faintest outlines of such an endeavor. It is only
in Nabokov's later works that the process of self re-creation
takes on such conscious properties.[35]

Ganin's intoxication with the re-creation of a vanished world
reflects a consistent impulse that runs throughout Nabokov's
œuvre – a persistent dissatisfaction with what *is* and a constant
yearning for what *is not*. This tension continues until the last
scene of the novel, when Ganin experiences an unanticipated

epiphany. Walking toward the railroad station to intercept Mary, he suddenly recognizes his fantasies about Mary for what they truly are – "the distant past" (*M* 113; *Mk* 166). He realizes now "with merciless clarity" that his affair with Mary had come to an end forever (*M* 114; *Mk* 168). Nabokov locates this epiphany in a setting dominated by the image system which had been so prominent earlier in the novel – the image of light and shadow. The narrative suggests that the "sober light" of early morning restructures the accustomed appearance of the shadows on the street and thus helps Ganin to recognize the spectral nature of his inner visions. Aside from these visual effects, however, one might ask what else has contributed to Ganin's revelation. What has triggered it?

A cynic might respond that as Ganin heads toward the railroad station to meet Mary, he is frightened off by the thought of having to confront reality. The consummate dreamer, he remains uncomfortable with the thought of trying to turn his dreams into life. Yet even if this be the case, Ganin may have learned something over the course of the novel. In turning away from his rendezvous with Mary he may be saving himself and Mary from the disenchantment he experienced when he transformed his idealized image of romance with Lyudmila into physical reality.[36]

Yet the narrative takes pains to assert that Ganin is ready to leave his fantasies about Mary behind: "the image of Mary ... now remained in the house of ghosts, which itself was already a memory" (*M* 114; *Mk* 168). He has "awakened," the novel suggests, to authentic physical life. As he watches workmen constructing a new building, the sheen of the fresh lumber seems "more alive than the most lifelike dream of the past" (*M* 114; *Mk* 168). This passage indicates that it is now the *past* which is recognized as a dream; real life is the world Ganin surveys in the present.

The episode suggests that Ganin has turned away from the world of inner fantasy and toward the world of external life. Perhaps he has at last absorbed the warning implied in Podtyagin's lament that he had put everything into his poetry that he should have put into his life and that now it was too late for him to start all over again (*M* 42; *Mk* 67). Just moments before leaving to meet Mary, Ganin observed the old poet on the verge of death. In that moment he may have glimpsed the peril of absorption with one's dreams, no matter how alluring those dreams might be.[37] At the end of the novel, then, Ganin steps out of the solipsistic world of creative vision and seems ready to rejoin the physical world. Nonetheless, a nagging question remains: what does Ganin's "awakening" actually mean?

Before answering that question it would be illuminating to consider a literary subtext with significant relevance to the novel. Nabokov introduces the subtext through his epigraph to the novel: "Having recalled intrigues of former years, / having recalled a former love" (*M* ix; *Mk* 7). This is a quotation from Stanza 47 of the first chapter of Pushkin's *Eugene Onegin*, where the poet-narrator states that he and Onegin used to relieve the burden of the present with memories of carefree love in the past. The stanza concludes: "As to the greenwood from a prison / a slumbering clogged convict is transferred, / so we'd be borne off by a dream / to the beginning of young life" (*EO* 1: 115). The *Onegin* subtext proves relevant on several levels.

Most obvious, of course, is the concern for the workings of memory which Nabokov's novel shares with Pushkin's. Beyond that, however, one notes a significant parallelism and divergence in the theme of lovers' separation and reunion. In Pushkin's verse novel, Onegin initially spurned Tatyana's love, only to pursue her years later when he discovers that she is married to another. Although Ganin and Mary had experienced some months of mutual affection, he too allows the relationship to erode, only to be seized with new feelings of attraction years later when he, like Onegin, discovers that she is the wife of another. Yet it is here that Nabokov diverges from Pushkin. Whereas Pushkin at the outset of *Onegin* depicts his hero in dynamic motion (driving to his uncle's country manor), he leaves the character at the end of the novel standing stock-still, dumbstruck by Tatyana's profession of fidelity to a husband she does not love. Nabokov, in contrast, begins his novel with a depiction of a static hero and concludes with an image of the character in dynamic action, riding a train out of Berlin. The *Onegin* subtext reinforces the dynamism of Ganin's choice at the end of *Mary*. He chooses not to cling to the past, or to try to restore it, but to move on in search of new adventures.

Nabokov's works often conclude on open-ended notes, depicting characters who have departed familiar territory for new lands. Here too, the reader may well wonder what the ultimate effect of Ganin's "awakening" may be. Although he seems more willing than before to embrace the reality of the present, one notes that he does not choose to return to the *pension* and to assist in the scene of disarray he left behind, with Alfyorov drunk and Podtyagin dying. His decision to board a south-bound train may reflect a desire to escape the reality of his present life as much as a desire to create something new.[38] His escapist impulses were noted at the outset of the novel when the narrator stated that Ganin's longing for other lands grew especially powerful in the spring (*M* 9; *Mk* 18).

What is more, the concluding scene in *Mary* contains an unsettling detail: "As his train moved off *he fell into a doze, his face buried* in the folds of his mackintosh, hanging from a hook above the wooden seat" (*M* 114, emphasis added; *Mk* 169). Although the final chapter has depicted Ganin awakening to life, the last sentence of the novel portrays him falling asleep again, perhaps to return to a state in which dreams and fantasies hold more charm than the external world.

For the reader, Ganin remains something of an equivocal character. He possesses an admirable capacity to re-create sensuous visions of nature and young love. Yet his casual attitude towards the feelings of those around him is disturbing. Toker's characterization of Ganin as "Nabokov's version of a charismatic villain" (*Nabokov* 40) has merit with its fusion of both positive and negative elements. Ganin represents a forerunner of a type which could be called the "indifferent aesthete" in Nabokov's work: one whose devotion to his inner creative designs renders him insensitive to the needs and weaknesses of others.[39]

Ganin's readiness to overlook the interests of others for the sake of his own wishes becomes even more pointed in Nabokov's next novel. In fact, Ganin's immersion in the world of inner vision seems relatively benign in comparison to the predilection for self-absorption which Nabokov's subsequent protagonists reveal. Having initiated his investigation into the dynamics of obsession with inner vision, Nabokov explores the subject in two directions. First, he delineates how one's pre-occupation with an internal image of another threatens one's relationship with the others in one's environment, and second, he explores how this pursuit of internal creativity fosters that fundamental bifurcation in identity which has been glimpsed in such characters as Mark Standfuss and Lev Ganin. Within just a few years, Nabokov's work provides striking views of the unusual forms this bifurcation can assume.

CHAPTER 2

Altering the themes of life

Nabokov's fiction in the years 1927 and 1928 expands upon the principles established in his earlier work and offers further illumination into the potential consequences of an individual's obsession with another. In certain works of this period, though, the other who is the object of such attention is not absent, but present, and this "presence" causes a shift in the dynamic of individual fixation. The protagonists seeking a desired goal in their relationship with another attempt to manipulate or control the lives of those around them. This endeavor offers an early form of what later emerges as an overt authorial aspiration.

Nabokov does not yet focus on protagonists who *consciously* try to shed their status as characters and to attain the powers of an author, but his fiction raises the issue in subtle ways, particularly in the English version of *King, Queen, Knave*. The brief sketch "The Passenger" discusses the urge that some would-be authors have to mold experience into neat aesthetic packages; "An Affair of Honor" illustrates this impulse at work within the life of a particular individual; and *King, Queen, Knave* demonstrates how this urge can dominate the lives of a whole series of characters.

"THE PASSENGER"

Published in March 1927, the sketch "The Passenger" ("Passazhir") is an early programmatic piece in which Nabokov deliberates on an aspect of the self–other relationship which he finds particularly significant – the relationship between writers and the subject of their art. The sketch consists of two elements: an unnamed writer's debate with a literary critic about the relationship between fiction and life frames an anecdote about a strange experience the writer had on an overnight train ride.

The writer's central premise is that everyday life has its own unfathomable designs that may be more elegant and subtle than the artificial plots dreamed up by would-be authors. Talking about life as if it were an author, the speaker chides his fellow writers for their opinion that life's "genius" is too untidy (*DS* 74; *VCh* 140) and for their urge to alter the themes of life in order to achieve some kind of "conventional harmony" and artistic concision (*DS* 73; *VCh* 140). While the speaker specifically targets artists striving too earnestly to devise neat plots with clever endings, his remarks have more important implications in the larger universe of Nabokov's works. Many of Nabokov's characters function as would-be artists in their relation to the surrounding world. Impatient with the arrangement of life as it is presented to them, they attempt to reshape their environment according to their own personal designs. Such would-be artists working in the medium of life inevitably run afoul of life's unpredictability, and thus suffer setbacks both in life and in their art.

Having delivered his didactic views, the writer illustrates them with an anecdote about an encounter on a train. Awakened at night by a passenger entering his compartment, the writer recalls his fascination with the sight of the stranger's foot, which was all he could see as the passenger prepared the upper berth. After describing the foot in graphic detail, the writer relates how he awakened later in the night to hear the passenger sobbing and muttering indistinct words.[1] Early the next morning several police board the train and begin a search for a man who had murdered his wife and her lover the evening before. The writer of course suspects that the unknown passenger is this murderer, thereby reflecting a fundamental proclivity among Nabokov's protagonists to project a desired identity onto unknown others.

As it turns out, however, the mysterious passenger is not the person the police want. Commenting on the way real life foiled his expectations, the writer expands upon the image of life as "author" introduced earlier. He states: "think only how nice it would have seemed – from the writer's viewpoint, naturally – if the evil-footed, weeping passenger had turned out to be a murderer ... Yet, it would appear that the plan of the Author, the plan of Life, was in this case, as in all others, a hundred times nicer" (*DS* 78–79; *VCh* 145). This statement raises an important question for the reader. Although the writer argues that the author Life is superior to ordinary authors in its designs, one must interrogate this premise more closely. Since "The Passenger" is itself a fictional work written by Nabokov, then the actual "Author" of the plan depicted in the sketch may not be life but rather Nabokov himself (or his agent, the implied author). Does the objective existence of the sketch itself subvert the message it contains?

The answer is two-fold, and requires a consideration of the sketch on two levels. Within the diegetic world of the narrative, the sketch supports the premise that life is unpredictable and that it defies attempts by individuals to control or manipulate it. On the other hand, when seen from an extradiegetic perspective, the world created in the narrative is not itself the "real" world: it is a fictional creation, subject to the authority of the author who has created it.[2] In a fictional text, then, the so-called Author Life is merely a mask worn by the authentic *auctor* or one of his agents, much like McFate in *Lolita*.[3]

Nabokov's subsequent work is built squarely on this two-fold structure, in which "life" and the vagaries of unpredictable "chance" depicted within the diegetic world serve to illustrate the control and cunning of the author's "choice" in the extradiegetic world. The meeting place between these two worlds is the narrative text itself. The critic seems to point this out when he declares that the "Word" is given the right "to enhance chance" and to make the transcendental into something that is not accidental (*DS* 79; *VCh* 146). Nabokov's subsequent texts invoke this duality in increasingly complex and intricate ways. Characters within the fictional world who try to manipulate others in their environment according to their own designs find themselves manipulated in turn by a more elusive other with powers vastly superior to their own. Indeed, it is in Nabokov's very next novel, *King, Queen, Knave*, that the author traces the first distinctive silhouette of this startling encounter between the diegetic and the extradiegetic mind. Before discussing that work, however, it would be illuminating to consider the short story "An Affair of Honor," a piece which offers a distinctive treatment of the urge to transform the designs of life into more appealing and comforting forms.

"AN AFFAIR OF HONOR"

Like numerous characters in Nabokov's fiction, the protagonist of "An Affair of Honor"("Podlets," written in 1927) – one Anton Petrovich – tries to replace a bleak reality with a soothing fantasy that is more to his liking. The cheerless situation confronting Anton Petrovich recurs often in Nabokov's work: Anton discovers to his anguish that his wife has been unfaithful to him. He challenges his rival Berg to a duel, and then spends the rest of the narrative dwelling on the consequences of his impulsive gesture. What makes this work distinctive is the way in which Nabokov blends narrative modes to foreground his protagonist's desperate attempt to transform the reality in front of him into something more satisfying. A basic third-person extrinsic narrative mode is frequently interrupted by segments that represent the character's personal perspective on events. These frequent shifts in narrative mode earmark Anton Petrovich as a character who is especially zealous in his desire to reshape the ongoing narrative that is his life.

One of the most striking aspects of Anton Petrovich's reflections on the duel he himself has instigated is his tendency to project roles for himself and for others. Characteristically, these projections founder on reality's unyielding reefs. Recalling his initial challenge to Berg, Anton laments: "He did not leave me his card. *According to the rules he should have given me his card*" (*RB* 90, emphasis added; *VCh* 111). Later, after brushing off an attempt by his sister-in-law to talk about his marital problems, he thinks: "How strange that she did not start imploring him not to fight. *By all rights she ought to have implored him not to fight"* (*RB* 95, emphasis added; *VCh* 116). He is also distressed with the men he has chosen as his seconds: "if it had come to choosing seconds, *they should in any case have been gentlemen"* (*RB* 93, emphasis added; *VCh* 114). In each of these passages, Anton Petrovich's concern with the failure of others to fill the roles he envisions for them is paramount, and it carries significant implications. Through this concern one discerns the framework of a central theme in Nabokov's work – the aspiration of a character to function as an author in relation to the lives of those around him. The aspiration which surfaces here will assume greater prominence in *King, Queen, Knave* and later novels.

A crucial element in the aspiration to attain authorial status in Nabokov's fiction is the need to deal with oneself as a potential character. Would-be authors must find a way of shedding the character dimensions of their identity; one way to do this is to assign a role to themselves in their fictional schemes. Much of Anton Petrovich's fantasizing is devoted to this process. When he first gives serious consideration to the fact that he has issued a challenge to Berg, he takes what could be called aesthetic delight in the prospect. His initial deliberations center on the emotional impact of the word "duel" itself: "A duel. What an impressive word, 'duel'! I am having a duel. Hostile meeting. Single combat. Duel. 'Duel' sounds best" (*RB* 94; *VCh* 115). Later, when he tries to imagine how the duel itself might unfold, he spends considerable energy thinking about his own appearance – what he should wear, what poses he might strike, and so on: "I must dress soberly, but elegantly . . . I must wear my new black suit. And when the duel starts, I shall turn up my jacket collar – that's the custom, I think . . . That's how they did it in that film I saw" (*RB* 101–2; *VCh* 123–24).[4]

The last phrase deserves note, for it offers insight into the source and quality of Anton Petrovich's creative inspiration. Drawing on prior works such as films, operas, and books, Anton Petrovich reveals himself to be a derivative epigone, not an original creator. In the English version of the story Nabokov

underscores the imitative nature of Anton Petrovich's inspiration by inserting several references to works such as Tchaikovsky's opera *Eugene Onegin*, which is itself an adaptation that
reworks (and deforms) Pushkin's novel in verse.⁵ Anton Petrovich wonders how Onegin behaves during the duel scene in the
opera and he recalls that in one performance the actor playing
Lensky fell down so realistically that his gun flew into the
orchestra (*RB* 102–3; compare *VCh* 124).⁶ Anton Petrovich's
fantasies, like those of Smurov in *The Eye*, exude an aroma of
overripe Romanticism.

Of particular interest in the passage quoted above (in which
Anton speculates on his conduct at the duel) is the degree to
which the character's thoughts are presented directly to the
reader. As Pekka Tammi has pointed out, this work reveals a
remarkable blending of what he terms narrator's discourse and
character's discourse (*Problems of Nabokov's Poetics* 77–78).
Those passages which transmit the character's impressions to
the reader often appear in the free indirect discourse mode (for
example "This accursed motion was somehow connected with
Berg, and had to be stopped." *RB* 89; *VCh* 110; or "Oh, if only
he could manage to disable Berg at the first fire. But he did not
know how to aim the thing. He was bound to miss." *RB* 99;
VCh 121); many of them are presented in the free direct
discourse mode as well (for example "The front door bell will
ring in a moment. I must keep perfectly calm. The bell is going
to ring right now. They are already three minutes late" *RB*
104; *VCh* 126).

When one studies the manipulation of narrative modes in
"An Affair of Honor," one notes an apparent increase over the
course of the work in the amount of narrative that is conveyed
through the free indirect and free direct discourse modes. The
effect of this increase becomes most dramatic in the final stages
of the narrative, when the narrator draws the reader directly
into one of Anton Petrovich's fantasies without providing
obvious markers that such a shift has occurred. After Anton
Petrovich has run away from the impending duel and taken
refuge in a seedy hotel, he realizes that his reputation will be
ruined forever. Disconsolate, he thinks that perhaps there is a

way out of his predicament. He then imagines leaving the hotel and going home. The next few paragraphs describe how he returns home to be greeted as a hero, for Berg too had fled before Anton's cowardice was revealed. Unfortunately for Anton Petrovich, this entire episode turns out to be just one more fantasy.

What sets this passage apart from the earlier ones, however, is that it not only contains segments of free direct discourse that are clearly meant to be recognized as the character's inner thoughts (for example "No, better take a taxi. Off we go" *RB* 114; *VCh* 137), it also contains several lines which are nearly indistinguishable from the extrinsic (and ostensibly objective) narrative mode that had prevailed earlier in the tale: "In the parlor, around the circular table, sat Mityushin, Gnushke and Tanya. On the table stood bottles, glasses, and cups. Mityushin beamed – pink-faced, shiny-eyed, drunk as an owl" (*RB* 114; *VCh* 137).[7] Thus the reader may be fooled into thinking that Anton Petrovich has in fact succeeded in avoiding disgrace. Only at the very end of the narrative does it become clear that this episode is merely a fantasy. Anton Petrovich smiles, gets up, and then ceases smiling: "Such things don't happen in real life" (*RB* 115; *VCh* 138).

Nabokov's use of what appears to be the extrinsic narrator's objective voice to convey a character's subjective impression recalls Mark's imagined return to Klara's house in "Details of a Sunset." Yet there is a significant distinction between the use of the technique in "Details of a Sunset" and its use here. In the earlier work, the episode of the imagined return arose out of the character's physical trauma: his accident plunged him into a realm of vision much richer than that to which he was accustomed. Here, in contrast, the central character has already demonstrated his penchant for creating elaborate scenarios in which he and others play assigned roles. Thus, the blending of markers of his own inner monologue with markers of the objective voice of the extrinsic narrator has a distinctive effect: it seems as though Anton has appropriated for himself the narrator's quasi-authorial role.[8] This is an impressive technical achievement with striking thematic implications.

Although Anton Petrovich evinces no awareness that he is trying to wrest control of the narrative discourse which presents him to the reader, "An Affair of Honor" takes an important step in that direction. During the next decade Nabokov develops this concept further until finally, in *The Gift*, he outlines the dramatic metamorphosis of created character into creating author.

Throughout "An Affair of Honor" Anton Petrovich struggles with issues of personal identity. He is tormented by the disparity he perceives between his involuntary role as a cuckolded husband and his desired role as dashing duellist. It is noteworthy that these two roles find an echo within the tale in the form of two separate characters who flank Anton Petrovich. Corresponding to the image of the dashing duellist is Berg, while corresponding to the image of cuckolded husband is Leontiev, a sorry individual whose wife is rumored to have cheated on him. The presence of these two figures merits attention: they may indicate a pair of potential identities for the central hero himself. Nabokov's manipulation of their names adds weight to this supposition. While Anton Petrovich is given no surname, neither Berg nor Leontiev has a first name or patronymic. At the outset of the story, then, Anton Petrovich's identity is perhaps still unfinished. Two paths lie open to him: he can become either a Berg or a Leontiev. The fact that he flees from his confrontation with Berg and encounters Leontiev near the end of the tale indicates which identity suits him better.

The presence of two figures who represent contrasting potential identities for the central hero anticipates the appearance of numerous other pairs in later Nabokov works, including *The Eye* and "Terra Incognita." Yet while the figures of Berg and Leontiev have concrete status as "real" characters in "An Affair of Honor," some of the subsequent character doublets have less concrete ontological status. Rather, they seem to be projections from within the protagonist's consciousness and emerge as possible alter egos for him, particularly when he is striving for authorial autonomy. The protagonist's creation of such alter egos becomes a staple of Nabokov's mature fiction.

Even in "An Affair of Honor," however, Nabokov's handling of Berg and Leontiev invests them with a certain dematerialized or imaginary air. To begin with, when recording Anton Petrovich's attempt to recall his first meeting with Berg, the narrator states that Berg "arose out of nonbeing," bowed in greeting, and then settled down again, not into his previous nonbeing but into an armchair (*RB* 83; *VCh* 103). Later, Leontiev materializes before Anton Petrovich just at a moment when the latter ponders his future course of action. The first indication of Leontiev's presence comes in the form of a disembodied voice that hails Anton Petrovich from above his ear (*RB* 110; *VCh* 133). Anton seems almost to have conjured the figure out of thin air at the moment of his deepest humiliation.

Faced with such a disheartening alter ego as Leontiev, Anton Petrovich retreats from the role assigned to him by "real" life into a world created in his imagination. As so often happens in Nabokov's fiction, however, external reality asserts its rights, and at the end of the narrative Anton surrenders his fantasy of triumph for the more material consolation of a greasy ham sandwich. The designs of external reality have a way of intruding upon the escapist fantasies of Nabokov's characters, and in the writer's next novel, the mind of the extradiegetic author who creates this external "reality" asserts its dominion over the narrow-minded and selfish schemes of the diegetic protagonists.

KING, QUEEN, KNAVE

Nabokov's second novel, written in the first half of 1928 and published later that year, strikes many readers as an abrupt departure from his achievement in *Mary*. Field writes that "*King, Queen, Knave* is a wholly new departure that has almost nothing in common with *Mashenka*" (*Life in Art* 152). Such an impression, however, stems more from the author's approach to his characters than from the introduction of radically new themes. In certain respects *King, Queen, Knave* represents an intensification of the central concerns of Nabokov's earlier work. Dominating the novel is Nabokov's exploration of the fatal consequences of a single-minded fixation with a desired other (and a concomitant blindness to the others physically present in one's environment). This theme, which first appeared in such works as "Details of a Sunset" and *Mary*, takes on sharp new definition in *King, Queen, Knave.*

Yet while Nabokov's concern with the problems of obsession with another carries over from *Mary* to *King, Queen, Knave*, the writer adopts a fresh approach to character depiction here. As he suggests in his foreword to the English version, he wished to move away from the "human humidity" permeating *Mary* (*KQK* viii), and he does so by associating his central characters with various types of inanimate objects such as department store mannequins, mechanical dummies, and of course, playing card figures. This device has led numerous critics, beginning with the novel's earliest reviewers, to speak of its protagonists as "cardboard characters" (Struve, "Notes on Nabokov" 51).[9] More recent critics, however, have modified this view, arguing that Nabokov's character portraits are extensive and well-rounded. Ellen Pifer asserts that Franz, "the young knave," is "far too intensely rendered a character to be dismissed, at the outset, as a paper figure" (*Nabokov and the Novel* 18); and Leona Toker argues that the characters are "fully realized" and "as rounded, or three-dimensional as the Inventor's automannequins"; what they lack is only the fourth dimension – the soul (*Nabokov* 57–58).

The real issue, however, is not how many dimensions Nabokov employs in creating his character portraits (David Rampton maps out the geometry of this issue in a different way than Toker does: in his view Nabokov makes Martha "a two-dimensional character in a three-dimensional world" [*A Critical Study of the Novels* 17]). What is important is the direction in which the characters move over the course of the novel. Broadly speaking, the process of "dehumanization" accelerates as the characters become enmeshed in the obsessions which enslave them.

A telling image of the ominous condition confronting the

central characters occurs in chapter 9, when Franz perceives that Martha's husband Dreyer had "divided in two": "There was the dangerous irksome Dreyer who walked, spoke, tormented him, guffawed; and there was a second, purely schematic, Dreyer, who had become detached from the first – a stylized playing card, a heraldic design . . . This Dreyer number two was very convenient to manipulate. He was two-dimensional and immobile" (*KQK* 177–78; *KDV* 173). Yet Dreyer is not the only one who evinces this inherent duality: all three main characters possess the capacity to "walk," "speak," and behave like human beings, but choose instead, by pursuing self-centered goals, to settle for the second condition – the status of playing cards. This choice shows up most obviously in their relationships to others. All three consistently view others as objects rather than as autonomous, independent entities. Ironically, the characters' predilection for objectifying others has the effect of reducing themselves to automatons too.

The character who demonstrates a tendency toward objectification in its crudest form is Franz, an unsophisticated country lad who journeys to the city with the most shallow of dreams for fame and fortune.[10] When he first sees Martha on his train ride to Berlin, he immediately transforms her into an object of erotic desire: "He bared the shoulders of the woman that had just been sitting by the window, made a quick mental test (did blind Eros react? clumsy Eros did, unsticking its folds in the dark)" (*KQK* 13; *KDV* 17). Even as he makes an object of her, however, he is not content to leave her with her individual features intact. Although he retains her "splendid shoulders" in his fantasy, he then "changed the head, substituting for it" the face of a seventeen-year-old girl with whom he had been infatuated. Yet even this substitution proves inadequate, so he makes one final substitution, attaching "the face of one of those bold-eyed, humid-lipped Berlin beauties that one encounters mainly in liquor and cigarette advertisements." Ironically, the substitution of a lifeless commercial image for that of a genuine individual encountered in the flesh has an uncanny effect: "Only then did the image *come to life*" (*KQK* 14, emphasis added; *KDV* 17). As this mental metamorphosis indicates, Franz is more comfortable with stylized two-dimensional images than with authentic individuals.

Indeed, an earlier passage indicates that Franz feels squeamish when confronted with the reality of the flesh in direct, unadorned forms. Upset by seeing a man with a disfigured face, Franz is overwhelmed by a flood of grotesque memories befitting a canvas by Bosch – "a chamber of horrors" – featuring such images as "a dog that had vomited on the threshold of a butcher's shop" and "an old man with a cough in a streetcar who had fired a clot of mucus into the ticket collector's hand" (*KQK* 3–4; *KDV* 7). This aversion to images of raw physicality later works to forestall any possibility of establishing true intimacy with Martha. At one point she asks him about his childhood, and he responds with a quick comment on the foul smell of her dog's breath: "That is how my childhood smells" (*KQK* 83; *KDV* 83). She does not grasp his remark, and she asks him to repeat it, but he declines to respond and instead goes on to describe his boating and drinking adventures with "mechanical" enthusiasm. For a moment, Franz had offered Martha a glimpse into his soul, but because of his own discomfort with coarse reality, he rebuffs her invitation to explore it with her.

Unable to appreciate the uniqueness of the other, Franz finds his affair with Martha gradually becoming a matter of deadening routine, and eventually Martha is transformed in his eyes from an erotic object into an object of revulsion. "In the inexorable light her skin looked coarser and her face seemed broader ... A complete stranger within Franz's consciousness observed in passing that she rather resembled a toad" (*KQK* 198; *KDV* 192).[11] Martha's transformation from beautiful woman into toad in Franz's eyes represents a striking inversion of the Russian folktale in which a prince marries an ungainly frog who turns into a beautiful princess with peerless skills in sewing, baking, and dancing.[12] Such fairy-tale elements occur frequently in Nabokov's work, and his inversion of the fairy-tale plot here underscores the degeneration of Franz's fantasy into a nightmare.

Nabokov further emphasizes the negative charge of this transformation through his manipulation of one of the most powerfully charged image systems in his work – imagery involving paradise and hell. When Franz first catches sight of Martha, he has just crossed over from the third-class section of the train to the second-class section. At that point, his passage seems to him to be a passage "from a hideous hell through the purgatory of the corridors and intervestibular clatter into a little abode of bliss. . . . He transformed the conductor's click into that of a key unlocking the gates of paradise" (*KQK* 11; *KDV* 14–15). This paradisal image recurs when Franz and Martha have intercourse for the first time: initially, Franz's bed is compared to a train gliding into motion; as the passion subsides, "the bed returned to Berlin from Eden" (*KQK* 98). Martha then exclaims: "'Franz, it was paradise!'" (*KQK* 98; *KDV* 97).[13]

Ultimately, however, Franz discovers what Nabokov's characters often find when they achieve the object of their desire: their paradise displays the hues of hell.[14] For Franz, the topography of the nether world consists of stark structures of confinement.[15] As his affair with Martha continues, he finds himself entrapped within a blind alley of sexual habit. Numerous passages underscore his lack of autonomy (see, for example *KQK* 156, 161, 167; *KDV* 153, 158, 163). The very room in which his trysts take place becomes a prison cell of lust, and the narrator's description of the wallpaper in the room makes a grim commentary on Franz's condition, once again invoking the paradise–hell imagery: the flowers in the pattern "arrived at the door from three directions but then there was no further place to go, and they could not leave the room, just as human thoughts . . . cannot escape the confines of their private circle of hell" (*KQK* 225; *KDV* 216–17. The phrase "of hell" was added to the English version.).

Franz's inexorable transformation from a vital, if crude, youth into a mindless dummy results not only from his own inability to find in Martha anything more than a sexual partner, but from her corresponding propensity to turn others into objects as well. *Her* predilection for objectification is unmatched in the novel. From the outset, she is determined to view external phenomena within the parameters of certain narrow categories. Thus she is offended by her husband reading a book of poems on the train, thinking to herself that a person who calls himself a businessman "cannot, must not, dare not act like that" (*KQK* 10; *KDV* 14).

Martha's insistence on keeping everything in its proper place recalls Tolstoy's Ivan Ilyich. Both characters transform their houses into the perfect emblems of their shallow, materialistic souls. As Ivan Ilyich "himself superintended the arrangements, chose the wallpapers, supplemented the furniture" (*Great Short Works of Leo Tolstoy* 265), so too, "Everything in the house . . . had been chosen by Martha" (*KQK* 36; *KDV* 37). The resulting effect is similar. Tolstoy writes of Ivan Ilyich's house: "it was just what is usually seen in the houses of people of moderate means who want to appear rich, and therefore succeed only in resembling others like themselves: there were damasks, dark wood, plants, rugs, and dull and polished bronzes – all the things people of a certain class have in order to resemble other people of that class" (266). As for Martha's house: "neither aesthetic nor emotional considerations ruled her taste; she simply thought that a reasonably wealthy German businessman in the nineteen-twenties, in Berlin-West, ought to have a house of exactly that sort, that is, belonging to the same suburban type as those of his fellows" (*KQK* 35; *KDV* 36).

More devastating than her desire to obtain the correct objects for her house is Martha's willingness to accept an element of alienation in her relationship with her husband. In this too she follows Ivan Ilyich. When Ivan Ilyich discovered that he and his wife did not share an emotional affinity, he was not dismayed: "This aloofness might have grieved Ivan Ilyich had he considered that it ought not to exist, but he now regarded the position as normal, and even made it the goal at which he aimed in family life" (261–62). Likewise, when Martha realized that she and Dreyer were emotionally estranged from each other, she accepted the situation as normal: "And Martha really did believe that her marriage was no different from any other marriage, that discord always reigned ... Therefore Martha never complained about her situation, since it was a natural and customary one" (*KQK* 65; *KDV* 66).[16]

Although members of Martha's set regularly take on extra-marital lovers, Franz's entrance into Martha's life offers her a sensation of breaking the stifling routines of her everyday existence. For a time, she relishes the novelty of this experience as an encounter with something joyful (see *KQK* 41; *KDV* 43), but within short order she begins to extend her manipulative tendencies toward Felix too. When deciding to let him kiss her for the first time, she chooses a day when she is menstruating; she will therefore have an excuse not to let things get out of hand (see *KQK* 86; this calculation does not appear in the Russian version). After they do become lovers, she persistently bends his will to her own, first teaching him to dance and to achieve "an automaton's somnambulic languor" (*KQK* 150; *KDV* 147), and later to become an obedient perfect accomplice in her schemes to murder Dreyer.

What Martha enjoys most in this relationship is her ability to manipulate and control Franz. Initially viewing him as warm "wax" that one can mold with pleasure (*KQK* 31; *KDV* 33), she glories in her ability to make him obey her commands (see *KQK* 167; *KDV* 163). Eventually, her need for his submissive presence becomes obsessive, and she feels she cannot live for more than a day without his obedient body (see *KQK* 199; *KDV* 193). Significantly, it is her inability to exercise a similar power over Dreyer that most vexes her in her dealings with him. She is dismayed that the man is "aflame" with life (*KQK* 205; *KDV* 198), and she is particularly perturbed by his "gross physicality" that seems to fill up her whole house and the whole world (*KQK* 199; *KDV* 193). She longs to turn Dreyer into a passive object, and in images that recur later in the novel (see note 22 below), the narrator describes Martha's ambitions with regard to Dreyer: "She needed a sedentary husband. A subdued and grave husband. She needed a dead husband" (*KQK* 197; *KDV* 191).

In her drive to reduce Franz and Dreyer to the status of

malleable automatons, Martha acts somewhat as authors do
when exercising control over their created characters. The
quasi-authorial element in Martha's personality is suggested by
the narrator himself when he discusses her plans to murder
Dreyer. He states that she unknowingly recalled details of
nonsensical shootings described in trashy novels, thereby committing a kind of plagiary (*KQK* 178; compare *KDV* 174), and
he reaffirms the association shortly thereafter (see *KQK* 180;
compare *KDV* 175). Yet Martha's authorial pretensions are
not confined to her schemes for murdering Dreyer. On the
contrary, she constantly tries to project her schemes onto the
live beings around her – in essence striving to transform them
into characters in her own invented plots.[17] In this she anticipates *Despair's* Hermann Karlovich who declares that "crime"
may be "art" and then tries to manipulate Felix as a character
in his mad design.[18]

Like Hermann, Martha evinces one fatal flaw, a fundamental blind spot in her vision. Commenting on her deliberations
with Franz about the murder, the narrator identifies the "blind
spot" as the victim himself. In Martha's limited imagination,
the victim shows "no signs of life" before he is to be deprived of
that life (*KQK* 180; *KDV* 176). Martha, like Hermann, fails to
take into account the independent life of her intended victim,
and she ignores the individual's physical reality for the illusory
image she projects onto him. This failure sabotages her plan,
for when Franz is ready to implement her murder plot, the
ostensibly lifeless victim speaks up and mentions an impending
financial windfall, thereby spurring her to postpone the murderous deed. In her quasi-authorial strivings Martha belongs to
that category of writers described in "The Passenger" who
would like to alter the design of life to suit their own inner
schemes. Characteristically, she falls victim to life's own tendency to thwart the neatest plans through the workings of
unpredictable chance.

The glaring discrepancy between Martha's inner vision and
the external reality in which she lives emerges at the seashore, a
setting which seems to expose each of the characters' inner
tensions. Before exploring the consequences of the novel's

change of venue, we must comment briefly on the character of Dreyer. Although he stands somewhat apart from Franz and Martha, he echoes their fundamental proclivities.

Critics have noted that Dreyer displays some characteristics associated with artist figures in Nabokov's works. (Carl Proffer even called him a "frustrated artist" ["A new deck" 301]). He is capable, for example, of soaring into the realm of "inutile imagination" (*KQK* 70; *KDV* 70). Yet Dreyer's artistic inclinations exhibit serious shortcomings. A major passage which Nabokov added to the English version of the novel points to the limitations of Dreyer's artistic aspirations. Commenting on Dreyer's unrealized ambition of becoming an artist and pursuing his inner visions, the narrator notes that a "fatal veil" would always come between Dreyer and those dreams which beckon to him (*KQK* 224).[19] What is this "fatal veil"? Pifer and Toker both point out that Dreyer's shortcoming is in part a failure of vision, an inability or unwillingness to examine the world closely or to break through the "film of familiarity" (*KQK* 106) with which he cloaks objects and people (see Pifer, *Nabokov and the Novel* 42–44 and Toker, *Nabokov* 51). Indeed, Dreyer proves remarkably similar to Martha in his predilection for objectifying the others he encounters in his life. He does this with both Franz and Martha, regarding the former as "a timid provincial nephew with a banal mind" and the latter as a "distant, thrifty, frigid wife whose beauty would occasionally come alive" (*KQK* 106; *KDV* 104).[20]

Although he does have opportunities to try to break through the film of familiarity in his interpersonal relationships, he does not pursue them. Once, after quarreling with Martha, he mentally urges her to let herself go and to cry openly; he imagines that she'll feel better afterwards. Yet although he prepares to speak aloud to her, he decides at the last minute not to say anything, thus repeating a long-established pattern in their relationship (see *KQK* 40; *KDV* 42). Dreyer's inability to extend himself here bars any chance of achieving true intimacy with his wife.

Most troubling in Dreyer is his lack of regard for the individual sensitivities of others. Sharing his creator Nabokov's fondness for coincidences, he enjoys the fact that Franz may have overheard Martha berating Dreyer in the train for his promise to give a poor relative a job, since it is Franz himself who turns out to be that poor relative. Yet it is not the coincidence alone that Dreyer relishes: he seems particularly pleased by the fact that something "nasty" may have been said by Martha in front of Franz (*KQK* 33; compare *KDV* 35). His amusement at someone else's potential pain indicates a palpable measure of self-centered insensitivity to others which his later actions confirm. After demonstrating to Franz the techniques of selling neckties the way they might be sold if the salesman were an artist, Dreyer leaves the store counter in utter disarray, neglecting to think that perhaps someone else might be held accountable for it (see *KQK* 73; *KDV* 73). Pifer characterizes Dreyer as "an amiable solipsist" (*Nabokov and the Novel* 42), but this may be too charitable.[21] Lurking within Dreyer's air of nonchalant self-absorption lie the makings of an indifferent aesthete or even a callous bully. He shares with Martha a disturbing urge to manipulate others for his own selfish ends. Having met Franz, Dreyer mentally implores Martha to allow him (Dreyer) "to play a little too;" he wants her to leave Franz to him for this purpose (*KQK* 40; *KDV* 41). Eventually, he does "play" with Franz in the literal sense of the word. He introduces Franz to the game of tennis in an episode that torments the youth as Dreyer exhibits "the thoroughness of an executioner" (see *KQK* 187–89; *KDV* 181–83).

Despite these traits, Dreyer's portrait undergoes a curious modification once the action of the novel moves from Berlin to the seashore. The narrative states that Dreyer had been at the seashore for less than a week, but had experienced several times already the onset of a "tender melancholy" (*KQK* 235; *KDV* 223). The reader senses a certain softening of the businessman's ebullient image. To account for this change, one could hypothesize that Nabokov wished to generate some sympathy for Dreyer on the eve of the murder attempt, but this explanation would not suffice to explain the kinds of changes that affect all three main characters at the seaside resort.

Since the characterizations of Franz, Martha, and Dreyer all shift somewhat during the novel's last scenes, it is possible that the change in setting plays a role. The novel opens with Franz's passage from the country to the city. At the outset, the city appears to Franz as a kind of fantasy world (see *KQK* 23–24; *KDV* 27) which slowly settles into the backdrop for a relentless nightmare. Nabokov's descriptions of the urban landscape emphasize its enclosed spaces, crowds, and repetitive routine. The seaside setting, however, offers a different atmosphere, one long associated in literature with freedom, creativity, and inspiration. Significantly, it is by the sea that all three characters exhibit traces of a new, two-pronged sensibility: they become dimly aware both of an enticing vision of autonomous existence and of their inescapable condition as figures trapped in an order not of their own making.

The first character affected by such a change is Dreyer. Although the narrative provides no specific explanation for his "tender melancholy," the environment in which it arises can be subjected to fruitful analysis. Delineating the possible factors behind the melancholy, the narrative states: "Perhaps it was the sun that had softened him up or maybe he was growing old, losing maybe something, and coming to resemble in some obscure way the pictureman whose services no one wanted and whose cry the children mocked" (*KQK* 235; *KDV* 223). The "pictureman" mentioned here is "an itinerant photographer" who was observed on the previous page walking along the beach and calling out into the wind: "'The artist is coming! The divinely favored, *der gottbegnadete* artiste is coming!'" (*KQK* 234; *KDV* 222–23). Perhaps when he hears this call Dreyer is reminded of his own creative potential, untapped and unappreciated.

At the same time, Dreyer is also drawn to a display of photographs in the shop windows: "Dreyer was touched by the many photographs going back to the preceding century: the same beach, the same sea, but women in broad-shouldered blouses and men in straw hats. And to think that those over-dressed kiddies were now businessmen, officials, dead soldiers, engravers, engravers' widows" (*KQK* 234; *KDV* 222). To the original Russian catalogue of subjects captured on film ("merchants, engineers, officials"), the English version adds such categories as "businessmen," "dead soldiers," and "engravers' widows." These emendations are significant, for they serve to engage Dreyer more directly in the photographic frame – he himself is a businessman, and has begun to feel the weight of age and death around him. Thus, in examining the subjects captured by the photographer's lens, he is actually looking at a kind of emblematic self-portrait. It is after his study of these photographs and other pictures (of "storm-tossed ships, foam-spattered rocks," etc.) that Dreyer suddenly feels "very sad" (*KQK* 234; *KDV* 222).[22]

Evaluating these two moments of melancholy together, one can attempt an interpretation of Dreyer's mood. The juxtaposition of the two scenes may allude to the fundamental split in Nabokov's protagonists between their inherent status as literary characters and their desired status as authors. Dreyer's melancholy may reflect the tension he feels between his aspiration to attain the status of a creator (like the itinerant photographer) – and his subconscious apprehension that he is little more than the object of some other creator's vision (like the figures in the photographs he views). This tension surfaces only in a muted form in *King, Queen, Knave*; it emerges more fully in Nabokov's later work.[23]

Dreyer is not alone in his melancholy. Franz too becomes aware of an agonizing disjuncture between the situation in which he has been placed and the state to which he aspires. At the dance in the *kursaal* Franz feels drunk and depressed. He resents being tormented by Martha, whom he now sees as a "reptile." The narrative continues: "A human being, *and after all he was a human being*, was not supposed to go on enduring such oppression" (*KQK* 254, emphasis added; compare *KDV* 239). This is the first time in the novel that Franz is described as viewing himself as a "human being," and it is immediately after this that he experiences a strange new sensation: "It was at that moment that Franz regained consciousness like an insufficiently drugged patient on the operating table. As he came to, he knew he was being cut open, *and he would have howled horribly if he were not in an invented ballroom*" (*KQK* 254, emphasis added; *KDV* 239). Like the phrase asserting Franz's sense of himself as a human being, the phrase indicating the invented nature of the ballroom was inserted into the English version. Taken together, the two phrases underscore the disparity Franz feels between his desire to be an authentic human being and his perception that he is situated in some kind of invented world.

Franz's anguish over his captive state finds a specific target in the figure of a haughty foreigner whose presence he notes at the resort. Although the English version provides more detail about the foreigner than the Russian, Franz's reaction to the figure is essentially the same in both versions. The first description of his reaction occurs during the dance mentioned above; phrases which are italicized occur only in the English version: "Franz had long since noticed this couple; they had appeared to him in fleeting glimpses, like a recurrent dream image or a subtle leitmotiv . . . *Sometimes the man carried a butterfly net* . . . and Franz felt envious of that unusual pair, so envious that his oppression, *one is sorry to say,* grew even more bitter" (*KQK* 254, emphasis added; *KDV* 239–40). The reference to the butterfly net makes it clear that the figure in question is a diegetic representative of the novel's author; numerous other details added to the English version (such as the anagrammatic auto-reference in the name Blavdak Vinomori, *KQK* 239) confirm this identification.[24]

Franz's bitter envy toward the foreigner, then, may reveal the resentment felt by a literary character who senses the presence of his maker (or his maker's representative) and who accurately perceives its implications for his own autonomy. The second mention of Franz's antipathy toward the foreign couple bears out this hypothesis. Imagining that the two are discussing him as they pass him on the promenade, Franz feels chagrin: "It embarrassed, it incensed him, that this damned happy foreigner . . . *knew absolutely everything about his predicament* and perhaps pitied, not without some derision, an honest young man who had been seduced and appropriated by an older woman" (*KQK* 259, emphasis added; *KDV* 244). Like Dreyer, Franz senses his true ontological status and experiences discomfort in the presence of another who has the power to define

him.[25] However, he lacks the will or the imagination to devise
any strategy of resistance, unlike certain later protagonists who
feel the defining presence of a powerful other in Nabokov's
fiction.

Of the three central characters, the one who comes closest to
actualizing her authorial aspirations is Martha, and ironically,
it is also she who experiences the strongest sensation of her
subordinate status, although she does not grasp the underlying
meaning of the sensation. Martha's display of quasi-authorial
impulses earlier in the novel has already been discussed, but it
is at the seashore that she gains the keenest glimpse of the
pleasure to be derived from exercising one's authorial potential.
While riding with Franz in the rowboat from which they plan
to throw Dreyer, Martha feels excited.[26] As the moment of the
planned murder draws near, Martha experiences a sense of
"blissful" peace, for she believes that her plan has worked and
that her "dream" has come true (*KQK* 245; *KDV* 231). Even
though she chooses to postpone the plan, she thrives on a
sensation that acts as an intoxicating drug for Nabokov's
would-be creators: "Everything was under control" (*KQK* 250;
compare *KDV* 236).[27]

Everything may be under control here, but the control
belongs to the authentic *auctor*, not Martha, and in the very
next scene she undergoes a curious sense of dissociation which
points to a truth more profound than she can fully comprehend. Suffering from a fever at the dance, Martha endures a
kind of separation from self during which she begins to see
herself from the outside: "She heard Martha Dreyer ask
questions, supply answers, comment on the horror of the
thundering hall . . . With an invisible hand she took Martha by
the left wrist and felt her pulse . . . She noticed that Martha was
dancing also" (*KDV* 252; *KDV* 237). This sense of dissociation
is noteworthy on two counts. First of all, such dissociation often
occurs with Nabokov's creative heroes during moments of
intense mental exertion (see, for example, "Terror" and
"Torpid Smoke"). Moreover, the specific form this dissociation
assumes – a bifurcation of the self into two entities (an internal
center of consciousness and an external, physical entity which

can be manipulated by others) – broadly corresponds to the
two basic dimensions of the self depicted in Nabokov's work:
the authorial and character dimensions. Martha has striven for
what might be called "authorial" control over the men in her
life. Now, for the first time, she sees herself just as the reader sees
her – as "Martha Dreyer," a figure whose actions are dictated
by others. In her own way then, she, like Dreyer and Franz,
catches a glimpse of the disparity between her desired status as
controlling author and her true status as controlled character.

That all three characters come to sense the limitations of
their beings at the end of the novel reflects a deliberate
maneuver by the authentic *auctor* himself. In the final scenes of
the novel he steps forward, as it were, into the text and uses
various devices to assert his authority over his fictional creations. Significantly, as the authorial presence asserts itself, the
characters begin to disintegrate or fragment, particularly in the
English version. Martha's delirium leads to her sense of dissociation, and Franz later has the impression that she has
spawned a double when he sees her sister Hilda and confuses
the two in his mind. He imagines: "Uncle, nephew, and two
aunts" (*KQK* 270; this is not in the Russian version). Likewise,
when he encounters Dreyer, he sees "not Dreyer but a demented stranger in a rumpled open shirt, with swollen eyes and
a tawny-stubbled trembling jaw" (*KQK* 271). Finally, Franz
himself seems to double and multiply. At one point the narrator
develops a resemblance that Dreyer had noted between Franz
and a hotel clerk and states: "The false Franz and the more or
less real one stood side by side" (*KQK* 270). In both versions of
the novel, Franz goes to pieces at the end of the text. Overcome
with hysteria, Franz is overheard by a woman in the next room:
she "heard through the thin wall what sounded like *several
revellers all talking together*, and roaring with laughter, and
interrupting *one another*, and roaring again in a frenzy of young
mirth" (*KQK* 272, emphasis added; *KDV* 260).

The apparent disintegration of the central personalities at
the end of *King, Queen, Knave* broadly echoes the disintegration
of the Inventor's automannequins at this point (see *KQK* 262–
63; *KDV* 246–47), as well as the collapse of the stick figure

"wife" created by Franz's mad landlord Enricht earlier in the work (see *KQK* 229; *KDV* 220). Indeed, the activity of these two diegetic "creators" parallels the work of the novel's extra-diegetic creator, and thus merits special attention as an indication of the kind of relationship the author establishes between himself and those who mimic his endeavor within the realm of the novel. In Nabokov's work, diegetic creators such as Enricht and the Inventor often serve both as distorted reflectors of the authentic *auctor*'s creative activity and as figures whose artistic shortcomings highlight the true skill of the *auctor* himself.

Neither the Inventor nor Enricht has attracted much critical attention, although Toker's study of the novel argues cogently that the Inventor appears in the novel as the agent of the force called "Fate" and is sent by Fate on Franz's trail to create a diversion that ultimately saves Dreyer from Franz's and Martha's murderous designs (*Nabokov* 54–56). Toker's discussion, however, does not address the fact that Enricht too serves as an agent of a higher force, one that assists Franz and Martha in their conspiracy against Dreyer. Thus, both the Inventor and Enricht stand in an intermediary position between the controlling consciousness of the authentic *auctor* and the programmed behavior of the central characters.

The two figures are linked in several ways, beginning with the manner in which they are presented to the reader. The Inventor is first depicted as "a nondescript stranger with a cosmopolitan name and no determinable origin. He might have been Czech, Jewish, Bavarian, Irish – it was entirely a matter of personal evaluation" (*KDQ* 88; *KDV* 87). The eccentric Enricht also has an enigmatic identity: "actually (but this of course was a secret) he was the famed illusionist and conjurer Menetek-El-Pharsin" (*KQK* 99; *KDV* 98); it is unclear whether this is only a private fantasy, or whether he once played such a role on the stage, practicing conjury like Shock.

Both men enter the novel as facilitators of others' fantasies. While the Inventor inspires Dreyer with enticing visions of the animated mannequins, Enricht inspires both Franz and Martha with visions of sexual activity. Enricht's assumption that Franz would bring his lady friend to his room "flattered and excited" the youth (*KQK* 59; *KDV* 59), and Franz's subsequent recollection of this assumption stimulates his sense of an erotic bond between himself and Martha (see *KQK* 63; *KDV* 64). Likewise, the picture hanging in Enricht's rented room of a "bare-bosomed slave girl ... being leered at by three hesitant lechers" (*KQK* 53; this image does not appear in the Russian version) inspires Martha to dream that "Three lecherous Arabs were haggling over her with a bronze-torsoed handsome slaver" (*KQK* 76). Just as the Inventor's mechanical dummies ultimately pave the way for Dreyer's salvation, literally serving as *dei ex machina*, so too does Enricht's room make possible the advancement of Martha's and Franz's destructive affair. It may be no coincidence, then, that as the Inventor bargains with Dreyer over the price of his mechanical mannequins, so too does Enricht bargain with Martha over the price of his room.

The connection between the Inventor's role in Dreyer's life and Enricht's role in Martha's life is underscored by the fact that both Dreyer and Martha embark upon their new "ventures" at approximately the same time. The Inventor enters Dreyer's life at the outset of chapter 5, and it is shortly thereafter in chapter 5 that Martha initiates her infidelity with Franz in Enricht's rented room. Subsequently, both Enricht and the Inventor appear when necessary to further their clients' enterprises. Indeed, Enricht's role as the secret protector of Martha's affair surfaces when Dreyer unexpectedly meets Franz on the street and accompanies him back to Enricht's lodging. Martha is waiting for Franz in his room, and the sudden arrival of her husband threatens to expose their affair. As Martha struggles to keep the door shut against the two men, she feels herself weakening: "Suddenly there was silence, and in the silence a squeaky querulous voice uttered the *magic anti-sesame*: 'Your girl is in there'" (*KQK* 221, emphasis added; compare *KDV* 212 – the emphasized phrase does not appear in the Russian version). If the Inventor is the agent of "Fate," as the novel suggests (see *KQK* 107–8; *KDV* 105–6), then Enricht represents the agent of an opposing force – perhaps that of blind passion or mechanistic lust. When Franz thinks back on

Dreyer's near-discovery of his wife's infidelity, he ruminates wistfully: "Last Sunday fate had almost saved him" (*KQK* 226; *KDV* 217).[28] Fate, however, was thwarted by Enricht and the force he represents. It is not until Martha, Franz, and Dreyer leave Berlin and the protective aura of the force Enricht supports that "Fate" has a free hand to save Dreyer and destroy Martha.

Nabokov's English revision of the novel underscores the fact that Enricht and the Inventor function like two pawns manipulated by higher forces arrayed in broad opposition to each other. The relevant passage reads:

> It is significant that Fate should have lodged him there of all places. It was a road that Franz had travelled – and all at once Fate remembered and sent in pursuit this practically nameless man who of course knew nothing of his important assignment, and never found out anything about it, as for that matter no one else ever did, *not even old Enricht*. (*KQK* 107–8; *KDV* 105–6)

Nabokov added the italicized phrase to the English version. With this passage and with his manipulation of Enricht's and the Inventor's roles in the novel Nabokov creates the outline of a structural device that will emerge more prominently in his subsequent work. Nabokov introduces into *King, Queen, Knave* a set of two forces that broadly oppose each other and battle for influence over the destinies of the novel's main characters. This type of structure also figures in *The Defense*, where the chess-like aspects of the conflict are overtly exposed. While secondary characters such as Enricht and the Inventor serve as unwitting pawns of higher forces such as "Fate," these higher forces, "Fate" included, are in turn controlled by the supreme entity in the novelistic cosmos – the authorial consciousness existing outside the text.

One effect of this structure is to emphasize the utter lack of control Nabokov's characters have over their own destinies. Not only are Martha's attempts to author the proper ending for her marriage ludicrous, but even those characters who are given a semblance of inventive skill (for example Enricht and the Inventor) are exposed as pretenders deluded by a sense of their own power. Their creative ventures pale in comparison to the structures created by the authentic *auctor*.

Enricht's "art" is marked by a sweeping proprietary attitude toward the "other." He believes that the whole world is merely a trick of his, and that all the people he encounters, including Franz and Martha, exist solely because of the power of his imagination and the dexterity of his hands (*KQK* 228; *KDV* 218). Enricht's claim takes the solipsistic tendency of a Mark Standfuss to its ultimate conclusion: he negates absolutely the other's autonomy. Nabokov exposes the fallacy of Enricht's claim by the mere fact that the created world continues to exist long after Enricht tries to dismiss Franz by saying: "You no longer exist" (*KQK* 229; *KDV* 220). In fact, it is not Enricht who has created Franz and the others, but an extradiegetic author, and Enricht himself is just one more of that entity's creations. This author literally "lays bare" the discrepancy between Enricht's inner fantasies and external reality when he has Franz catch sight of Enricht standing on all fours with his rear toward a mirror. This figure, who believes that he can change shapes at will, now chuckles as he peers "through the archway of his *bare* thighs at the reflection of his *bleak* buttocks" (*KQK* 87 emphasis added; compare *KDV* 86). Equally suggestive of the insubstantiality of his fantasies is the fate of his "wife," who turns out to be nothing more than a gray wig and a shawl mounted on a stick. When Franz discovers this, he knocks the entire contraption on the floor (*KQK* 229; *KDV* 220). Enricht's elaborate fantasies collapse at the merest contact with the "reality" of the authentic *auctor*'s creations.

Similar in conception is the Inventor's dream – to create a band of lifelike mechanical dummies. Unlike Enricht, the Inventor expresses an awareness of the artistic implications of his endeavor. Although the narrator states that the Inventor is "neither an artist nor an anatomist" (*KQK* 194; *KDV* 187), he himself tells Dreyer that his achievement would be an "artistic" one (*KQK* 91; *KDV* 90). Yet the Inventor's own creator – the authentic *auctor* – does not share the view that there is something inherently artistic in making one's creations precise replicas of real life, and he signals this through the episode where the Inventor puts his automannequins on display. In the English version of the scene, there are only two figures instead of the promised three, and these two collapse much like Enricht's dummy wife: the female model's career ends "in an ominous clatter" offstage, while the male model's attempt to doff his hat results in his arm coming off as well (*KQK* 262–63; *KDV* 246).[29] The dummies' disintegration occurs not only because they are no longer needed by Fate to save Dreyer's life; it exposes the folly of the original conception as well.

This scene presents the basic design of a pattern utilized frequently in Nabokov's mature work. Nabokov, the creator of the fictional world, toys with the aspirations of his characters to highlight both their limitations as characters and his own powers as creator. It is also typical that while the Inventor strives and fails to give a semblance of real life to his artificial dummies, Nabokov himself succeeds in the opposite endeavor: he takes figures who might seem "real" according to the conventions of nineteenth-century fiction (specifically, the *Bildungsroman* and the novel of adultery) and exposes their artificiality.

Nabokov returns to this pattern in such works as "Lips to Lips" and *Despair*. In his later work Nabokov enlarges the self-reflexive and metaliterary dimensions of his fiction. His heightened predilection for exposing the artificiality of his created world becomes obvious when one compares the English version of *King, Queen, Knave* with the Russian original. Overt references to the fictional nature of the characters and transparent references to the identity of the author abound in the revised version.[30]

The presence of the author is most apparent at the end of the novel, when he steps into the text through the surrogacy of the exotic foreigner with the butterfly net. Throughout the English version of the novel, though, the author demonstrates his control over his material through the image of the movie theater being constructed on the street where Franz lived in Berlin. When finished, the cinema is to feature the premiere of a film entitled *King, Queen, Knave*, a film based on a play of the same name by a writer named Goldemar (another mask for

Nabokov?). The play, the film, the movie house, and Nabokov's novel are all linked together in a series of overlapping fictional constructs. The transformation of the live action of the play into the celluloid animation of the film is analogous to the transformation of the "realistic" characters of nineteenth-century fiction into the animated dummies of Nabokov's novel. Likewise, the construction of the movie house which will exhibit the finished film is analogous to the construction of Nabokov's verbal text to exhibit his created characters. The premiere of the film is scheduled to take place at approximately the same time as the action of the novel comes to an end. The overt metaliterary implications of the cinema-film-play image clearly mark it as a product of Nabokov's late artistic consciousness; his work of the late 1920s does not reveal such a high degree of self-reflexivity. Nonetheless, even in its original form the novel points the way toward Nabokov's future interests.

King, Queen, Knave reveals a significant increase in the complexity of Nabokov's artistic design when measured against his achievement in *Mary*. As in his first novel, Nabokov underscores the debilitating disjuncture from everyday reality that overwhelms those preoccupied with images of a desired other. In contrast to that work, however, he does not focus on a single character obsessed with an absent other, but rather brings a set of three characters to the front of the stage, illuminating, as it were, that Berlin setting which had seemed to be merely a world of shadows for the protagonist of the earlier novel. Yet even though it is not an absent other who forms the target of the characters' obsessions, the mere *presence* of the desired other does not alter or diminish the effects of alienation produced by the characters' obsession with the other. The same dynamic which blinded the characters in Nabokov's earlier works to the surrounding reality operates here, and the results may be even more tragic.

King, Queen, Knave also displays a heightened awareness of the degree of artifice involved in the construction of the fictional world. Joining the three central characters are two secondary figures who serve as diegetic agents of the extra-diegetic author and who exert a hidden influence on the destinies of the main protagonists. When the central characters encounter these figures, they unwittingly come into contact with the visible representatives of an enigmatic higher power whose actual presence they can sense only in muted forms. At the end of the novel, Nabokov partially lifts the veil separating his world from the world of his characters, and in moments of lucidity that ironically strike the characters more like the visions of delirium, they confront the possibility that their lives are framed by an unknown other. It is just this sensation – the apprehension of an omnipotent other in the character's everyday world – that forms the subject of Nabokov's next novel and first masterpiece, *The Defense.*

CHAPTER 3

The evil differentiation of shadows

In Nabokov's fiction at the end of the 1920s, that obsession with images of the other seen in *Mary* and *King, Queen, Knave* takes on ever more serious tones. Confounded in their relationships with others, his protagonists begin to see the other as an enigmatic, even hostile entity. Gradually, the entire world becomes transformed before their eyes, and the resulting vision often arouses terror in their souls. As Franz discovered "horror" in his solipsistic affair with Martha, so too the protagonists of "Terror" and *The Defense* find horror in the cosmos they perceive around them. Having lost the ability to view others without distortion, they find themselves locked in a realm of nightmarish transformation. To chart the contours of this delirium, Nabokov draws on the fantastic art of Nikolai Gogol, adapting those idiosyncratic narrative techniques which edge the readers away from their accustomed viewpoint on the narrated event.

While Nabokov's works highlight the dangers of failing to see the other in proper perspective, they also underscore the importance of forging intimate relationships with others in one's environment. Those characters bedeviled by an uncertain sense of personal identity require close contact with another to help them fix their moorings in life. Yet the narratives of this period demonstrate how difficult it is for Nabokov's protagonists to forge such relationships. Those notes of insecurity found in Franz's reaction to the foreign couple in *King, Queen, Knave* turn into an outright fear of others during this period. One thus arrives at a Dostoevskian dilemma: while needing others to help define their place in the cosmos, Nabokov's characters fear the very prospect of such external definition. The two works examined in this chapter focus on characters who need support from others but who are, for different reasons, unable to achieve the kind of sustained relationships with others necessary for personal security and growth.

"TERROR"

Published in 1927, the brief story "Terror" ("Uzhas") proved a seminal work in Nabokov's development. Though just ten pages long, it highlights concepts that form the nucleus of his major novels for the next two decades. Here the author reveals for the first time the profound horror that springs up when one experiences a complete disjuncture between the world of inner vision and the world of external reality. At the same time, it underscores the vital necessity of maintaining a close relationship with another to help locate one's place in a world of seeming formlessness.

The story divides into two parts. In the first, the autobiographic intrinsic narrator attempts to evoke for the reader the kind of sensation he unveils in the second part. He begins by discussing the sense of dissociation he feels after hours of intense mental concentration at night. Turning on the light and looking into a mirror, he fails to recognize the image in the glass as his own. During those hours of creative labor (he is a poet), he had "grown disacquainted" with himself, and he is unable to make the external image in the mirror merge with his own internal sense of self. This experience of dissociation is noteworthy on two counts. First, it sets up the more horrifying experience the narrator will describe in the second part of the story, when he finds himself unable to recognize the identity of *anything* in the external world. Second, it foregrounds a concept that will become of increasing importance in Nabokov's work: the potential disjuncture between one's inner sense of identity and the image one presents to the outside world. This passage represents an early formulation of the intriguing idea that one may not only be an "other" from someone else's perspective, one can even be an "other" to oneself.

In subsequent works, confrontation with a mirror is often

associated with that latent bifurcation of identity existing
within Nabokov's creative personalities. In his lecture on "The
Art of Literature and Commonsense" Nabokov made a revealing comment about mirrors: "A madman is reluctant to look at
himself in the mirror because the face he sees is not his own: *his*
personality is beheaded; *that of the artist* is increased" (*LL* 377,
emphasis added).[1] Mirror scenes often accompany a character's sense of disjuncture between the inner and outer selves;
this disjuncture may lead either to artistic creation or to chaotic
madness.

The premise that one's external identity may not coincide
with one's internal conception of self figured marginally in
Nabokov's earlier work (for example Ganin traveled under a
false name). It is only after "Terror" that the concept attains
major significance in Nabokov's fiction, especially in works
such as *The Defense*, *The Eye*, and *Despair*. The narrator's
description of his sense of dissociation prefigures later develop-
ments, particularly in *The Eye*. He compares his experience to
meeting an old friend after years of separation: "you see *him* in
an entirely different light" (*TD* 113, emphasis added; *VCh*
196). The narrator's sense of personal dissociation leads him to
envision an entirely separate entity – the imaginary friend in
his comparison.[2] His creative act, of course, occurs only for
rhetorical purposes here, but in *The Eye*, such rhetoric assumes
more substance and propels the plot of the work itself.

The Eye also develops a premise suggested in the concluding
scene in "Terror" – that every person creates a personal image
of a specific other which may not coincide with that other's own
sense of self. When the narrator of "Terror" visits his girlfriend
on her deathbed, he realizes that she does not recognize him
standing there. As he recounts this experience, he introduces an
important image of doubling:

She did not recognize my living presence, but . . . I knew that she saw
me in her quiet delirium, in her dying fancy – so that there were two
of me standing before her: I myself, whom she did not see, and my
double, who was invisible to me. (*TD* 121; *VCh* 204)

In works such as "Details of a Sunset," "The Potato Elf," and
Mary Nabokov had depicted characters who formed images of

another that did not correspond to genuine reality: Mark
Standfuss saw his Klara as a loving fiancée; Nora saw Shock as
a poet; and Klara saw Ganin as a thief. "Terror," however, is
the first work in which Nabokov draws explicit attention to the
process; he introduces here the essential concept of the
"double" created by the other's perspective. Subsequently, the
narrator of *The Eye* pursues this line of creation: he collects and
catalogues the various images of himself fashioned by everyone
he encounters.

To return to the scene of the narrator's sense of dissociation
before the mirror, one finds additional insight into the fluidity
and ambiguity of human identity. The narrator declares: "the
more insistently I told myself 'This is I, this is so-and-so,' the
less clear it became *why* this should be 'I'" (*TD* 113–14; *VCh*
196–97). Nabokov's narrator exposes the seemingly arbitrary
nature of personal identity in a manner reminiscent of the
narrator in Gogol's "The Diary of a Madman." Gogol's hero
wonders why he is a titular councilor and asks: "Why precisely
a titular councilor?" (*The Complete Tales of Nikolai Gogol* 1:
252).[3] The arbitrariness – and potential fluidity – of personal
identity becomes an appealing concept to those Nabokov
heroes who are dissatisfied with their current roles; many test
the boundaries of identity and attempt to change them. Thus
Hermann Karlovich makes a muddled stab at assuming Felix's
identity in *Despair*, while the narrator of *The Real Life of
Sebastian Knight* declares that any soul may be yours if you find
and follow its "undulations" (*SK* 204).

The narrator's uncertainty over the essential meaning of his
identity in the opening pages of "Terror" has an important
corollary. Unsure about his *own* identity, he becomes anxious
about the presence of an "other" in his environment. This
occurs even when the other is his girlfriend. At one point, he
recalls, he suddenly became terrified of her presence in the
room with him. It was not, however, *her* specific presence that
bothered him; rather, he was terrified by the very notion of
"another person" itself (*TD* 115; *VCh* 198). The narrator then
links this sensation with the earlier one, remarking that he had
forgotten that he had experienced something quite similar on

lonely nights in front of the mirror (*TD* 115–16; *VCh* 199). Both experiences stem from a fluid sense of self. Those who are unsure about the parameters of their own identity will feel puzzled or even threatened by the presence of an enigmatic other. Having uncovered this latent source of uncertainty, however, "Terror" goes on to indicate that an intimate relationship with another can play a significant role in helping to anchor one's place in the world.

In the second part of "Terror," the narrator moves from a discussion of his difficulty in relating to specific individuals to a description of his sense of alienation from the cosmos at large. The circumstances which lead up to this experience are noteworthy. First of all, the sense of dissociation occurs in a "foreign" city – a place where the narrator is separated from familiar settings. More importantly, he is *alone*, cut off from the support of that other who had become so important to him – his girlfriend. The woman here plays a role in the narrator's life similar to Mme. Perov's role in the life of the pianist Bachmann in the story "Bachmann": she provides the high-strung artist with a grounding in everyday reality. She is simple and unassuming, and as the narrator puts it, it was precisely that "gentle simplicity" that protected him (*TD* 116; *VCh* 199). This figure represents the prototype for the protective female characters who will appear in *The Defense* (Luzhin's wife) and *The Real Life of Sebastian Knight* (Clare Bishop).

The narrator's separation from his beloved may serve as the catalyst for his experience of "supreme terror." He states that the experience was preceded by four nights of near-sleeplessness, which he attributes to the fact that he had lost "the habit of solitude" in recent years. Now those solitary nights cause him relentless anguish (*TD* 117; *VCh* 200). Separation from his beloved, then, leads to a sense of dissociation from the world at large. Declaring that he suddenly saw the world "as it really is," he attempts to define the sensation of alienation more precisely. He explains that when he stepped out into the foreign city after another sleepless night, he saw houses, trees, cars, and so on, but did not recognize them as such. He continues: "My line of communication with the world snapped, I was on my own and the world was on *its* own, and *that* world was devoid of sense" (*TD* 118–19; *VCh* 202).

The narrator's sudden inability to recognize the conventional meaning of the people and objects he sees in his environment has numerous echoes in Nabokov's work, from Luzhin's paranoid visions to Kinbote's inspired fantasies. The narrator's experience here, however, has a prototypical character, for unlike the later visionaries who see the world stripped of its everyday meaning and charged with new, *personal* meaning, the narrator here sees the world stripped of *all* meaning.[4]

Just as he was perplexed by his external image in the mirror and troubled by the arbitrary nature of personal identity, so too does the narrator view the outside world as a random collection of objects whose significance is unknown to him. He has attained a perspective that some might call transcendent, but rather than being able to discern the ultimate interconnectedness of all phenomena, he can find *no* connections whatsoever. In effect, the narrator has lost the ability to decode the system of signs which surrounds him. For example, when he sees a dog sniffing in the snow nearby, he feels tormented by his efforts to recognize what "dog" might mean (*TD* 120; *VCh* 203).[5] His plight is similar to that of the young man depicted in "Signs and Symbols," only in the reverse direction. Whereas the youth in "Signs and Symbols" suffers from "referential mania," believing that everything happening around him provides a covert reference to his life and personality (*ND* 69), the narrator here suffers from what might be called "non-referential mania," believing that *nothing* in his environment has any reference to him. In both cases, the inability to find a balanced level of meaning in the outside world proves terrifying.

Significantly, what terminates the narrator's experience of cosmic alienation is his renewed concern with a specific other. Handed a telegram stating that his girlfriend is dying, the narrator snaps back to the realm of ordinary sensation: he feels both astonishment and a pain that he labels as "quite human" (*TD* 120; *VCh* 204). As he travels to her bedside, he notes that he had ceased to analyze the meaning of being and nonbeing, and he was no longer terrified by such thoughts (*TD* 120; *VCh* 204). Emotional involvement with a beloved other breaks down the walls of personal isolation and the torment of an existential lack of self-definition in life.

It is of course ironic that it is the death of the narrator's girlfriend that restores him to sanity; as in "The Potato Elf," Nabokov often endows death with such multivalent significance. For while the woman's death temporarily preserves the narrator's sanity, that same death now deprives the narrator of his one link to the everyday world. The narrator concludes his account with the ominous prediction that his brain is "doomed" and that someday this fearful terror will overtake him again: when that happens, there will be "no salvation" (*TD* 121; *VCh* 205).[6]

The death of his girlfriend leaves the narrator bereft of a specific other who can ground him in the reality of everyday life. Yet it may be the narrator's very recognition of this loss that leads him to reach out to a more anonymous other – the reader of his tale. Several times in his discourse he attempts to establish a bond between his own experience and that of the unknown reader. When trying to explain his sense of dissociation from his reflection in the mirror, he uses a second-person pronoun in the English version (and a second-person singular verb form in the Russian version): "*you* see him in an entirely different light ... " (*TD* 113, emphasis added; *VCh* 196; see also *VCh* 197).

When he later begins his description of his dissociation from the external world, he is so concerned about getting through to his audience that he calls for a special typographical form to mark the enormity of the experience. Wishing first that the passage be set in italics, he concludes that not even italics would do: he needs "some new, unique kind of type" (*TD* 118; *VCh* 201). Later he tries to establish a bond with his readers by using the first-person plural form "we" (*TD* 118; *VCh* 201). A poet, he anticipates Cincinnatus in his awareness of the difficulty of precise verbal expression (see his chagrin over the poverty of his store of "ready-made words," *TD* 115; *VCh* 198), as well as his belief in its importance. Asserting that he feels human speech to be a "clumsy instrument," he concludes: "Still, I would like to explain" (*TD* 115; *VCh* 198). The narrator's desperate desire to find a responsive audience for his impressions becomes a major concern for subsequent Nabokov narrators such as Hermann in *Despair* and Humbert in *Lolita*.

Although Nabokov published "Terror" separately in 1927, he republished the story as the concluding work in the prose portion of the 1930 collection *The Return of Chorb* (*Vozvrashchenie Chorba*). Its position there may have been calculated. The collection opens with the title story, which provides a poignant portrait of a man devastated by the death of his wife. As the final story of the cycle, "Terror" also depicts the death of a loved one. In both works, the central character is alienated from those around him, and the separation from a cherished other plays a crucial role in this alienation. Chorb's predicament, however, is presented to the reader at a certain remove. The third-person narrative, for all its psychological eavesdropping, situates the reader outside the character's consciousness, and the conclusion of the narrative even locks the reader out of the room where Chorb and the parents hold their tense confrontation. In "Terror," on the other hand, the reader experiences *with* the narrator his moment of supreme terror and alienation from the surrounding world. More importantly, the story does not finish with a moment of psychological detachment as in "The Return of Chorb." Rather, the narrator ends his account with a chilling view of his personal future, predicting an inescapable descent into insanity. Nabokov's 1930 collection concludes, then, with a baleful image of impending madness, and it foretells the future direction of his art. From *The Defense* to *The Eye* and *Despair* Nabokov explores the alienation produced by the inability to balance transforming vision with meaningful interaction with others.

THE DEFENSE

In his short book on Nikolai Gogol Nabokov makes the assertion that great literature "skirts the irrational" (*NG* 140). He goes on to say that at this high level of art, literature does not concern itself with social issues, but rather appeals to "that secret depth of the human soul where the shadows of other worlds pass like the shadows of nameless and soundless ships" (*NG* 149). Prompted by Nabokov's appreciation of Gogol's short story "The Overcoat," these comments (and particularly their image of "shadows of other worlds") prove apt for a consideration of *The Defense* (*Zashchita Luzhina*) as well. This work is the first of Nabokov's novels to offer a glimpse into what the writer called "those other states and modes which we dimly apprehend in our rare moments of irrational perception" (*NG* 145). Among his Russian fiction, only *Invitation to a Beheading* surpasses this novel in its exploration of such states.

The Defense represents Nabokov's earliest major attempt to chart the effects of a full-scale transformation of reality. He believed that an ability to seize upon and recombine perceived elements of the visible world was an essential element in the artistic endeavor (see, for example, his comments in the lecture "Good Readers and Good Writers," *LL* 2). Yet he also believed that one must temper such inspiration with "cool and deliberate work," not permitting a creative fantasy to reach the stage of "morbid exaggeration" (*LL* 377). In "The Art of Literature and Commonsense" he provides a formulation of madness that proves quite pertinent to *The Defense*: "Lunatics are lunatics just because they have thoroughly and recklessly dismembered a familiar world but have not the power – or have lost the power – to create a new one as harmonious as the old" (*LL* 377).

This is precisely the misfortune that befalls the protagonist of *The Defense*, the chess grandmaster Aleksandr Luzhin. Luzhin's creative vision dismembers the familiar world of his everyday environment, but he lacks the power to sustain a world of harmony in its stead. He is finally driven to suicide by his terrifying perception that the entire world is a kind of cosmic chess game in which he must match wits against an invisible yet infinitely cunning opponent. Nabokov's utilization of the motif of chess competition is itself a "strong move." It points to a critical shortcoming in Luzhin's basic relationship with the "other" as such. Not only is he tormented by his fear of an intangible other in the cosmos, he is further handicapped by his inability to establish intimate contact with any of the more tangible others in his world. His failure to balance his flights of creative fancy through a solid relationship with another proves his undoing: he becomes a solitary captive in the riveting yet horrifying realm of transforming personal vision.

The specter of human alienation raised in "Terror" emerges as a pervasive force poisoning Luzhin's existence in *The Defense* as well, and Nabokov depicts the process of alienation at work in two distinct periods in Luzhin's life.[7] From his childhood to early adulthood Luzhin fends off the attentions of almost everyone he encounters, from parents to schoolmates alike. After his breakdown in chapter 8, his reluctance to permit true intimacy is directed at one specific target – the woman who nurses him back to health. Luzhin's formative years should be considered first.

The reader's initial glimpse of Luzhin depicts the child drawing a caricature of his governess "as horribly as possible" (*Df* 16; *ZL* 24). Ironically, the very horror (*uzhas*) nesting in the word "horribly" (*pouzhasnee*) will come back to haunt Luzhin later in life when he plunges into his paranoid fantasies about chess. Luzhin's problems with others, both visible and invisible, began long before he discovered the game of chess. His relationships with his parents are particularly strained. Since the parent–child bond may be the most cherished in Nabokov's work, Luzhin's evident sullenness in his parents' presence portends trouble. When his father visits him at school, Luzhin reacts to his father's smile by turning away as if he had not seen the man (*Df* 28; *ZL* 36). When the boy returns from school, his father wants to take him by the shoulders and kiss him on the cheek, but again, he is confronted by a child who turns his face away (*Df* 31; *ZL* 39). A similar reserve marks Luzhin's relationship with his mother. On the evening when he hears about chess for the first time, he retreats to his room and puts out the light; when his mother comes in and bends over him, he pretends to be asleep (*Df* 43; *ZL* 51).

Luzhin avoids the caresses of those who love him, and he is repulsed by the raucous antics of his schoolmates. He tries to escape from them physically and mentally, hiding in the school woodpile (see *Df* 29; *ŽL* 37) and retreating into the cerebral realms of geometry (*Df* 36–37; *ŽL* 44; see also *Df* 17; *ŽL* 25) and magic. In the last pursuit, Luzhin seeks "harmonious simplicity" (*Df* 36; *ŽL* 44). The "real" world is complex and confusing; Luzhin longs for order and precision.

These are the very qualities he discerns in the game of chess. When he first hears the game characterized as the "game of the gods" with "infinite possibilities" (*Df* 43; *ŽL* 51), Luzhin perceives in it the refuge from life he has been seeking. Later, the narrative elucidates the reason for his fascination with the game: "Real life, chess life, was orderly, clear-cut, and rich in adventure, and Luzhin noted with pride how easy it was for him to reign in this life, and the way everything obeyed his will and bowed to his schemes" (*Df* 134; *ŽL* 144). As the language of this passage indicates, what Luzhin seeks in the realm of cerebral fantasy is a sense of order and control, and this aspiration for control links him to many of the other visionary characters in Nabokov's Russian fiction. Such characters retreat from the unpredictable world of everyday life in order to construct a new world where they hope to exercise absolute authority.

As Ganin discovered in *Mary*, however, absorption with the world of inner vision dissevers one from the external world, and such an experience may not be entirely comforting. From the first day of Luzhin's discovery of chess, a fissure between Luzhin's inner world and the external world opens up. While that April day "froze forever," the movement of the seasons continued "in different plane" and barely affected him (*Df* 39; *ŽL* 47). This is true not only in the temporal dimension, but in spatial dimensions as well. The many cities in which Luzhin played were all "identical," and the specific setting – hotels, taxis and so on – are viewed by him as "external life" of no interest to him (*Df* 94–95; *ŽL* 104). Like Franz in *King, Queen, Knave*, Luzhin finds himself living a mechanical life, "automatically" winding his watch at night and eating haphazardly out of some kind of "melancholy inertia" (*Df* 95; *ŽL* 104).[8]

Even when he meets a woman who wishes to love and care

for him, he is only momentarily gratified that "here talking to him . . . was *a real live person*" (*Df* 99, emphasis added; *ZL* 109). As she herself realizes, he never asks her any questions about herself; apparently he takes her "for granted" (*Df* 88; *ZL* 97). Luzhin, then, is in a more extreme condition than the narrator of "Terror." Whereas the latter was able to engage in an empathic relationship with one external other, Luzhin avails himself of his fiancée's services as a caretaker, but never extends himself to consider her needs for intimacy or communication. Consequently, while the narrator of "Terror" is able to stave off the onset of madness while his girlfriend still lives, Luzhin cannot manage even that.

Luzhin's dissociation from the external world reaches its climax during a tournament in Berlin, and although Luzhin's immersion in the world of mental fantasies parallels Ganin's immersion in his recollections of Mary, he goes far beyond Ganin in the degree to which his alienation affects his relationship to the outside world. At first, he merely experiences a delay in making the transition from the inner world of chess strategies to the world of everyday life (see *Df* 123; *ZL* 133), but soon a full-fledged split develops. Describing this phenomenon, Nabokov introduces an image that will become highly significant in his subsequent fiction – that of the double: at night, "the Luzhin who was wearily scattered around the room slumbered, but the Luzhin who visualized a chessboard stayed awake and was unable to merge with his happy double." This division grows worse as the tournament continues, so that the "unpleasant split" begins to appear even in daytime (*Df* 126; *ZL* 136). Luzhin's dissociation here represents an evolution of that process first depicted in *Mary* and "Details of a Sunset" – the creative individual's sense of bifurcation between his physical self and his inner, cerebral self. It is this very bifurcation that provides the basis for Nabokov's subsequent exploration of the authorial and character dimensions of his protagonist's identities.

Like Ganin, Luzhin sinks deeper and deeper into his inner world, until he finally discovers that the external world has dissolved into a "mirage" (*Df* 134; *ZL* 144). For Luzhin now,

"Real life" is "chess life" (*Df* 134; *ZL* 144). Luzhin's perception here recalls Ganin's attitude toward his memories of Mary. Ganin viewed his memories not merely as a process of reminiscence, but as "a life that was much more real ... than the life lived by his shadow" (*M* 55; *Mk* 86). Luzhin's condition, however, carries more threatening implications. His intoxication with the realm of chess strategies has entirely fractured his relationship to the outside world. During his final match, the external world – represented in the form of a burning match – asserts its presence, thereby triggering a crucial epiphany within Luzhin:

The pain immediately passed, but in the fiery gap he had seen something unbearably awesome, the full horror of the abysmal depths of chess ... But the chessmen were pitiless, they held and absorbed him. There was horror in this, but in this also was the sole harmony, for what else exists in the world besides chess? Fog, the unknown, non-being ... (*Df* 139; *ZL* 149–50)

The "horror" Luzhin feels here echoes the fear felt by the narrator of "Terror." Alienated from the everyday world, both men confront a new realm of haunting mystery and complexity. Luzhin's perception, however, is more nuanced. As the passage above indicates, he sees harmony as well as horror in this realm. Unfortunately, that which prevents him from fully savoring the harmony is also responsible for his horror: he cannot control or direct the workings of his creative imagination or find a way out of its entrancing labyrinths. Thus he cannot recognize in the external world the proper road back to the apartment of the one being in that world who truly loves him, and he collapses on the Berlin streets, the victim of a mental breakdown.[9]

Before considering the second phase of Luzhin's alienation from the external world – his relationship with his fiancée – it would be illuminating to examine the origins of his obsession with chess and the specific influences shaping his idiosyncratic attitude toward his "spectral art." Brian Boyd argues in "The Problem of Pattern" that Luzhin is subject to the influence of two incorporeal forces: on one side is a chess force directed by Luzhin's dead grandfather, and on the other is a

force directed by Luzhin's dead father who encourages Luzhin
away from chess and toward family life. This interpretation has
much to recommend it. It is likely that Nabokov creates in *The
Defense* an ontological hierarchy similar to that discerned in
King, Queen, Knave: beyond the conventional existential level
inhabited by the central characters lies a higher world of
intangible opposing forces, which in turn serve as agents for the
master creator – the novelist himself.

Boyd's analysis concentrates on the way the opposition
between grandfather and father affects Luzhin's *life*. It is worth
noting that these two forces also affect Luzhin's *art* – his
approach to chess. In the chess realm the two forces commingle
to create a charged amalgam that stays with Luzhin throughout his life. The grandfather's influence on Luzhin is relatively
straightforward, although mystical in origin. As Boyd notes,
Luzhin's earliest encounters with chess occur in contexts associated with the grandfather's presence. Although the grandfather played chess, his real talent lay in music: he was a
virtuoso violinist and composer. Luzhin's first conscious awareness of chess occurs during a concert of the grandfather's music
held on the anniversary of the man's death; the person who
excites Luzhin with images of chess's "infinite possibilities" is a
violinist who muses, "Combinations like melodies. You know, I
can simply *hear* the moves" (*Df* 43; *ZL* 51). The association of
chess with music becomes a fixed element of Luzhin's subsequent chess experience, and it represents the grandfather's
specific contribution to Luzhin's chess encounters.[10]

The influence of Luzhin Senior on Luzhin Junior's attitude
toward chess is more complex and emotionally potent. To
understand this in full, one must look at the way Luzhin Junior
is initiated into the game. The most striking feature of Luzhin
Junior's exposure to chess is the element of sexuality or
eroticism connected with it. Luzhin first hears of the game from
the violinist in his father's study. Before the violinist speaks to
Luzhin about chess, Luzhin hears the man talking on the
phone to a woman, apparently his mistress. Once the mistress
theme is associated with Luzhin's discovery of chess, it becomes
more pervasive. That night, when Luzhin's mother comes into

his bedroom, he pretends to be asleep and thereby prevents her from caressing him. The very next day, his mother is horrified to discover that her husband has become involved in an illicit affair with her second cousin, and while Luzhin's father tries to reassure her of his fidelity, little Luzhin "stealthily" asks this woman – his aunt – if she will teach him how to play chess.[11]

The scene of Luzhin's first chess lesson contains numerous images of physical contact. For example, after the aunt has arranged the pieces on the board, Luzhin wants to encourage her to continue her instruction: "'now,' said Luzhin and suddenly kissed her hand." His aunt takes note of this uncharacteristic display of affection and says she never expected such "tenderness" from him (*Df* 46; *ZL* 54). Luzhin, who has rebuffed his mother's attempts at intimacy, spontaneously expresses affection toward his aunt. In this, of course, he follows his father's example, and he continues to do so in the days ahead, even skipping school to visit his aunt surreptitiously. This period comes to an end when the school telephones his parents. Although his mother does not know where he has been, she instinctively perceives in his behavior a parallel to her husband's behavior, and she cries to his father: "'He cheats . . . just as you cheat. I'm surrounded by cheats'" (*Df* 53; *ZL* 61).

The point of the connection drawn between sexuality and Luzhin's early fascination with chess is not to affirm some quasi-Freudian hypothesis that Luzhin's impulse to play chess represents a sublimation of his sexual drive, as his manager Valentinov believes (see *Df* 94; *ZL* 103). Rather, the erotic motif alerts the reader to the fact that Luzhin's obsession with chess is a powerful passion which, like any passion in Nabokov's work, leads to destruction when left unchecked. The affair that Luzhin's father conducts with his mistress serves as a model for Luzhin's "affair" with chess, and there is a palpable overlap in the attitudes of father and son toward the object of their obsession. Luzhin Senior's relationship with his mistress fuses irresistible passion with a corrosive awareness of its alarming intensity. A similar complex of emotions develops within Luzhin Junior's passion for chess as well.[12]

Due to these two influences, Nabokov's descriptions of

Luzhin's chess matches contain not only the musical imagery associated with Luzhin's grandfather, but also that blend of dismay and rapture that Luzhin Senior experienced when dealing with his passion for his mistress. This fugal interlacement structures Luzhin's final match with Turati. The description of the match begins with numerous musical images: "At first it went softly, softly, like muted violins ... Then, without the least warning, a chord sang out tenderly" (*Df* 137; *ZL* 147). Soon, this imagery grows more pronounced: "a kind of musical tempest overwhelmed the board and Luzhin searched stubbornly in it for the tiny, clear note that he needed in order in his turn to swell it out into a thunderous harmony" (*Df* 138; *ZL* 149). In these images one perceives the legacy of Luzhin's grandfather.

As the game progresses, however, elements of the father's legacy of emotional ambivalence begin to surface, as in the line: "Luzhin's thought roamed through *entrancing* and *terrible* labyrinths" (*Df* 138, emphasis added; *ZL* 149, in Russian the key epithets are *upoitel'nyi* and *uzhasnyi*). The two opposing registers conjoin and confront Luzhin with their stark irreconcilability when Luzhin burns his hand and experiences his epiphany, realizing: "There was horror in this, but in this also was the sole harmony." Harmony and horror – these are the contrasting squares of Luzhin's chess consciousness, a consciousness molded by the dual influences of his grandfather and father. It is interesting that the "scorching pain" of Luzhin's burn revives an image introduced into the description of Luzhin Senior's first game of chess with his son: confused by the play, Luzhin Senior took his move back, "slowly stretching out his fingers toward the Queen and quickly snatching them away again, *as if burned*" (*Df* 65, emphasis added; *ZL* 73). Applying Boyd's approach, one could speculate that the spirit of Luzhin Senior may have arranged his son's burn during the match with Turati in an effort to make his son realize the dangers of the path he had taken.

The contradictory confluence of forces experienced by Luzhin in his fateful match with Turati resurfaces when Luzhin again hears the siren call of the chess gods while recovering from his breakdown. As he listens to Valentinov's voice near the end of the novel, he re-experiences that wrenching duality of feeling, and the description of his reaction combines images both from the realm of music (the legacy of his grandfather) and from the realm of fatal passion (the legacy of the father). The passage begins: "To the sound of this voice, to the music of the chessboard's evil lure, Luzhin recalled, with the exquisite, moist melancholy peculiar to recollections of love, a thousand games that he had played in the past" (*Df* 246; *ŽL* 257). It continues: "there were tender stirrings in one corner of the board, and a passionate explosion, and the fanfare of the Queen going to its sacrificial doom . . . Everything was wonderful, all the shades of love, all the convolutions and mysterious paths it had chosen. And this love was fatal" (*Df* 246; *ŽL* 258). Both legacies – the grandfather's and the father's – appear in this passage, but the legacy of the closer relative – the father – is perhaps stronger. Studying both the beauty and the peril of his attraction to chess, Luzhin finds the latter more potent, and the passage concludes: "The aim of the attack was plain. By an implacable repetition of moves it was leading once more to that same passion which would destroy the dream of life. Devastation, horror, madness" (*Df* 246; *ŽL* 258). Passion for chess, in Luzhin's view, leads only to horror (*uzhas*) and destruction.

What is fatal here, though, may not be the complex of feelings that swirl within Luzhin, but rather his inability to find an outlet for them. In this, perhaps, one finds the most troubling sign of Luzhin Senior's legacy – an inability or unwillingness to extend himself and to communicate these inner contradictions to a loving other – in both cases, a wife. Boyd argues that Luzhin Junior's wife is sent to him by his father's spirit in an effort to usher the young man into the safe sphere of family life, and the hypothesis is plausible.[13]

Luzhin's fiancée tries to create a secure environment for Luzhin during his recovery from his breakdown. The early stages of his recovery return him to a child-like state, and Luzhin feels so secure that he even begins to review his childhood with fondness (see, for example, *Df* 164; *ŽL* 174–75). Boyd suggests that this type of softening toward the past may indicate a fundamental transformation within Luzhin's psyche, leading ultimately to a reconciliation with his past and particularly with his father in the world beyond death: "From the blank of death, perhaps, he will awaken to a world where the past becomes both his haven, home, defense, *and* the new domain of his art where he can endlessly explore the pattern of time" ("The Problem of Pattern" 600).

This is a very optimistic reading of the conclusion of *The Defense*, and not all readers may accept it. While it is true that Luzhin seems more comfortable with his past, one should note that this degree of comfort is only possible because he holds the past at a considerable remove: "It seemed as though that distant world was unrepeatable; through it roamed the by now completely bearable images of his parents, softened by the haze of time" (*Df* 165; *ZL* 176).[14] While the transformation of life into the radiant realm of timeless art has positive connotations in Nabokov's work, such a transformation proves successful only when it does not seek to escape or ignore the realities of life – its pains as well as its pleasures. Unfortunately, there is no indication that Luzhin can look upon the pains of the past with understanding, nor does he show any inclination to honor the memory of his father with a visit to his grave; indeed, he avoids even this small gesture.

Sadly, Luzhin remains vulnerable to despair in the face of what he perceives to be the inescapable pain of life, and he remains unwilling to share his inner anxiety with his wife. Mrs. Luzhin is partly responsible for Luzhin's isolation. She has impressed upon him her own conviction of the dangers of the chess world. In this she follows the example of Luzhin Senior, who feels ineffectual when confronted with forces beyond his understanding and who chooses to turn away from such difficulties rather than deal with them. Mrs. Luzhin does not understand Luzhin's imaginative world, and she is frightened by it. She therefore tries to channel Luzhin away from his inner reveries by surrounding him with the distractions of the material world. Still, Mrs. Luzhin possesses an abundance of love for Luzhin, and if, as Leona Toker puts it, she "is guided by pity rather than by understanding" (*Nabokov* 75), she remains one of the most sympathetic and positive female figures in Nabokov's *œuvre*.[15] Consequently, Luzhin's repeated rejection of her attempts to comprehend his anguish seems especially heartless.

During the second half of the novel, Luzhin becomes obsessed by his perception that events in his life represent a pattern of recurrence from the period leading up to his mental breakdown. Despite his vigilance in seeking out such patterns, he misses the most tragic repetition of all. His decision to lie to his wife and to conceal from her the corrosive passion gnawing at his soul reproduces the behavioral pattern his father had shown toward *his* wife. This pattern of avoidance or rejection of the other leads to the final isolation of both men.[16]

Luzhin's predicament during the second half of the novel recalls the state afflicting several protagonists in Nabokov's early fiction. He becomes so obsessed with the image of an intangible other that he fails to value properly the tangible others in his environment. Of course, the intangible other in this novel is not an absent love or a dead spouse, but rather an enigmatic entity who has the power to manipulate events in the plane in which Luzhin lives. During the onset of Luzhin's mental breakdown in the first part of the novel, the character had perceived a bifurcation between two worlds: the chess world had seemed to him to be "real" life, while the physical world was merely a dream or shadow world. Now, however, this simplistic dichotomy has collapsed. The external world is no longer an insubstantial shadow realm. Rather, it has become for him the tangible field for a cosmic chess match in which he is both opponent and playing piece. Luzhin experiences life in a manner recalling Baudelaire's vision in the poem "Correspondances": the world has become a "forest of symbols" which observe him "with a familiar gaze." For Luzhin, everything in the world is a material signifier of an immaterial yet oppressive higher consciousness.

Luzhin's perception of an unknown other manipulating events in his life exposes a recurring apprehension in Nabokov's work: the anguish felt by a fictional character when confronted by the specter of the more powerful entity which defines him – the author himself. Franz felt an inexplicable resentment toward the foreign couple he saw at the seaside resort in *King, Queen, Knave*, but his resentment represented only an unconscious reaction to the presence of his creator's surrogate. While Luzhin never realizes that the "other" he senses is actually his author, his perception of the other's influence brings him closer to an authentic understanding of the situation in which he has been placed.[17]

Luzhin also distinguishes himself from Franz in his reaction to the existence of this other who seems to know and define him. He does not slip into a passive state of resentment, but rather attempts to defend himself against the dominion of the other by actively exercising his own powers of imagination. Commenting on Luzhin's behavior, Pekka Tammi declares that the novel presents: "the rare spectacle of a fictive hero trying to 'defeat' his maker by constructing an imaginative structure of his own" (*Problems of Nabokov's Poetics* 143). This declaration may need modification, since Luzhin does not seem to know that it is his "maker" that he is up against. Nonetheless, his behavior does indicate an unconscious aspiration to shed that aspect of his identity which functions as a character and to attain the autonomy and sovereignty of an authentic artist.

Luzhin's resistance to being perceived as a character first emerged when he was a child. His father tended to see him in such terms, for he would connect Luzhin Junior to fictional characters in the inscriptions he wrote in his books: "*I earnestly hope that my son will always treat animals and people the same way as Tony*" and "*I wrote this book thinking of your future, my son*" (*Df* 33; *ZL* 41).[18] At the time, Luzhin Junior reacted to this with a feeling of shame. Yet Luzhin Junior's schoolmates reinforce the association when they call him "Tony" thereafter (*Df* 30; *ZL* 38). Then, when Luzhin is an adult and recovering from his breakdown, he meets an old classmate at an émigré ball. The man again associates Luzhin with a literary character: "Tell me, Luzhin ... Your first name and patronymic? ... Ah, I seem to remember – Tony ... Anton ... What next?" Luzhin responds with a shudder: "You're mistaken" (*Df* 197; *ZL* 209).

He continues to reject any attempt to link his identity with that of a literary character.

The countervailing impulse – to strive for the power of an autonomous creator – is more pronounced in Luzhin's life, showing up, for example, in the pleasure he takes in "reigning" over the chess board (*Df* 134; *ZL* 144). It is here, however, that the basic relationship established between authentic *auctor* and character in *King, Queen, Knave* comes into play. Although Luzhin seeks to prove that he is the equal of his invisible rival, Nabokov employs numerous techniques to underscore the character's deficiencies. *The Defense* is a characteristic Nabokov text in that it exposes the artistic shortcomings of its protagonists while asserting the skill of the author in the same arena.

Although one can point to several episodes that reveal defects in Luzhin's aesthetic capacities,[19] it is instructive to focus on those elements of weakness which can be directly contrasted with his creator's strengths. One such test of artistic proficiency is aesthetic mobility, the ability to glide effortlessly across the linear channels of conventional thought. In his Gogol book Nabokov points out the prominence of dramatic focal shifts in the writer's prose. Suggesting that such shifts have the effect of simultaneously "blurring" the sentence and disclosing a "secret meaning," Nabokov affirms that these shifts form the very basis of Gogol's art (*NG* 140). Yet Nabokov fills his own fiction *The Defense* with wondrous focal shifts of this type: he creates daring leaps in chronology, point of view, and narrative structure.[20]

One example of this mobility should suffice to indicate the tenor of Nabokov's technique. The narrator describes the efforts Luzhin's future wife makes as she tries to find something to talk about with the taciturn Luzhin: "she began to rummage in her handbag, searching agonizingly for a topic and finding only a broken comb" (*Df* 87; *ZL* 97). This is a remarkably facile shift, guiding the reader from the realm of abstract concepts to that of concrete objects in the course of a single sentence. It is representative of the fluidity of Nabokov's discourse in *The Defense* and it serves to highlight a certain affinity between his technique and Gogol's. In "The Overcoat," for example, the narrator states that Akaky Akakievich's absorption with the lines he copied at work was so deep that "it was only if a horse's muzzle, appearing from goodness knows where, would come to rest on his shoulder ... that he would notice that he was not in the middle of a line, but in the middle of the street." Gogol's sentence displays the same ease of transition from one state to another – from the psychological to the physical – that is found in the Nabokov sentence. Both writers aspire to blur the distinctions between physical and psychological "reality," and they use their verbal media to do so.

What, one may ask, is the ultimate point of such bold shifts in *The Defense*? The answer strikes to the core of Nabokov's artistic design. The author orients his art in the realm of the human consciousness, exploring the way the individual consciousness perceives and orders experience. In *The Defense* his elaborate narrative shifts expose the fundamental difference between the relatively limited perspectives of his characters and the relatively unlimited perspective of that other which surrounds and gives life to the characters – the author himself. Nabokov's art celebrates a freedom of movement in consciousness that is inaccessible to his invented characters.[21] The ease with which the narrator of *The Defense* floats over the boundaries of time and space forms a sharp contrast with the way Luzhin desperately dashes to and fro at the end of the novel. The character's frantic shifts in movement and intention represent a pathetic parody of the elegant shifts discernible within his creator's discourse.

Nabokov asserts in his Gogol study that great art skirts the irrational, but it is precisely the irrational that terrifies Luzhin. As a consequence, he suffers both as an artist and as a man. As the narrative indicates, a central defect in Luzhin's artistic aspirations is the gradual calcification of his imagination (see *Df* 97; *ZL* 106). Once an original strategist, he has become increasingly rigid over the course of his life. In highlighting this process of increasing rigidity Nabokov utilizes another technique which also underscores Luzhin's essential status as literary character: the manipulation of literary subtexts to connect his hero with previous figures in Russian literature. Again, it is Gogol who provides a forerunner for Nabokov's conception of Luzhin. *The Defense* contains distinct echoes of Gogol's story "The Portrait," from the appearance of a strange portrait with mysterious powers to a pointed commentary in each text on how the protagonist's artistic originality has atrophied into well-worn, conventional patterns.[22]

Through these techniques Nabokov flaunts the control that he as author exerts over his creation Luzhin. While several critics have discussed the relationship between author and character in terms of the chess imagery which pervades the novel,[23] the text presents another image that encapsulates the aesthetic relationship between the creator and his creation – the image of pictorial framing. At least two incidents occur in the novel in which actual or imagined scenes are transformed into framed pictures. Before running away from his parents in chapter 1, Luzhin Junior sees "a small girl . . . on an enormous bale eating a green apple, her elbow propped in her palm" (*Df* 20; *ZL* 28). This scene reappears as an oil painting in the entranceway to the apartment of Luzhin's future in-laws: "A village girl in a red kerchief coming down to her eyebrows was eating an apple" (*Df* 119; *ZL* 129). Likewise, Luzhin Senior's dream of his son as a musical *Wunderkind* described in chapter 2 (*Df* 25; *ZL* 33) becomes transformed into a woodcut in the bedroom of Luzhin Junior and his wife (*Df* 174; *ZL* 185). The image of framing is also evoked in a declaration by Luzhin's fiancée that before the couple can be married, they must "hang on the wall" for two weeks. In other words, their intention to marry must be officially displayed (*Df* 172; *ZL* 182–83). Later, their future apartment is characterized as the "frame" for her mother's mental picture of their sexual life (*Df* 172; *ZL* 183).

To what end does Nabokov include these images of pictures and framing? In each case one finds an example of "real" or imagined activity being transformed into frozen aesthetic objects. In part, this transformation parodies the aspiration of both Luzhin Senior and Luzhin Junior to reduce unruly life into neat, circumscribed frameworks.[24] At the same time, the device reminds the reader of the dominion of the authorial consciousness over the world of the novel. From the point of view of the author and reader, the only distinction between the scenes perceived by Luzhin Junior or Luzhin Senior and the pictorial representations of these scenes hanging on the wall of the characters' apartments is the *degree* of fictionality they display: all are the fictive creations of a human author.

It is also important to realize that the transformation of "life" into "art" gains impetus over the course of the novel. This is often the case in Nabokov's fiction. As his characters become more desperate to resist the influence of the mysterious "other" they perceive around them, the authorial consciousness becomes increasingly overt in making its presence known. In *The Defense* this is accomplished both through the increasing density of patterns of recurrence and through the steady transformation of animate scenes into inanimate pictorial representations.

Given the increasingly overt nature of the author's demonstration of control over Luzhin's life, one may question whether Luzhin's attempts to escape the moves of the invisible other will lead him to a harmonious afterlife. The evidence of Luzhin's final vision is ambiguous at best. Just as he is about to release his grip on the window sill and fall to his death, he experiences a revelatory sight: "the whole chasm was seen to divide into dark and pale squares, and at the instant when Luzhin unclenched his hand ... he saw exactly what kind of eternity was obligingly and inexorably spread out before him" (*Df* 256; *ZL* 266). Whether this vision promises entrance into a world where Luzhin's creative fancy can roam unfettered, or whether, on the contrary, it heralds his imprisonment in a realm of circumscribed maneuvers remains a matter for readers to debate. Nonetheless, both the starkness of Luzhin's perception, and the sardonic tones in which it is conveyed (for example, "obligingly and inexorably"), contrast sharply with the triumphant experience depicted at the end of *Invitation to a Beheading*. Whereas Cincinnatus casts off the shackles of those who try to circumscribe his moves and then strides purposefully toward a realm of beings akin to him, Luzhin gazes at an afterworld filled only with a vast chessboard pattern.[25] No matter what the outcome, it is clear that *within* the world of the novel, Luzhin's encounter with the invisible other whose will predefines him has crushed his spirit. His feeble attempts to escape the influence of the other result in tragic destruction. Subsequent Nabokov protagonists will attempt more elaborate maneuvers to evade the influence of the other, whether that other is physically present or not. Their striving for autonomy takes on ever more startling and unusual forms.

Luzhin embodies a particularly interesting stage in the evolution of Nabokov's visionary heroes. On the one hand, his perception of a cosmic chess opponent seems to be generated by the collapse of an overwrought psyche. An obsessive chess strategist, he projects onto an untidy world the more structured designs of a chess match. Since he fears everyday life, the image he conjures up is a threatening one. On the other hand, his perception of the influence of an intangible intellect in his world is not just a mad delusion; it displays a tantalizing apprehension of authentic reality. However, he has misinterpreted the specific nature of this higher power. Locked into the psychology of chess maneuvers, he can only imagine the entity in terms of chess, and thus he plunges to his death without discovering his true ontological status.[26]

Nabokov's works in the late 1920s indicate the writer's increasing interest in the consequences of transforming the external world according to the dictates of inner vision. The first characters to experience a full-scale perceptual transformation – the narrator of "Terror" and Luzhin – find the experience horrifying. As Nabokov explored the process further, though, he began to probe the implications suggested earlier in Anton Petrovich's escapist fantasies: that one's imagination might transform the world into a more harmonious and congenial realm. In this next stage, represented by works such as *The Eye* and *Despair*, we find a further evolution in the depiction of the relationship between the self and the other. As Nabokov's characters become more self-serving in their visionary transformation of the world, they become more narcissistic and eager to minimize their vulnerability to the opinions or control of others. The insecurity evident in such characters as

Luzhin or Anton Petrovich returns in Nabokov's next works, but the protagonists' response to their perception of the other's influence changes dramatically. Nabokov's subsequent protagonists employ unprecedented strategies in their attempt to establish their sovereign independence from the other.

CHAPTER 4

A fondness for the mask

THE EYE

With the publication of *The Eye* in 1930, Nabokov's work embarks upon a new direction. Elaborating on the situation he treated in *The Defense*, where the central character's obsession with the other was less a matter of desire than of fear, Nabokov explores in *The Eye* and again in *Despair* the ways in which creative individuals attempt to cope with their anxiety about the power of others to evaluate or define them. Like certain of Dostoevsky's heroes, Nabokov's protagonists look to others for validation in self-definition, yet they fear others precisely because the others possess this defining power. To utilize a concept Mikhail Bakhtin articulated in reference to Dostoevsky's work, these characters long to retain for themselves "the final word" about themselves and their identities (*Problems* 43). Nabokov's works in this period resonate with Dostoevskian subtexts. Although Nabokov had grave reservations about the aesthetic qualities of Dostoevsky's art, the latter's early work offers penetrating treatments of psychological situations that now engage Nabokov's own attention.

In "Terror" Nabokov depicted for the first time a character's trepidation when confronted with the abstract notion of "other" as such. *The Defense* developed this theme further, providing a concentrated view of one man's fear of an abstract, invisible other. With *The Eye* and *Despair* Nabokov depicts two related responses to this basic fear. In each work an autobiographic intrinsic narrator tries to defend himself against the threat of others by wresting control of the levers of creation: he

attempts to "author" himself and the others in his world. These
narrators hope to actualize the aphorism discussed by Steven
Kellman in "The Fiction of Self-Begetting": "*scribo, ergo sum*"
(1248).

The narrator of *The Eye* takes the preliminary step in this
venture. A deeply insecure individual, he attempts to defend
himself against the potentially damaging evaluations of others
by creating a fictitious alter ego, although he never acknowledges the degree of artifice involved in his vision. His account
of the experience divides into three parts. In the first section he
describes his life as an émigré in Berlin, and he exposes the
salient character traits that motivate the subsequent events of
the novel. These traits are a pervasive insecurity about how
others perceive him, and an obsession with self-observation. He
notes the "humiliating constraint" he feels in the presence of
the two boys with whom he lives as a tutor (*E* 13; *S* 5), and he
laments his propensity for watching himself: "I was always
exposed, always wide-eyed; even in sleep I did not cease to
watch over myself, understanding nothing of my existence,
growing crazy at the thought of not being able to stop being
aware of myself, and envying all those simple people – clerks,
revolutionaries, shopkeepers – who, with confidence and concentration, go about their little jobs" (*E* 17; *S* 8). The envy
which the narrator articulates here echoes the emotions
expressed by Dostoevsky's underground man when the latter
confesses to experiencing bilious envy over the "spontaneous
man – the real, normal man" (*Notes* 96; pt. 1, ch. 3) as opposed
to men of "heightened consciousness," such as he, who are
paralyzed by the inertia of self-analysis (*Notes* 102; pt. 1, ch. 5).

The narrator's extreme self-consciousness suffers a crushing
blow when his mistress's husband thrashes him under the
implacable gaze of his two young charges, a gaze that the
narrator mentions several times in his account of the incident
(see *E* 22, 24, 26; *S* 12, 14, 16). This moment of humiliation
leads him to a shocking external view of himself: "A wretched,
shivering, vulgar little man in a bowler hat stood in the center
of the room, for some reason rubbing his hands. That is the
glimpse I caught of myself in the mirror" (*E* 27; *S* 16). As in

"Terror" the mirror scene is associated with a profound element of dissociation. In the earlier work, the narrator simply could not connect what he saw in the mirror with his own sense of inner self. Here, the narrator is shocked by the external image he sees in the mirror. He intuitively seeks to dissever himself from that image and, if possible, to eradicate it. Thus he rushes to his old apartment and shoots himself.[1]

The second portion of the novel recounts the narrator's impressions of existence after he has supposedly killed himself. All the people he encounters are, according to him, merely figments of his consciousness which has survived his death. A major part of this experience consists of cataloguing various opinions about a certain figure named Smurov who, the reader gradually realizes, is none other than the narrator himself. The final portion of the novel depicts the apparent reintegration of the narrator and Smurov, but this new union does not represent a precise return to the psychological state which opens the novel. On the contrary, the lack of true integration between the narratorial consciousness and the external image of Smurov continues in a new and perhaps even more debilitating form.

It is ironic, though, that the narrator's suicide attempt does not bring an end to the extreme self-consciousness he laments in the opening section. On the contrary, it liberates his penchant for self-observation, only in a new, more distanced form. The narrator's gunshot wound plays a role analogous to Mark Standfuss's accident in "Details of a Sunset." The physical trauma stimulates his creative vision and leads to a state of bifurcation between the realm of inner consciousness (the narrating "I") and the experiences his physical form (Smurov) undergoes in the outside world.

In setting the stage for the process of bifurcation depicted in *The Eye*, Nabokov may have drawn inspiration from Dostoevsky's novella *The Double*, which he regarded as Dostoevsky's best piece (*LRL* 100), even terming it "a perfect work of art" (*LRL* 104). In *The Double*, as in *The Eye*, the main character is an insecure individual who experiences a sensation of doubling after a moment of intense public humiliation. In a passage that anticipates the narrator's self-destructive gesture in *The Eye*, the narrator of *The Double* says of his protagonist after the moment of humiliation: "Golyadkin had been killed – actually killed in the full sense of the word, and if he at this moment preserved the ability to run, it was only through some kind of miracle" (*Polnoe sobranie* 1: 138; the translation is mine). It is immediately after this impression of being killed that Golyadkin begins seeing his double.

One can identify several points of correspondence between Dostoevsky's Golyadkin and Nabokov's narrator,[2] but what is more important than these points of correspondence is a crucial difference between the two – their attitude toward their projected doubles. For Golyadkin, the perception of a double is primarily a source of torment and anguish: he feels his place in society preempted by a more clever and skillful alter ego. For the narrator of *The Eye*, however, the perception of a double is a source of potential enjoyment. He hopes to savor the successes of his alter ego without suffering any negative repercussions.

Even in this, however, Nabokov may have expanded upon the traces of a strategy devised by Golyadkin when he sought to buffer himself against the judgments of others. Startled by an embarrassing encounter with one of his superiors, he wonders: "should I pretend that this is not I, but someone else who looks remarkably like me, and act as if there's nothing going on? Exactly: it's not I, not I, and that's all there is to it!" (*Polnoe sobranie* 1: 113). Later, he attempts to forestall further embarrassment by a variant of the same strategy: "I'll be an outside observer, and that'll be the end of it ... whatever happens there, it's not I who's guilty" (*Polnoe sobranie* 1: 223). This is precisely the tack that the narrator of *The Eye* pursues in his post-suicide state. By detaching himself from the externalized figure of Smurov, he can cloak himself in an air of non-involvement or non-responsibility. Moreover, once he has created this external surrogate, the narrator can project onto the figure any identity or background he finds appealing. By "finalizing" Smurov himself, he hopes to preempt any denigrating finalization by others.

Of course, a central source of irony in the novel is the degree to which others *do* finalize Smurov, and the degree to which the narrator's claim of objective disinterest crumbles before the impact of these independent views. The middle portion of the novel consists of a series of oscillations in which the narrator's positive perception of Smurov is overturned by a disillusioning contact with reality. Each setback spurs the narrator to try to generate a new, positive image once again. Evaluating these oscillations, D. Barton Johnson notes that the psychological distance between the narrator and Smurov varies according to the quality of the reflected image of Smurov: when the image is positive (in the narrator's eyes), the psychological distance is large; when the reflected image is negative, the distance shrinks (see "Eyeing" 335). Johnson's observation is accurate, but it merits further qualification. The reflected image of Smurov seems most positive when it is most removed from "reality" (for example Smurov as military hero in Yalta, Smurov as Vanya's beloved), and seems most negative when authentic reality irrupts into the fantasy. Any encroachment of reality upon the narrator's fantasy jeopardizes his illusions and confronts him with the disturbing truth about a self-image that he is trying to flee.[3]

Over the course of the novel, the oscillations in the narrator's relationship toward Smurov become more exaggerated and uncontrolled, reaching a climax when the narrator finds Vanya alone on her balcony and declares his love for her. Here he effectively takes over the role he had earlier projected for his surrogate – that of Vanya's successful suitor. His attempt, of course, meets with a resounding rejection. The narrator's momentary fusion with the role he had projected for Smurov, coupled with Vanya's inevitable rejection of his advances, diminishes the distance between the narrator and Smurov to zero, and it brings the narrator face to face with that very reality he has been trying to avoid since his initial suicide attempt.[4] The very next scene provides a visual emblem of the reunification of the narrator with his externalized projection. After leaving Vanya's apartment, the narrator passes a mirror in the entrance to a flower shop. He recalls: "I noticed the reflection in the side mirror: a young man in a derby carrying a bouquet, hurried toward me. That reflection and I merged into one. I walked out into the street" (*E* 107; *S* 82). The act of self-observation in a mirror here echoes the initial episode of self-observation discussed above (*E* 27; *S* 16). Yet although the narrator is visually rejoined with his physical alter ego Smurov, this reunification does not indicate an authentic acceptance and reintegration of the original self. On the contrary, the narrator resists the restoration of physical reality. He returns to the room where he shot himself, finds the mark left by the bullet he fired, and declares that this mark is the proof that he had really died. Immediately, he says, the world regains its "reassuring insignificance" and he is ready now to evoke "the most fearsome shade from my former existence" (*E* 109; *S* 83).

Through this recreation of the initial suicide attempt the narrator works a further metamorphosis in his relationship to himself, and he arrives at a fresh strategy for defending himself against debilitating encounters with others. This new strategy is revealed when he confronts that "most fearsome shade" – the irate husband who had thrashed him at the outset of the novel. This man, identified now as Kashmarin, accosts the narrator, addresses him as Smurov, and offers him a promising lead for a job. Yet the narrator refuses to be moved by Kashmarin's kindness. Instead, he asserts: "Kashmarin had borne away yet another image of Smurov. Does it make any difference which? For I do not exist: there exist but the thousands of mirrors that reflect me . . . Somewhere they live, somewhere they multiply. I alone do not exist. Smurov, however, will live on for a long time" (*E* 112–13; *S* 86).[5]

This assertion reveals an entirely new approach to the potential difficulties of life. Previously the narrator had claimed that he was the creator of the world in which he appeared to live, and that everyone else, including Smurov, was merely an illusion created by him. Now, however, he takes the opposite tack. He claims that it is he alone who does *not* exist, and that what truly exist are only the multiple images of Smurov. He suggests that his "existence" consists only of external masks and that there is no authentic, immanent core to his being.[6]

The name Kashmarin rings with a certain irony here. The name itself is derived from the Russian word for "nightmare" (*koshmar*). On the surface, it would appear that this Kashmarin has become a benign figure, and that the nightmare has been stripped of its terrors. In actuality, however, the light "dream" (*mechta*) with which his post-suicide fantasy began, a dream in which Vanya was attainable "at your dream's disposal, your dream-cornered prey" (*E* 39; *S* 26), has turned into a true nightmare in which the narrator has cut himself off from all meaningful contact with those around him. He has stepped into an emotional void.

The last lines of his narrative, however, contain an unexpected revelation about the narrator's orientation toward the other. Having expressed his indifference to what others may think of Smurov, he suddenly discloses a fresh concern for the opinions of a different kind of other – not one who lives in the immediate world of the novel's characters, but someone who stands outside the text – its disembodied reader. He exclaims: "I am happy – yes, happy! What more can I do to prove it, how to proclaim that I am happy? Oh, to shout it *so that all of you believe me* at last, *you cruel, smug people*" (*E* 114, emphasis added; *S* 87). This Dostoevskian outburst is the first moment in the novel when the narrator evinces an awareness of an outside audience, and it represents a masterstroke on the part of Nabokov, the real author. After apparently devising a strategy to ensure his invulnerability against the potential insults of his *visible* world ("The world, try as it may, cannot insult me. I am invulnerable" [*E* 114; *S* 87]), the narrator now displays a fresh anxiety over the judgments of those who live in an *invisible* world, the world of his reader.

With this shift of focus from the diegetic to the extradiegetic world, Nabokov redirects *his* readers' attention from the dynamics of story to issues of literary creativity. He now encourages the reader to consider the narrator's creation of an alter ego in a fresh light – not only as a strategy for deflecting the attacks of others onto an external surrogate, but also as a way of gaining power and autonomy for himself by assuming a new role – that of author.[7]

The narrator's sudden address to his anonymous audience,

together with a remark he makes about his "literary gift," challenges the reader to return to the narrative to evaluate the narrator's artistic expertise. Although critics have commented on the link between the narrator's fantasy and the workings of artistic creation since the novel's first appearance (see, for example, Weidle's review in 1930), they have not analyzed the narrator's authorial aspirations in the context of his relationship to two specific "others" – his creation Smurov, and his creator the authentic *auctor*. While one can measure the narrator's artistic competence in terms of such issues as perceptual acuity and originality of artistic inspiration, one must examine the narrator's relationship to these two crucial others in order to arrive at a proper evaluation of his authorial strivings.[8]

The narrator's creation of Smurov represents an important development in that fundamental bifurcation of identity noted earlier in Nabokov's work. To actualize their authorial potential, Nabokov's protagonists must shed that aspect of the self which functions as a character. The narrator's vision of a post-suicide existence displays just such an attempt at divestment. Reserving for his inner consciousness the powers of authorial creator over those around him, he creates the externalized surrogate of Smurov and assigns to him certain attributes of a literary character, such as a fictional pre-history and the capacity to be defined by outside interpreters.[9] His attitude toward Smurov is like that of a nervous author agonizing over the public response to his creation: he assiduously collects and catalogues all the various "readings" of his creation. Of course, by giving new life to Smurov as a created character, the narrator also hopes to give new life to himself as an author too. Thinking of Smurov as the narrator's "work," one could apply Heidegger's affirmation: "The artist is the origin of the work. The work is the origin of the artist" ("The Origin of the Work of Art" 17).

As he collects the various readings of his surrogate's personality, the narrator encounters the same type of polarity that occurred in "An Affair of Honor," where Anton Petrovich was flanked by two contrasting potential identities – the daring Berg and the ineffectual Leontiev. The narrator finds a similar duality in Smurov's latent identity too. On the one hand he imagines (in notably florid and hyperbolic terms) that Smurov is "capable, in a moment of wrath, of slashing a chap into bits, and, in a moment of passion, of carrying a frightened and perfumed girl beneath his cloak . . . to a waiting boat" (*E* 46; *S* 32). On the other hand, he reads in Roman Bogdanovich's letter that Smurov is a "sexual lefty" incapable of a physical relationship with a woman (*E* 94; *S* 70). The narrator himself is torn between these two potentials – he longs to be the former, but fears the perception that he may be the latter (thus he dreams of Smurov wearing a fur coat with a "feminine collar" and with hands bedecked in rings; *E* 96; *S* 73).[10]

If the narrator indeed seeks to achieve a new identity as authorial creator by fashioning an externalized, fictitious alter ego, how successful is he in this endeavor? Andrew Field is willing to consider the possibility that the narrator's evident confusion masks his ultimate genius (*Life in Art* 171), while Susan Fromberg Schaeffer finds the narrator very skillful in his attempt to replay and redeem his difficult past ("The Editing Blinks" 9–28). On balance, however, the evidence suggests that the narrator achieves less success than he himself would like, and one can point to several specific traits of his creative product to bolster this opinion.

In addition to the deficiency in perceptual skills noted above, one of the narrator's most glaring defects is his failure to maintain the illusion of separation between himself and his creation Smurov. Unlike Nabokov, who insisted upon a rigid distinction between himself and his fictional representatives (see, for example, his proclamation that he is not Fyodor Godunov-Cherdyntsev in *The Gift*, *G* 9), the narrator often encounters a blurring of boundaries between himself and his imagined alter ego. He cannot maintain his detachment from his projection; his own personality and emotions bleed into the figure of his externalized creation.[11] In the end, the distinction between Smurov and the narrator collapses altogether. When Kashmarin hails the narrator as Smurov, he accepts the designation. He has lost the will to sustain the illusion that Smurov is a physical entity separate from himself.

The narrator's inability to supply Smurov with a vital, independent identity highlights his shortcomings as a creator. As in other Nabokov works, the would-be artist's own inadequacy finds a powerful counter in the prowess of the authentic artist who has created him. The text of *The Eye* represents a major advance over a similar design evident in *The Defense*, for here, Nabokov utilizes the narrator's very own *discourse* to indict his character. *The Eye* represents the most accomplished example thus far of a dual-voiced narrative mode, in which the fictional narrator's discourse unwittingly conveys the authentic *auctor*'s message along with his own. This covert message undermines the very message the narrator wishes to promote.

One could point to several examples of such divergent messages embedded within the narrator's discourse. Perhaps the most significant of these revolves around the issue of authorship itself. While the narrator seeks to demonstrate that he is an autonomous center of consciousness, the creator of the world described in his discourse, his activities signal his true status as fictional character, one who is dependent on others for inspiration and life itself. For example, the long tale of military valor which he ascribes to Smurov is stitched together from elements lifted from the works of Lermontov and Pushkin.[12] By having Smurov relate activities experienced by literary characters of the past, the narrator both exposes his own derivative imagination and accentuates Smurov's (and his own) kinship with the fictional creations of others.[13]

The narrator's naive introduction of literary antecedents into *The Eye* serves as one technique which points to his essential status as a literary character, but Nabokov also utilizes other, more unusual techniques to stress the fictional status of his narrator. One of the most striking features of *The Eye*, in fact, is the degree to which the narrative itself points to the fictional essence of the characters it presents. In several places, the appearance of one character seems to be generated out of the discourse of another. This process may be expected in the case of the narrator's relationship to Smurov. After the narrator has speculated that Smurov "was obviously a person who ... concealed a fiery spirit" (*E* 46; *S* 32), it is no surprise that

Smurov would later narrate an action-packed tale of his heroic
exploits during the Russian Civil War.

Even more noteworthy, though, is the fact that this process
occurs with *other* characters too. In several places the words of
one character conjure up the life or conduct of another. The
narrator's lover Matilda initially describes her husband as a
"savagely jealous" man who would beat his rivals and was
"beautiful in his cruelty." The narrator comments on how he
found it difficult to reconcile the "*image she created* of her
husband" with the figure he had met, but that he could
imagine the man "acting the banal *role* assigned to him by his
wife" (*E* 16–17, emphasis added; *S* 7–8. The last phrase does
not appear in the Russian original.) Soon, this very figure
appears, and acts out the precise scenario narrated by his wife
and contemplated by the narrator.[14]

The subsequent metamorphosis of this fierce husband into a
benign benefactor may also be prompted by another's words.
Roman Bogdanovich tells of an acquaintance named Kashmarin who once thrashed a man nearly to death out of
jealousy. Hearing the details of the story, the reader recognizes
that this Kashmarin is Matilda's husband. Roman Bogdanovich further states, however, that although Kashmarin was an
"extremely rough and quick-tempered fellow," he "did cool off
fast and was kind in his own way" (*E* 46; *S* 31). This latter
characterization then comes true at the end of the novel when
the narrator encounters Kashmarin and finds him generous
and apologetic.

Of all the examples of "spontaneous generation" found in
The Eye, perhaps the most dramatic is a figure whose sudden
entrance into and departure from the narrative mark him as an
authorial agent – Vanya's Uncle Pasha. The first mention of
Uncle Pasha occurs when the narrator searches Vanya's apartment for clues about her feelings for Smurov. He finds an
envelope lying on the table "like an old useless mother," and
the sheet it contained "seemed to be sitting up like a robust
babe." Scanning its contents, he remarks with dismay, "The
letter was from a person unknown to me, a certain Uncle
Pasha. It contained not a single allusion to Smurov! And if it

was coded, then I did not know the key" (*E* 68; *S* 49–50). Truly, the narrator does not understand the coded significance of this letter. The sole purpose of the letter is to give birth to "a robust babe" – the character of Uncle Pasha.

Once born from the verbal medium of the letter, Uncle Pasha grows to assume a major, if fleeting, significance in the narrator's life.[15] He arrives in Berlin "unexpectedly," and then turns up even more unexpectedly in the waiting room of a doctor visited by the narrator on the day after Pasha's arrival. The narrator comments: "On the following day occurred one of those coincidences involving new arrivals that for some reason are so frequent, as if there existed some tasteless prankish Fate not unlike Weinstock's Abum who, on the very day you return home from a journey, has you meet the man who had chanced to be sitting opposite you in the railway car" (*E* 72; *S* 53). The narrator's reference to "tasteless prankish Fate" reminds one of the figure of "Fate" in *King, Queen, Knave* who had sent the Inventor in pursuit of Franz. The narrator's subsequent reference to meeting the man "who had chanced to be sitting opposite you in the railway car" reinforces the association, for Franz had just such an encounter in the earlier novel.

Although he himself refers to the concept of "Fate," the narrator seems unaware of the true significance of Uncle Pasha in his world. Pasha exists not merely to provide the narrator with the most positive image of Smurov – Smurov as happy bridegroom; Nabokov could have achieved the same result by using a more enduring character in the novel. On the contrary, the very artificiality of Pasha's arrival and disappearance (which the narrator himself characterizes as "magical" *E* 78; compare *S* 58) marks him as an authorial agent like prankish Fate, and it signals the presence of a calculating consciousness that orders phenomena in the fictional world.[16]

In some respects, the narrator of *The Eye* seems less perceptive than his predecessor Luzhin, for he, unlike Luzhin, does not detect the influence of a more powerful other manipulating events in his world, although signs of such manipulation are evident to the attentive reader.[17] On the other hand, he is acutely aware of the potential of external others to define him, and he seeks, like Luzhin, to thwart the others' power of definition through the preemptive exercise of his own creative power. Luzhin's attempt to defend himself against the influence of the other led him to commit suicide. Ironically, it is the narrator's own urge to commit suicide that leads to his creative breakthrough in *The Eye*. His "suicide" spurs him to posit an imaginative defense against the threatening influence of others in his world. Yet he too, like Luzhin, proves unable to sustain his defensive illusion, and the causes of his failure are similar to those which befell Luzhin. Both men are unable to distinguish properly between internal and external reality, and thus neither can construct an imaginative world that will not be susceptible to the vagaries of external events.[18] What is more, since both characters are beset by a fundamental fear of the influence of others, neither is able to find a channel of meaningful interaction with those around them, and thus they are doomed to wander in a maze of distorted projections and deceptive reflections.

Given the narrator's difficulty in dealing with others, it is illuminating to examine his attempt to create a fictional alter ego from the standpoint of a literary theoretician whose work foregrounds issues of dialogism and the other in the process of creation – Mikhail Bakhtin. Bakhtin's early essay "Author and Hero in Aesthetic Activity" (written circa 1920–23) provides an interesting perspective on the narrator's endeavor in *The Eye*. In this essay Bakhtin expounds the theory that when an author creates a literary hero, the very process of creating the *other* serves as a means of defining the *self*. As he articulates it: "The artist's struggle for a defined and stable image of the hero is to a large degree a struggle with himself" (8). Commenting on Bakhtin, David Patterson writes: "The role of the hero, in short, is to bring the author to life" (*Literature and Spirit* 82).

According to Bakhtin's essay, aesthetic creation is essentially a two-stage process. In the first stage the author must step outside himself and achieve a state of identification with his hero. In the second stage, he must return to his own place and give completed form to the material gleaned in the identification process. In *The Eye* the narrator's evolving relationship to his alter ego Smurov can be analyzed according to this scheme. The first stage occurs when the narrator originally creates the Smurov persona and then attempts to discover his underlying identity (or, to use the narrator's term, "to dig up the true Smurov" [*E* 64; *S* 47]). This process occupies the central part of the novel. The second stage – the "return to one's self" – occurs when the narrator suspends his investigative activity and re-merges with his external image. A closer examination of this process should elucidate these stages.

Bakhtin declares at the outset of his discussion that the author "must stand outside himself, to experience himself not on the same plane in which we actually experience our life ... he must become an *other* in relation to himself, to look at himself with the eyes of an other" (16). He states that this is particularly important when the hero coincides with the author in life, "that is when he is in essence autobiographical" (16). This is precisely the situation that prevails in *The Eye*, where the ostensible "author" (the narrator) and his hero (Smurov) are one and the same. Thus, the narrator seems to achieve an important preliminary step when he stands back and looks at himself from the outside, as if looking at another.[19]

Once he has taken up this outside perspective, the narrator is ready to begin the first stage of aesthetic activity proper. Describing the process of aesthetic contemplation at large, Bakhtin attempts to lay out the necessary ingredients to achieve a truly "aesthetic" position. He states that if one wishes to experience and to "complete" (*zavershit'*) someone observed outside oneself, one must begin with identification (*vzhivanie*): "I must experience – see and learn – that which he experiences, I must put myself in his place, and coincide with him" (24). This identification process is evident in numerous passages in *The Eye*. The narrator often tells the reader what Smurov's inner experience must be ("Yes, he must be a former officer, a daredevil who liked to flirt with death, and it is only out of modesty that he says nothing about his adventures" *E* 45; *S* 31). At the same time, however, one must recognize that these passages reveal a certain insincerity on the part of the narrator.

He does not really want to uncover (or to reveal) what Smurov has experienced and felt, for he himself knows that Smurov's authentic experience has been humiliating. To identify with Smurov, then, means to identify with himself, and this is something he cannot bear. Thus, the narrator does not really complete the process of authentic "identification" that is the necessary first stage of aesthetic activity. This is highly ironic, since the narrator and Smurov are one and the same. Nonetheless, as a would-be author, the narrator fails to achieve a state of common experience with his hero, and thus is left only with a series of half-finished masks and false identities.[20]

Having only partially fulfilled the first stage of aesthetic activity, the narrator utterly fails to complete the second as well. According to Bakhtin, "the aesthetic activity begins, properly speaking, when we return into ourselves ... and begin to give form and completion to the material of identification" (26). Far from returning to himself and then giving "form and completion" to Smurov's experience, however, the narrator first seems to merge with him, and then loses interest in him. The merger occurs on the psychological plane when he usurps Smurov's place as Vanya's suitor during the scene on her balcony, and it finds physical confirmation when he merges with his external mirror image outside the florist's shop.

From the Bakhtinian perspective, however, what is more troubling than the narrator's failure to "return" to a position distinct from his created hero is his refusal to give "completion" to Smurov's identity. Indeed, the narrator professes a complete lack of interest in his supposed creation. As he says of his encounter with Kashmarin: "Kashmarin had borne away yet another image of Smurov. *Does it make any difference which?*" (*E* 112–13, emphasis added; *S* 86). His failure to give completion to the Smurov character means that Smurov is doomed to remain a fragmented, diffuse entity. Of course, by failing to give *Smurov* an integral identity as a character, he fails to give *himself* an integral identity as an author as well. Thus he too is doomed to remain in a state of fragmentation. He himself seems to suggest this when he comments: "I do not exist: there exist but the thousands of mirrors that reflect me" (*E* 113; *S* 86).

Bina Freiwald aptly sums up the narrator's haunting insubstantiality when she remarks that the "detective-story plot line" concerning the identity of Smurov is resolved, but the "epistemological query" of the narrator's identity "progresses toward dispersion, plurality, and absence" ("A Pliable Reality" 116–17).

From the point of view of Bakhtin's theory, then, the narrator's failure to complete his character Smurov represents a serious flaw in his attempt to attain authorial status. Bakhtin, however, later modified his views on the importance of the author providing his character with a finalizing, transgredient response. In his 1929 study *Problems of Dostoevsky's Poetics* he suggests that Dostoevsky's innovative strength lay in his willingness to leave to his characters their "independence, inner freedom, unfinalizedness and indeterminacy" (51). Yet even under this new standard the narrator's treatment of Smurov exhibits serious shortcomings. His failure to finalize Smurov does not imply that he has conferred upon Smurov genuine autonomy or a voice of his own. The open-ended quality of his portrait of Smurov derives not from its richness and depth but rather from its sketchiness and fragmentedness. The resulting portrait is quite different from Nabokov's own handling of his characters. While on the one hand Nabokov provides each of his protagonists with a specific, well-defined personality, in his finest works – *Invitation to a Beheading*, *The Gift*, *Lolita*, *Pale Fire* – he also endows his protagonists with a stimulating complexity and open-endedness that invite the reader to engage them further.

What then, has the narrator of *The Eye* achieved at the end of his narrative? The suspension of his quest to find out what others think about Smurov represents the cessation of even his minimal and oblique mechanism for engaging in a dialogue with those around him. He claims to have discovered that "the only happiness in this world is . . . to be nothing but a big, slightly vitreous, somewhat bloodshot, unblinking eye" (*E* 113; compare *S* 86–87), but this condition of passive watchfulness seems sterile and empty. One recalls that the narrator of "Terror" felt horror when he discovered that he was "no longer a man, but a naked eye, an aimless glance moving in an absurd world" (*TD* 120; *VCh* 203. See also the poem "Oculus" *PP* 101). To be nothing more than an observer, devoid of genuine human interaction, is to die spiritually and to be imprisoned in a solipsistic void, stripped of identity, meaning, life. The narrator himself seems to sense this when he suddenly turns to his invisible audience and says: "Oh, to shout it so that all of you believe me at last, you cruel, smug people." Having rebuffed the attentions of those around him, he still has an instinctual craving for external validation.

At the end of *The Eye* the narrator has neither succeeded in creating a new, life-affirming identity as an autonomous center of creative consciousness nor managed to enter into relation-ships of mutual understanding with others. He is, in short, trapped in a kind of emotional limbo. He longs either for the ability to stand on his own, or for acceptance by someone outside the borders of his self, but he lacks the means to attain either of these ends. His situation represents a nuanced evolu-tion from the state of stark horror felt by the narrator of "Terror" or Luzhin in *The Defense*. It points the way toward the restless striving of Hermann Karlovich, who will respond to the failure of one attempt at gaining authorial status by a series of other attempts, each of which is doomed to fail as well. A way out of the existential impasse glimpsed in *The Eye* and explored in *Despair* is not discovered by the protagonists of Nabokov's major novels until *Invitation to a Beheading* and *The Gift*, where the protagonists learn to nurture the spark of authentic artistry within themselves and thereby light a path out of the desolation of the insular ego. *The Eye* is a remarkable work, rich in ambiguity and allusiveness. It provides a sugges-tive framework from which Nabokov's subsequent fiction takes its unique shape.

LAUGHTER IN THE DARK

Nabokov did not match the unusual innovation in narrative technique found in *The Eye* in either of his next two novels, *Glory* (*Podvig*) or *Laughter in the Dark* (*Kamera obskura*).[21] He did not resume his investigation of the implications of viewing oneself as an other until he began work on *Despair*. In some respects, *Laughter in the Dark* retraces ground traversed in *King, Queen, Knave*, and critics have noted a marked similarity between the two novels. Andrew Field states that one could profitably think of *Laughter in the Dark* as "an adaptation or free translation from the Russian of *King, Queen, Knave*" (*Life in Art* 158–59). As in the earlier novel, the central characters are German natives living in "a smug German world" (*LD* 14) and involved in a sexual triangle in which the pivotal female figure is a calculating, materialistic poseur. The driving emotions here, as before, are a destructive passion and a tendency to objectify others, viewing them only according to one's own personal needs. Nabokov's narrative underscores the shabbiness of these individuals' fantasies using techniques familiar from *King, Queen, Knave*, including sardonic narrative asides and the incorporation of cinematic and paradise–hell imagery.[22] Nabokov himself signals the affinities between the set of characters found in *Laughter in the Dark* and those in *King, Queen, Knave* when Albinus receives an invitation for lunch from a couple named Dreyer (*LD* 86; *KQ* 58).[23]

Laughter in the Dark does, however, contain two important elements which distinguish it from the earlier novel. First of all, to the basic triangle involving sexual misconduct Nabokov has added a second triad of characters whose relationships provide a compelling counterpoint to the first group: this triad consists of Albinus's wife Elisabeth, his daughter Irma, and his brother-in-law Paul. This group is bound together not through self-serving passions, but through altruistic love. Secondly, the novel expresses an overt concern with another dimension to the self–other relationship of increasing importance to Nabokov at this time: the relationship between the would-be artist and the subject of his art.

As in so many of Nabokov's early works, the central dynamic of the novel is a character's obsessive desire for a specific other, a desire which blinds the character to the needs of the rest of the people in his world. The destructive nature of Albinus's passion for Margot is evident from the outset. Albinus tells himself that he's going "mad" in chapter 1 (*LD* 13), and he thinks of shooting the woman even before he has formally met her (see *LD* 13; *KO* 9). Later, when he is enthralled by desire for her, he imagines possessing her and then killing himself (*LD* 62). G. M. Hyde has aptly noted that Albinus's dismay over his infatuation recalls Irtenev's dilemma in Tolstoy's "The Devil" (*America's Russian Novelist* 59–63). Hyde does not point out, however, that Albinus echoes Tolstoy's hero even to the extent that he finds himself torn between two opposing ways to eliminate the cause of his desire: either to kill the woman who arouses his feelings, or to kill himself.

The potent charge buried within Albinus explodes when he discovers that Margot has deceived him with Rex. In a passage whose language recalls the vitiating disjuncture between the reality of inner vision and the reality of everyday life described in *Mary* and *The Defense*, the narrator observes that even though Albinus has returned to live with his wife, he takes no note of her: "*Real life*, which was cruel, supple and strong like some anaconda, and which he longed to destroy without delay, *was somewhere else*" (*LD* 283, emphasis added; *KO* 198). When he finally has an opportunity to destroy Margot, however, it is he who dies, not she. That passion, which Nabokov's English version of the novel describes as "lust burning a hole in his life" (*LD* 19; compare *KO* 12) eventually consumes Albinus. His death, indeed, has the air of a self-destructive act. It is his own gun that discharges into his body during his tussle with an unseen Margot; perhaps it is even he who pulls the trigger.

Yet it is not only *self*-destruction that results from Albinus's "morbid passion," as was the case with Martha's obsession with Franz, or with Luzhin's obsession with his invisible chess opponent. Albinus's desire ravages other people's lives as well. His disregard for the others who care for him is not a case of simple neglect. Rather, it involves an active process of negation or elimination. Thus he decides that "if he was not to go on tormenting himself, he *must erase the image of his family from his memory*" (*LD* 92, emphasis added; *KO* 62). Here we see that Albinus's destructive energies are directed against that most cherished bond in Nabokov – the familial tie – and against memory itself. Albinus's crime surpasses ordinary infidelity. Although his wife suffers from his selfish pursuits, her response to his infidelity both underscores her own selflessness and points to an even more innocent victim. As the narrator notes when discussing Elisabeth, she views Albinus's abandonment of Irma as "far more monstrous" than his desertion of her (*LD* 109; compare *KO* 74). Obsessed with Margot, Albinus abandons his daughter physically and later suppresses his memories of her.

Irma herself demonstrates a spirit of altruism and compassion for others that her father lacks, and it is this compassion that leads to her ruin. Hearing someone on the street whistling in a way that recalls her father, Irma knows that this cannot be her father, but she is still troubled. She thinks that it may be her father after all, and she worries that no one will let him in (*LD* 159; *KO* 108). Going to the window, she opens it and exposes herself to a fatal blast of frigid air. Albinus's lust, which burns a hole in his life, also drains the warmth from his daughter's cosmos. Opening her window and her heart to her love for her father, she is felled by the icy touch of his abandonment.[24]

Albinus compounds the injury he has done to his daughter when he fails to attend her funeral. Reflecting on her loss, he enters her former nursery, but instead of thinking of his child he envisions another figure – a "lively, wanton girl" (*LD* 178; *KO* 121). His desire to remain with this other child – his mistress Margot – conquers his impulse to go to Irma's funeral. Several passages in the novel make it clear that Margot has replaced Irma in Albinus's life, and their sexual relationship represents a coarse parody of the precious parent–child relationship in Nabokov's works.

Adding to the pathetic nature of Albinus's obsession with Margot is the fact that she remains essentially an object formed by his desire. The two never establish a relationship of mutual understanding and intimacy. Margot appears before Albinus's eyes only in a sequence of alluring images – the untouchable beauty of first encounter (*LD* 20–21; *KO* 13–14) becomes the chaste maiden to whom he will introduce the joys of sex (*LD* 49). When he discovers that she is not as innocent as he first thought, he then finds himself stirred by *externals*, such as the childish lines of her body and the way her eyes grow dim during erotic moments. (*LD* 92; *KO* 62–63). For her part, Margot has no interest in Albinus's inner world. Although he himself is "amazed" at her lack of curiosity and wonders why she never questioned him about his former life (*LD* 93; *KO* 63), this is entirely natural for her: she views him only as a means of financial support. A master manipulator, she captivates Albinus with her shallow tricks. In a neat emblem of their true relationship, she locks him in his bedroom early in their acquaintance: Albinus never does gain entrance to her inner world, nor does he ever escape the *camera obscura* of his own desire.

Albinus's blindness to the inner world of those he loves (Margot) and of those who love him (Elisabeth and Irma) finds an ironic counterpoint in his profession as art critic. As one who should possess a discerning eye for authenticity, he displays an egregious flaw: he cannot tell the difference between genuine masterpieces and artistic forgeries in his own collection. In the initial description of Albinus in Nabokov's English version, the narrator writes that Albinus would amuse himself by imagining that a scene or face he encountered in real life was drawn by a famous Old Master. The narrator comments on the overall effect: "it turned his existence into a fine picture gallery – *delightful fakes*, all of them" (*LD* 8, emphasis added). This form of amusement has serious implications: it has the effect of creating an aesthetic distance between Albinus and the everyday world, a remove that becomes ever more damaging over the course of the novel. Margot, of course, is one of the "delightful fakes" that Albinus encounters in life, but her performance hardly measures up to the work of an Old Master. When she manipulates Albinus with her poses of innocence or injury, she displays no spark of originality: her roles are hackneyed and stereotypical.

Neither Albinus nor Margot rise above the roles assigned to them in the script of the novel. One character who does, however, manifest a spirit of directorial ambition is Axel Rex. It is Rex who initiates such actions as locking another in a room: when he runs off with Margot, he locks her landlady in her lavatory (*LD* 35; *KO* 24). Later, Margot will mimic this action with Albinus. Moreover, it is Rex who directs the dumb show at the Swiss chalet after Albinus has become blind. Of all the characters in the novel, he comes closest to actualizing that fundamental bifurcation of personality discussed previously. On the one hand, he evinces the authorial dimensions of his personality when he directs the actions of others: he even provides the colors in which the blind Albinus pictures his world (*LD* 261; *KO* 182). At the same time, he creates roles for himself to play out in the eyes of others. Thus he represents himself to Albinus as a homosexual with no interest in Margot, and later he acts as Albinus's spiritual confidant (*LD* 181; *KO* 122–23). As shall be noted below, however, Rex never succeeds in casting off the essential character dimensions of his personality, and he is ultimately revealed to be more of a puppet than he imagines.

Through Rex's character, as well as through the writer Udo Conrad, Nabokov delves into the ethical issues connected with an artist's relationship to his art. Though he had touched upon the topic in previous works, Nabokov explores the subject of ethical responsibility in *Laughter in the Dark* to an extent unmatched earlier. His initial point of departure is Rex. Rex is depicted as a cruel and sadistic creature in his personal life: as a child he used to set fire to mice and did unspeakable things to cats simply out of cold curiosity (*LD* 142–43; *KO* 97). At the same time, however, the narrator states that "this dangerous man was, with pencil in hand, a very fine artist indeed" (*LD* 143). What does this juxtaposition of attributes imply? Does the narrator mean to suggest that one can separate the aesthetic merit of an artist from his personal ethics?

While this might be true in theory, in Rex's case the narrative suggests that such a distinction is spurious, for Rex's "art" is intimately bound up with his callous attitude toward others. The narrator provides a telling example: "if, in real life, Rex looked on without stirring a finger while a blind beggar, his stick tapping happily, was about to sit down on a freshly painted bench, he was only deriving inspiration for his next little picture" (*LD* 144; compare *KO* 98). The "aesthetic" rationale for Rex's refusal to help the blind beggar here contains a glaring fallacy. Rex could easily have grasped the irony of the beggar's predicament without allowing the physical mishap to reach its unfortunate denouement. Not only is Rex's art parasitical, feeding on the misfortunes of others, but a spirit of sadism informs its very core.

This incident also points to a disturbing blurring of the line between life and art in Rex's mind. Misfortune in *life* affords him a kind of *aesthetic* pleasure that is very different than Nabokov's own "aesthetic bliss," a state charged with such qualities as "tenderness" and "kindness" (*L* 316–17). Not only does Rex derive inspiration for his art from the misfortunes of others, he is willing to tamper with others' lives in order to stimulate his perverse sensation of aesthetic pleasure. Rex's manipulation of Albinus's suffering provides a preview of Hermann's manipulation of Felix in *Despair*.

Also noteworthy in this example of Rex's inspiration is the narrator's choice of the epithet "little" for Rex's intended picture: it reminds the reader to consider precisely what kind of art Rex produces. His greatest success comes in two genres – cartoons, and forgeries of the work of Old Masters (*LD* 146). While the first tends to trivialize human life, reducing the complexity of suffering into flat, schematic outlines, the second blandly imitates the original genius of others. If Rex is a "fine" artist, this can only be true of his technical skills. The art he produces is both derivative in conception and heartless in spirit.[25]

Nabokov's final evaluation of the merits of Rex's approach to art emerges out of his depiction of Rex at Albinus's Swiss chalet. Although Rex is the ostensible director of the action there, the reader's first view of Rex at the moment of Albinus's arrival is telling: "Rex, meanwhile, leaned out of the window and made droll gestures of greeting to Margot ... it was a capital imitation of Punch" (*LD* 253; *KO* 173–74). Despite his directorial aspirations, Rex fills neatly the role of a puppet. Although he believes that he can torment Albinus with impunity, his reign is abruptly ended with Paul's arrival. Seizing Albinus's cane, Paul strikes Rex, and Nabokov uses one of his more charged image systems to describe the result: "suddenly something very remarkable occurred: like Adam after the Fall, Rex, cowering by the white wall and grinning wanly, covered his nakedness with his hand" (*LD* 278; *KO* 195). Rex is chased out of his self-centered paradise ("a rather gross Paradise," to quote Udo Conrad; *LD* 222) by a benign spirit sent by a higher deity (the authentic *auctor*) to punish him for his arrogant attempt to appropriate for himself the rights of authorship over the others in his world.[26] The last view of Rex presented in *Laughter in the Dark* emphasizes his actual status as a puppet figure. As Paul leads Albinus away from the chalet he says: "There's no one here. Only that naked wretch looking out of the window" (*LD* 279; *KO* 196). This returns the reader to the scene of Albinus's arrival at the chalet. Rex's status as puppet, not puppet master, is established here once and for all.[27]

Rex erroneously assumes that he can control "real" life, the life of those around him. He underestimates the fact that others *do* exist and have their own autonomous existences in his world. Paul's unforeseen arrival underscores the fallacy of Rex's worldview. In his eagerness to direct Albinus's life according to his own whims, Rex repeats the mistake outlined by the writer in "The Passenger": impatient with the "untidy" genius of life, Rex attempts to alter its themes to achieve his own "conventional harmony" and "artistic conciseness" (*DS* 73; *VCh* 140).

Although Rex's attempt to manipulate the others in his environment is exposed as a perversion of the aesthetic impulse, the question of how genuine artists ought to relate to others in their world remains open. Nabokov's handling of the character of Udo Conrad sheds additional light on this issue. As several critics have noted, Conrad seems to serve as a kind of "authorial self-portrait" (Rampton 23). Described by Albinus as a writer with "an exquisite vision and a divine style" but with "contempt for social problems" (*LD* 132; compare *KO* 90 – Conrad's prototype Segelkranz is disparaged for his penchant for "complex psychology"), Conrad later delivers a diatribe against "Freudian novels" and literature that subsists on "Life and Lives" (*LD* 216). These characteristics and opinions distinctly resemble those of Nabokov himself.[28] Moreover,

Conrad's role in the novel is essentially that of authorial agent. Aside from delivering the opinions quoted above, his only function is to confirm Albinus's suspicions about Margot and Rex. Conrad learns that Rex and Margot are having an affair through a technique described earlier in the novel as "fate's classical method: eavesdropping" (*LD* 71). As "fate" is so often associated with authorial design in Nabokov's work, Conrad's role as eavesdropper marks him as an authorial agent. Significantly, Conrad drops out of the novel as soon as he has delivered his essential piece of news to Albinus. Having done his turn, he completes a "vanishing trick" much like that evoked in the title of his own novel (*LD* 133).

What is especially interesting about the figure of Conrad, though, is not the fact that he confirms Albinus's suspicions about Margot, but the reaction he displays when he does so. Realizing that Albinus has rushed off in a state of agitation, Conrad muses: "I wonder whether I haven't committed some blunder (... nasty rhyme, that! '*Was* it, I *won*der, a – *la*, la, la – *blun*der?' Horrible!)" (*LD* 222). Having perceived that he may have caused Albinus some anguish, he immediately retreats into a reflection on the aesthetic shortcomings of an accidental rhyme. This immediate withdrawal from the specter of human pain is noteworthy, and it raises serious questions about the artist's relationship to the suffering of his fellow humans. Nabokov's narrator delivers no overt commentary on Conrad's escape into aesthetics, but one can read the last word of this chapter – "Horrible!" – not only as a direct quotation from Conrad about his rhyme, but also as an oblique comment from his creator on Conrad's attitude of aesthetic detachment.

On the other hand, in the portrait of Conrad's prototype that appeared in the Russian original Nabokov presented an alternative reaction to the writer's realization that he has inflicted pain. In the original version of this scene, Nabokov depicted the writer Segelkranz (Conrad) reading to Kretschmar (Albinus) a scene from his new novel in which two lovers are overheard conversing in a dentist's office (*KO* 149–51). Kretschmar recognizes in this dialogue the voices of Magda and Robert Horn (Margot and Rex). After Kretschmar leaves, Segelkranz learns that Kretschmar has been blinded in an automobile accident. He is so distraught over his role in this situation that he tears up the offending manuscript (*KO* 177). Segelkranz's sense of responsibility and guilt here contrasts sharply with Conrad's impulse toward aesthetic retreat.

The two opposing approaches taken by Nabokov's artist figures when confronted with human pain point to a source of unresolved tension in the novel between the ability to view such scenes with aesthetic detachment and an ability to feel compassionate empathy for the one in pain. This tension, which first surfaces in the discussion of Rex's art, is not resolved through any one character in *Laughter in the Dark*.[29]

Yet Nabokov not only addresses this issue through the fictional artist figures in the novel, he also touches it through the handling of pain by the narrator himself. The narrator begins his discourse with a biting treatment of Albinus, particularly in the revised version of the novel. Early in the text he comments that Albinus was not "particularly gifted" (*LD* 8; *KO* 7) and had "a slowish mind" (*LD* 14; compare *KO* 9). Later he inserts a telling narratorial aside: "'You're a liar, a coward and a fool,' said Margot (*summing him up rather neatly*)" (*LD* 54, emphasis added). Yet the narrator's attitude toward Albinus shifts somewhat over the course of the novel; he seems to treat Albinus more sympathetically toward the end, especially during his torment at the hands of Rex.

An important feature of the narrator's treatment of Albinus is his handling of the character at moments of extreme emotional distress. The first of these occurs when Albinus enters the nursery in Paul's apartment where Irma lies dying. The narrative reads:

The man who had entered halted a couple of feet from the bed. He could only dimly discern his wife's fair hair and shawl, but with agonizing distinctness he saw Irma's face – her small, black nostrils and the yellowish gloss of her rounded forehead. He stood like this for a long time, then he opened his mouth very wide and somebody (a distant cousin of his) seized him under the armpits from behind.

He found himself sitting in Paul's study. (*LD* 174; *KO* 118)

One notes first of all the detached perspective with which Albinus is presented to the reader. The narrator refers to him not as "Albinus" but as "the man who had entered" (though his name occurs in the Russian version). The ensuing passage presents a mute scene depicting actions and postures, not emotions.

The effect of this detachment is complex. On the one hand, one is reminded of the insularity of grief experienced by Chorb, who did not wish to "taint" his grief by sharing it with any other soul (*DS* 60; *VCh* 6). Yet Albinus's situation is different from Chorb's. He is not guarding his grief from philistine inlaws like the Kellers. Rather, he has chosen to exclude his own wife from his inner world. Thus, his utter alienation from his family is reproduced by the reader's estrangement from Albinus's inner world at this moment.[30]

At the same time, however, the narrator's evocation of Albinus's estrangement does not represent the same kind of retreat into aesthetics suggested in Conrad's reflection on a bad rhyme. On the contrary, the inclusion of a few key details adds incisiveness to the reader's perception of Albinus's condition. Only one word denoting emotion, the epithet "agonizing," appears in this passage, but its placement is significant. The word is used to describe Albinus's vision of his daughter: "with agonizing distinctness he saw Irma's face." For perhaps the first time in the entire narrative Albinus seems to see another person clearly – not as a fantasy projection, but as a real individual, suffering and in pain. The sensitive reader does not need a highly charged passage of emotional description to understand the enormity of this experience for Albinus. More authentic feeling may be suggested in this externalized perspective than in those passages where hyperbolic pseudo-grief is on display, as for example when Albinus sees Margot weeping. After the narrator states that Margot "*managed* to burst into sobs" and was "sobbing nicely" (emphasis added), the narrator provides Albinus's perspective: "he had never before seen tears of that size and brilliance" (*LD* 119; *KO* 81). Other such evocations of Margot's "grief" include the exaggerated comment: "The world was swamped in tears" (*LD* 192; *KO* 130), and the sarcastic observation that Margot was "smiling through her tears, which was difficult, seeing there were no tears to smile through" (*LD* 100; *KO* 68).

A second occasion when the narrator pulls away from an expected moment of visible suffering occurs at the moment of Albinus's automobile accident. This passage offers a stunning display of narratorial manipulation. Beginning with the perspective of an old woman gathering herbs on a hill above the road where Albinus's car is about to encounter two bicyclists, the narrator shifts from the woman's perspective to that of a pilot flying above the road. Continuing this arc of elevation and remove, the narrator comes to rest in Berlin, where he depicts Elisabeth feeling unaccountably restless and uncomfortable; she wonders what is going on and why she feels all "a-tingle" (*LD* 238; *KO* 163–64). Now the narrator begins a return journey, ultimately reverting to the old woman on the hillside. The narrator never provides an objective account of the automobile crash: the nearest approximation is Albinus's noticeably detached recollection of the scene, "a picture that was, in its gaudy intensity, like a colored photograph on glass" (*LD* 240; *KO* 164).

What might Nabokov's aim here be? He perhaps has a dual purpose. On the one hand, his withdrawal of narrative focus on Albinus's automobile as the car heads into its climactic crash clearly eschews the kind of rapt voyeurism demonstrated by someone such as Rex, who takes great delight in watching life's accidents unfold. At the same time, though, its suggestion of narrative virtuosity does not represent the sort of escape into aesthetic play found in Conrad's reflection on unintentional rhymes. On the contrary, through his dramatic sequence of perspectives (and through the camera imagery in the novel as a whole) Nabokov foregrounds the concept of vision itself, contrasting Albinus's self-absorbed, self-inflicted blindness with a very different mode of vision – Elisabeth's empathic "second sight." Nabokov raises here the possibility of developing a new way of seeing, one different from the conventional mode utilized by the average viewer. Such vision would go beyond the mere visual registration of surface detail or the projection of desired images onto a neutral subject. It would look beneath the surface level into the deeper essence of things, and would entail seeing with the emotions and the spirit as well as with the eyes. Nabokov thereby transforms his *camera obscura* into a *camera lucida*.[31]

Nabokov's manipulation of narrative perspectives in *Laughter in the Dark* points to a resolution of the tension raised by the transformation of the overly emotional Segelkranz into the coolly detached Conrad. To be an artist necessarily entails an exploration of human pain – separation, loss, and death. Yet in confronting these events one must neither remove oneself entirely from them by reverting to verbal play, nor dwell on them in passages of unfiltered emotional excess. Rather, one can create a distinctive blend of methods which will encourage readers to apply their own sensitivities to the material at hand. Instead of serving as passive spectators whose responses have been entirely preselected and arranged, such readers will experience the intricate richness of human emotion *within* themselves. Nabokov's readers, in short, will share the imaginative process with the author, adding their own personal vibrancy to the suggestive outlines traced by the author on the page.

Laughter in the Dark provides a complex examination of the tension between conflicting attitudes of engagement and detachment, both in relationships among individuals and in the relationship between artists and the subject of their art. Nabokov will explore this tension further in his subsequent fiction, arriving at an intricate synthesis in his last Russian novel, *The Gift*. In the works which precede *The Gift*, however, Nabokov continues to stress the danger – and the ease – of retreating from difficulties with others into aesthetic constructs of one's own making. Nabokov's next novel, *Despair*, depicts the sobering consequences of just such a capitulation to the lure of narcissistic self-absorption.

CHAPTER 5

Dimming the bliss of Narcissus

During the early 1930s Nabokov probes more deeply into the mercurial realm of personal identity, with its capacities for specular self-absorption and solipsistic projection. In his fiction of this period he invents a memorable series of characters who attempt to transcend their everyday positions by creating imaginary alter egos or projecting elements of identity onto external entities. Nabokov's work examines these core processes from several angles. While "Terra Incognita" provides a model of imaginative creation in what is almost its freest form, three other works depict the operation of personal projection channelled onto specific targets. "Lips to Lips" ("Usta k ustam") features a would-be writer who projects elements of himself onto a character he creates in a work of literary fiction; "The Admiralty Spire" ("Admiralteiskaia igla") depicts an individual whose projections are directed onto a literary character created in someone else's work of fiction; and *Despair* (*Otchaianie*) presents the chronicle of a man who combines both of these approaches. Hermann Karlovich engages in a massive episode of projection onto an external entity, but this entity is not a literary character in a work of fiction read by Hermann, it is a living person in Hermann's world. Hermann, however, treats this other as if he were his own literary creation. His proprietary attitude toward the external world both recalls the solipsistic visions of the narrator of *The Eye* and echoes the callous manipulations of Axel Rex. The resulting mix leads to one of the most memorable portraits in Nabokov's work.

"TERRA INCOGNITA"

Published in November 1931, "Terra Incognita" presents a remarkable variation on the process by which a character replaces a drab, everyday identity with a more exotic vision of the self. Ostensibly the account of an autobiographic intrinsic narrator's expedition with two European companions into a remote tropical jungle, the story raises intriguing questions about perception and projection. As the narrator (named Vallière in the English version) recounts his impressions of this ill-fated journey, the reader comes to suspect that the narrator is not actually participating in a jungle expedition, but rather is imagining all this as he lies in a delirious fever in a European bedroom. The effect of this recognition is much like that occurring in *The Eye*, where one slowly realizes that the narrator of the tale is Smurov himself.

What makes this work particularly interesting is not only the demands it places on the reader's powers of perspicacity, but also the insights it offers into the core consciousness's penchant for creating imaginary alter egos. Throughout the work the narrator adamantly insists that authentic reality lies in the tropical jungle through which he moves (see *RB* 128; *S* 127) and not in his "supposedly real" existence in a European bedroom (*RB* 127; *S* 117).[1] At the end of his narrative he makes a desperate gesture that points to his underlying creative impulse: "My last motion was to open the book, which was damp with my sweat, for *I absolutely had to make a note of something*; but, alas, it slipped out of my hand. I groped all along the blanket, but it was no longer there" (*RB* 128, emphasis added; *S* 128). This final gesture may be emblematic of the narrator's fundamental urge – to channel his creative impulse into a written medium.

When Nabokov's protagonists strive to attain the status of author, the process involves two crucial elements. First, the protagonist attempts to demonstrate authorial control by envisioning a plot and manipulating his "characters" according to the dictates of inner vision. Secondly, the would-be author tries to shed that aspect of the self which functions as a character. In this narrative, the first element is obvious: the narrator envisions an exotic jungle setting and animates it with a plot involving treacherous natives, fatal illness, and so on.[2] The second element is also present, but in a subtle guise.

If one looks closely at the two central characters who accompany the narrator, one notes that they exist in a distinctive relationship to each other. Gregson is courageous and adventuresome. The narrator states that although Gregson fully realizes the dangers of their situation, he boldly plunges into the uncharted wilderness, catching butterflies as avidly as ever (*RB* 121; *S* 118). Cook, on the other hand, is an obvious coward, and squeamishly begs the others to suspend their explorations and to return home (*RB* 121–22; *S* 119–20). The two characters form a typical Nabokovian pair of complementary opposites, much like Berg and Leontiev in "An Affair of Honor," and Smurov as audacious lover versus Smurov as "sexual lefty" in *The Eye*. In each case, the central character is flanked by two figures who function as potential alter egos for the core self: one figure is perceived to be powerful and courageous, the other timorous and weak. If the jungle expedition described by the narrator here is actually the product of his creative fancy, then Gregson and Cook represent external projections of two opposing tendencies within the narrator's mind. On the one hand, he seeks to be like Gregson, capable of disregarding danger and exploring the realm of the unknown. On the other, he feels a fear of the unknown and seeks to return to the security of his accustomed surroundings, his home.

The narrator's creation of potential alter egos in "Terra Incognita" represents a major development over the appearance of such doublets in the above-mentioned works. Whereas Berg and Leontiev were "real" people in Anton's world, and the different versions of Smurov were alternate views held by people who encountered him, the two alter egos here are doubly fictitious. They are the products of the narrator's own creative fantasy.

Many of Nabokov's subsequent protagonists will also follow a pattern of projecting their inner propensities (especially the negative ones) onto some type of external entity. As Nabokov's comments on his own artistic method suggest, such a process has links with literary creation. Remarking on the unattractive heroes of *Laughter in the Dark*, he compared them to the "mournful monsters" found on the facades of medieval cathedrals. They are placed there merely to show that they have been "booted out" of his inner self (*SO* 19). The key, however, to the success or failure of such projection lies in the way the impulse is carried out. As the novel *Despair* indicates, the choice of one's medium is crucial, as well as the degree of control one exerts during the process.

The "terra incognita" of the title denotes not only the unexplored jungle depicted in the narrative, it stands for the uncharted realm of the liberated imagination. In order to explore this realm, the narrator recognizes the necessity of killing that part of his psyche which fears the unknown. Thus he says of Cook: "He had to die" (*RB* 121; *S* 119. The Russian version reads: "Ego nado bylo ubit'." A more literal translation would be: "He had to be killed."). To a certain degree this recognition parallels the narrator's reaction in *The Eye* to his humiliation at the hands of Matilda's husband: that aspect of his personality which is fearful and weak had to be killed off in order to give birth to a new, independent center of creative consciousness. In killing Cook, the narrator of "Terra Incognita" might rid himself of that aspect of his personality which functions as a character – helpless and dependent – and it would thus liberate that element within him which displays authorial inclinations – self-directed, inquisitive, and comfortable with the unknown.

Significantly, neither the narrator nor his positive alter ego Gregson have the will to kill Cook at the appropriate moment, and thus Cook lives on long enough to kill Gregson, in a fatal struggle that leaves both characters dead. If Gregson and Cook represent products of the narrator's creative consciousness, then it is no coincidence that their joint death signals the imminent cessation of the narrator's consciousness as well. Throughout the narrative, reminders of the narrator's unwanted European bedroom become increasingly prominent, testifying to the weakening of the narrator's inventive powers. The deaths of his two projected alter egos signal the ultimate collapse of his creative fantasy.

The narrator's commentary on the gradual disintegration of his jungle vision leads to a sobering reflection on the shape of life after death. As the narrator sees it, the increasing persistence of what he takes to be his "hallucinations" of a European bedroom is a symptom of his impending end. He states that he recognized that the obtrusive room was fictitious, "since everything beyond death is, at best, fictitious: an imitation of life hastily knocked together, the furnished rooms of nonexistence" (*RB* 127; *S* 127). This somber vision becomes starker as the tale ends: "Everything around me was fading, leaving bare the scenery of death – a few pieces of realistic furniture and four walls" (*RB* 128; *S* 128). As these two passages indicate, death appears to the narrator as a kind of prison cell knocked together out of "realistic" but imitative objects derived from everyday life.

This is a forbidding image of death, matched in Nabokov's Russian-language fiction only by Luzhin's glimpse of the afterworld at the conclusion of *The Defense*. It offers a stern view of the limitations imposed by a suspension of creative potential, and it contrasts dramatically with the conceptualization of death evoked in such works as *The Gift* and *Invitation to a Beheading*. Indeed, it is instructive to read "Terra Incognita" in comparison with the latter novel, for the two works share many motifs (see Connolly, "Nabokov's 'Terra Incognita'"). That which the narrator attempts in "Terra Incognita" – to channel his creative vision and transcend the confines of his banal sickroom cell – becomes the very triumph Cincinnatus achieves at the conclusion of *Invitation to a Beheading*.

The apparent death of the narrator at the end of "Terra Incognita" raises the question of how he is able to narrate the story of his own demise. Is it possible that he is narrating the tale from beyond the grave? Since it seems clear that the narrator of *Transparent Things* is a ghost, one might argue that the same situation prevails here. On the other hand, *Transparent Things* was written several decades after "Terra Incognita" and the novel contains several elements indicating that the narrator is the recently deceased author Mr. R. Written in 1931; "Terra Incognita" does not display the same kind of internal evidence that its narrator is a ghost, and there is no compelling reason to hypothesize that Nabokov was exploring such a device at this stage of his career. The matter could be debated at length, but the parameters of the present study do not permit a detailed discussion.

If one assumes that the tale is not narrated by a narrator who is dead, then two further alternatives arise: either the narrator died after he finished narrating his tale, or he did not actually die after all. Pekka Tammi supports the first alternative when he argues that the narrator "discourses, in effect, on his own death and actually *dies* at the precise moment of uttering the final clauses" (*Problems of Nabokov's Poetics* 41).[3] His discourse, according to Tammi, would be one which is conducted in his own mind "simultaneously with the progression of the narrative" (41). This is an intriguing hypothesis, but it is also possible that the text represents the recollection of a narrator who did not die, but rather recovered from his delirium and later tried to provide a record of the fabulous sensations he experienced during the illness itself.[4] If this be so, the tale echoes the narrative situation in *The Eye*, where the narrator claims to have succeeded in killing himself, but more likely has survived to spin out a fantasy of death and inertia-bound consciousness.

In any case, the story itself does not foreground the issue of who narrates the tale or how it is narrated, but rather challenges the reader to address the question of what *within* the narrative represents authentic reality and what represents the narrator's projections. In its exploration of the creative projection of alternative selves, it manifests an important advance in the development of self–other issues. Like *The Eye* which precedes it and *Despair* which follows it, "Terra Incognita" reflects a shift away from a concentration on characters who are obsessed with *external* others to an exploration of the way in which characters turn *inward* and make *themselves* the object of their perception, thereby opening the door to potential self-transformation. As Nabokov's protagonists pursue the process of viewing themselves as an other, they become more purposeful in their efforts to gain the autonomous stature of an author, and to leave behind the subordinate status of a literary character. From the tentative strivings of such beings as the narrator of "Terra Incognita" will come the liberation of such figures as Cincinnatus and the narrator of *The Gift*. During the years immediately following the writing of "Terra Incognita," however, Nabokov's fiction continues to illuminate the shortcomings of those characters who try to overstep the confines of their ordained roles but fail to gain the status of authentic authors.

"LIPS TO LIPS"

"Lips to Lips," a humorous and touching account of an elderly émigré's attempt to animate his drab life by writing a novel, represents a milestone in the evolution of Nabokov's prose fiction.[5] The story's protagonist is Ilya Borisovich Tal, the director of a firm that installs bathrooms. A widower, Tal has experienced a touch of "writer's itch" and he longs for the kind of attention or "warmth" he might find from readers of his work (*RB* 49; *VF* 254). The story depicts Tal's labor over a wretched novel entitled *Lips to Lips*, and his subsequent victimization at the hands of one Galatov, the editor of an avant-garde literary journal who promises to publish the work but needs a subsidy from Tal to keep the journal afloat. Tal's discovery that his work is to be serialized to support the journal wounds his ego, but at the end of the story he gathers up all "the crumbs of praise" he had recently received and decides to acquiesce in the ignoble arrangement.

Nabokov scholars have demonstrated that the story reflects an actual incident in the émigré literary community: it represents a Nabokovian jibe at the circle of figures associated with the journal *Chisla* (*Numbers*).[6] For current readers, however, Nabokov's treatment of the relationship between author and hero – both on the diegetic level (Tal and his protagonist Dolinin) and on the extradiegetic level (authentic *auctor* and his protagonist Tal) – may be more compelling than the settling of old literary feuds.

In writing his novel, Ilya Borisovich strives to escape the routines of his mundane life. Through this act he hopes to create a new identity for himself. Thus, at his office his employees know that he is not only "an excellent person" but also "a *Schriftsteller*" (*RB* 58; *VF* 264). As previous Nabokov works have suggested, the aspiration for authorial status involves a mechanism of dissociation and divestment of one's attributes as a character. Tal's creation of Dolinin as an externalized alter ego displays this impulse for divestment. By creating a fictional surrogate in the character Dolinin, Tal tries to re-create himself as an author too.

Dolinin transparently serves as Tal's alter ego in fiction. Both Tal and his hero are elderly, well-to-do, and single. They both experience infatuation in their later years – Dolinin for a young woman he meets at the theater, and Tal for a vision of recognition as an author. (It is typical of Tal's obtuseness, however, that he does not recognize that Dolinin's lack of success with Irina portends the ultimate failure of his own dream.) The transfigurations of self-image that Tal works into his portrait of Dolinin manifest a clear attempt to retouch a bleak and threadbare canvas. These transfigurations remind one of the narrator's initial representation of Smurov in *The Eye*, and later of Hermann's self-representation in *Despair*. In all three cases, the protagonist tries to provide an attractive image of himself through his narrative discourse. Tal, however, is more traditional (and less duplicitous): while he sets out to write a conventional piece of fiction – a novel – his predecessor and successor wish to convince their readers that their representations are faithful to life as well as artistic.

Despite Tal's authorial aspirations, however, Nabokov's narrative demonstrates that not only does Tal lack the aesthetic sensitivity to become a genuine author (for example, he is familiar with Pushkin mainly through opera – *RB* 50; *VF* 255), he also lacks any possibility of shedding his status as a character. The text exposes numerous affinities between Tal and his character Dolinin. Aside from a broad resemblance in identity

– age, economic, and marital status – Tal and Dolinin are linked through Nabokov's manipulation of their names. In the Russian original, Nabokov endows Ilya Borisovich with no surname while providing Dolinin with no first name or patronymic. A complete identity emerges only when the two are combined. This device recalls "An Affair of Honor," where a similar relationship exists between Anton Petrovich and his potential alter egos Berg and Leontiev. When translating the work into English, Nabokov gives both Dolinin and Tal a surname, but he forges a new link in that both names evoke one English equivalent: *Tal* in German and *dolina* in Russian both mean "valley."

A more striking connection between Tal and his hero is their mutual ineptitude with a cane. The narrator notes at the outset that while Ilya Borisovich "naively delighted" in the appearance of an elegant cane which he would present to his hero, he did not foresee what problems the cane would cause him when he later wished to depict Dolinin carrying Irina (*RB* 48; *VF* 252–53). Tal's failure to cope skillfully with the cane he invents in *his* narrative anticipates his subsequent difficulty with the cane provided him in *Nabokov's* narrative. Overhearing Galatov discuss his exploitation of Tal in a theater lobby, Tal rushes out of the theater, only to realize that he has left his cane behind. Torn between his anger at Galatov and his desire to recover his possession, he swallows his pride and returns to the theater. Not only does this mishap with the cane signal Tal's status as character by linking him with Dolinin, it also portends his future exploitation by the others in his environment, and this state of subordination itself echoes the position of a literary character manipulated by an external author.[7]

Yet Tal's subordination to Galatov and the littérateur Euphratski pales in the reader's eyes before his subordination to the designs of the authentic *auctor*. As Davydov points out ("*Teksty-Matreshki*" 22–23), Nabokov sets up a direct polemic between his "word," represented by the story "Lips to Lips" and Tal's "word," represented by the novel *Lips to Lips*. Not only do the two works share the same title, but in the Russian version of the text, the passage from Tal's novel which opens the text of Nabokov's story is not set off from the subsequent text in italics. In the opening section, then, Tal's text and Nabokov's text share the same language, but as frequently happens in Nabokov, this dual-voiced text conveys two very different messages. From Tal's point of view, the passage indicates the "surprising facility" with which descriptions of emotions come to him (*RB* 48; *VF* 252), but from Nabokov's (and the reader's) point of view, the passage serves to demonstrate how badly the character writes. His work reveals a proclivity for bathetic clichés, a lack of stylistic and lexical precision, and a consistent inability to cope with "routine items," those crucial "trifles" which Nabokov's own art celebrates.

The fact that this introductory passage, which is drawn from Tal's novel, and the concluding passage of the story, which represents Nabokov's authorship alone, both deal with an encounter in a theater further indicates that Nabokov wishes his word to polemicize with Tal's. Once again, the theme of the cane settles the authorial competition decisively in Nabokov's favor. While Tal as a writer is tormented by his inability to incorporate a cane smoothly into his narrative, Nabokov as a writer uses that same item as the axis around which the very denouement of his story pivots. In effect, he drubs Tal with the very cane which Tal admires but does not know how to manipulate.[8]

Nabokov's use of the cane as the badge of authorial sovereignty is characteristic of the writer's relationship toward those of his protagonists who have vain pretensions to authorial status: he manipulates those specific elements which confound his characters to demonstrate his own facility as author-controller. Moreover, he further accentuates the character status of his would-be authors by connecting them to earlier characters in Russian literature. As critics have noted, "Lips to Lips" contains many intertextual references. Davydov recognizes aspects of Akaky Akakievich and the tradition of the ridiculed clerk in the figure of Tal ("*Teksty-Matreshki*" 29–35), and John Barnstead detects an elaborate network of allusions to characters from Mikhail Kuzmin's fiction in the story (see "Nabokov, Kuzmin, Chekhov, and Gogol").

In "Lips to Lips" Nabokov provides a variant on the situation he treated in *The Eye*: a man who is dissatisfied with his lot in life attempts to transform that lot by creating a fictional alter ego and a new reality to accompany it. In the short story, the protagonist attempts this through conventional means by writing a novel in which his fictional representative appears. In *The Eye*, however, the text which introduces the fictional representation of self is not presented by the narrator as a novel, but rather as a chronicle of actual experience. Nabokov combines these two approaches in *Despair*. Hermann's narrative is ostensibly a record of actual events, but he repeatedly refers to its aesthetic qualities as well. Nabokov's manipulation of the boundaries between his characters' fictions and his own fictions grows increasingly complex: his fictions soon grade into metafictions.

"THE ADMIRALTY SPIRE"

This brief story, published in June 1933, provides an engaging treatment of the issues of projection and narrative reliability that occupy center stage in *Despair*, excerpts of which had begun to appear in 1932 and 1933. The story consists of a letter written by an unidentified writer to "Serge Solntsev," the author of a novel entitled *The Admiralty Spire*. Perceiving in this novel a distorted version of his own adolescent love affair with a woman named Katya, the protagonist writes to scold Solntsev for having trivialized his treasured experience. As he attempts to set the record straight, however, he becomes increasingly agitated by his own recollections, and he finally bursts out with the declaration that his addressee is not an unknown lady novelist but Katya herself.

After an emotional appeal to Katya to cease her authorial endeavors, the writer abruptly shifts direction, and in a Gogolian gesture of emotional withdrawal, he concludes: "perhaps, after all, Katya, in spite of everything, a rare coincidence has occurred, and it is not you that wrote that tripe, and your equivocal but enchanting image has not been mutilated. In that case, please forgive me, colleague Solntsev" (*TD* 139; *VF* 232). This shift in tone recalls the last entry of Gogol's "Diary of a Madman," in which the demented narrator reveals for the first time that a sensitive soul lies beneath his mad delusions ("Mother, save your poor son! Drop a tear on his sick head! . . . Mother, have pity on your sick child!" 1: 258–59). After having exposed his vulnerability in this way, he suddenly retreats into his former madness: "And do you know that the Dey of Algiers has a boil just under his nose?" A Gogolian presence in Nabokov's work during the early 1930s has already been noted; this particular story by Gogol also casts prominent shadows in *Despair*.

Even more than Gogol's tale, however, Nabokov's short story offers a wondrous range of emotional registers. The letter writer begins his discourse in a tone of brittle jocularity, but he gradually becomes more lyrical as he immerses himself in his memories of the affair. Finally, after breaking his pose of detachment and making his frank appeal to Katya's emotions, he resorts to that remarkable "loophole" declaration with which his discourse concludes.[9]

In addition to its stylistic richness, the text addresses a significant aspect of the self-other relationship: the issue of projection in interpersonal encounters. This issue surfaces in the central question raised in "The Admiralty Spire": who *is* the "other" to whom the narrator writes his letter: a male writer named Solntsev, a female writer using Solntsev as a pseudonym, or Katya herself? This question cannot be answered with certitude. To judge by numerous other Nabokov works, however, one may guess that Katya is not the author of the book and that the letter writer's assumptions reflect his personal projections. Although he states that his addressee is Katya, the narrator expresses doubts about this at the end of the letter, and many of his observations point out significant discrepancies between his personal romance and the banal affair depicted in the novel. It is typical of Nabokov's characters to fix upon another's external features and then to endow

them with their own personal content. Solntsev's novel provides the letter writer with a neutral text onto which he
inscribes his own individual traits, just as Hermann Karlovich
does with Felix in *Despair*.

The writer's approach to his addressee evinces a palpable
element of solipsism. The following passage is representative:
"Do you wish to know what happened? Glad to oblige" (*TD*
127; *VF* 219). Here, he both posits a question for the other and
provides his own answer to it. In effect, his gestures in the
direction of dialogue are mere ripples in a seamless monologue.
Reinforcing the impression that his image of his addressee
represents personal projection, he ascribes to her his own
physical features. He imagines her as a woman lying "massive-
ly" in her hammock, and then he states that he too is a massive
person and that therefore they are *both* out of breath (*TD* 127;
VF 219).

In fact, he creates a whole sequence of identifications for his
unknown addressee, all of which are derived from his reading of
the literary text. Examining the style of the novel, he declares
that he can easily tell that the author's masculine name is
merely a pseudonym for a woman writer. As he sardonically
notes: "Every sentence of yours buttons to the left" (*TD* 126;
VF 218). It is ironic that he makes such a claim, since he had
earlier warned against drawing erroneous conclusions about his
own identity from a study of his handwriting. Noting that his
handwriting is "slender" and that his commas display a
"youthful flourish," he reveals that he is actually "stout and
middle-aged" (*TD* 125; *VF* 217).

Yet even though he cautions his addressee against the
dangers of projective interpretation, he himself provides a series
of speculative characterizations for the putative author of the
novel. First claiming that she is a massive individual, he later
asserts that the writer is not at all heavy, but rather is the same
narrow-shouldered Katya he once loved. This series of shifting
identifications seems to support the hypothesis that the letter
writer is engaged in an episode of projection, but at the
same time it draws attention to the hermeneutic challenge
faced by any reader when trying to evaluate the identity

and reliability of an individual who has produced a written discourse.

The major thrust of the letter writer's missive is to refute the portrait of himself and Katya which he discerns in Solntsev's novel. Behind this attempt we recognize a recurrent concern in Nabokov's fiction – the resentment felt by a literary character toward the author who has generated its fictional identity. In this story, of course, the literary character in question is meant to be a "real" person who reacts against a distorted portrayal of himself in a work of fiction that he has read. Yet the sense of injury this individual experiences is only one step removed from the rebellion of a literary character against an authentic *auctor* who has given the character life in a work that is ultimately directed to the extradiegetic human reader. This type of resentment flares up in Nabokov's later work and becomes a common theme in postmodernist fiction (see Waugh *Metafiction* 119–21). In "The Admiralty Spire," however, it is important to note that the letter writer does not merely protest against the image of himself created in Solntsev's novel. By creating his own set of characterizations for the Solntsev persona, the writer attempts to out-author that author; in effect, he transforms Solntsev into his own fictional character.

With its protagonist's concern for the word of the other and his concomitant desire to put forth a word of his own, "The Admiralty Spire" stands as a noteworthy companion piece to *Despair*. In both texts an autobiographic intrinsic narrator seeks to establish a state of aesthetic autonomy from the finalizing categorizations of others, yet in each case, this posture of seeming independence belies a deeper insecurity and dependence on the word of the other. "The Admiralty Spire," however, depicts the confrontation between self and other in a relatively benign form, whereas in *Despair* the situation escalates out of control, resulting in violence and death.

DESPAIR

With *Despair* Nabokov presents the culmination of a dynamic he had explored in works from "An Affair of Honor" to *The*

Eye: the desperate attempt of a character to defend himself against the potential influence of others by arrogating to himself the powers of a creative artist.[10] The novel moves beyond *The Eye* in its treatment of the perverse way its protagonist strives for authorial status by exorcising the character dimensions of his identity. Hermann Karlovich, the autobiographic narrator of *Despair*, is more self-conscious about his aspiration for authorial status than the narrator of *The Eye*, but even this literary-minded figure (who claims that there is not a thing about literature that he does not know [*D* 55; *O* 45]) does not perceive the full implications of his actions or how they reflect his true ontological status.

Hermann evinces his authorial impulse in two disparate but interconnected realms in the novel – the realm of everyday life and the realm of verbal narrative. In his life, Hermann Karlovich attempts to manipulate and control the visible beings around him, while in his narrative, he attempts to manipulate an invisible other – his presumed reader. Hermann himself links the two realms at the very outset of his narrative: "If I were not perfectly sure of my *power to write* and of my marvelous ability *to express ideas* with the utmost grace and vividness . . . *nothing at all would have happened*" (*D* 13, emphasis added; *O* 5). Here he affirms that it was his confidence in his powers of verbal creativity that led to the decisive events in his physical life. Even in these first lines, however, the reader discerns a glaring deficiency in Hermann's ability to control his creative energies: he interrupts his own discourse after the word "vividness" and launches into a Gogolian digression ("So, more or less, I had thought of beginning my tale"). It is not until several lines later that he concludes his original thought with the words "nothing at all would have happened."

This ruffle in the texture of his verbal discourse reflects more egregious flaws in his other creative endeavor: the attempt to refashion the living world around him into a personal work of art. Encountering a man named Felix who he believes is his exact physical double, Hermann murders the fellow, assuming that the police will think that it is he, Hermann, who has been murdered, and that his wife Lydia will receive an insurance settlement. This crime, he asserts, should be considered an artistic work of "genius." The reader learns, however, that the endeavor is marred from the outset: according to the press accounts, the murdered man did not resemble Hermann "in the least" (*D* 201; *O* 183). As in *The Eye*, the reader of *Despair* must deal with a narrator who is notoriously unreliable in regard to his perceptions about himself and his surrounding reality.

At the core of Hermann's attitude toward the other lies a deep-rooted insecurity. To delineate his response to this insecurity, one can examine his approach to others in each of the two realms illuminated in the novel. We will look first at the relationships Hermann establishes with the others in his world, and then turn to the narrative through which he tries to elucidate those relationships. Although the following discussion treats the two realms separately, the interconnections between them will be readily apparent.

Hermann's story

Hermann's dealings with others are dominated by an arrogance fuelled by his profound insecurity. Anxious over the power of others to judge him, he attempts to forestall any negative evaluations by defining the other first. His treatment of his wife is characteristic. Quick to label her "my unobservant wife" (*D* 59; *O* 48) and "my fool of a wife" (*D* 60; *O* 50), he declares that she loved him faithfully (*D* 39; *O* 28) and that to her he was the "ideal man" (*D* 35; *O* 27). This self-image is crucial for Hermann, for he longs for adulation and approval. Yet the reader soon realizes that Lydia is having an affair with an impoverished painter, her cousin Ardalion.[11] Hermann's insistence on Lydia's love for him may testify to his blindness to the reality in which he lives, but it is equally probable that his insistence masks a deeper recognition of an unpalatable truth he does not wish to acknowledge.

In similar fashion, Hermann rejects an unflattering portrait of him drawn by Ardalion as entirely lacking any semblance of a likeness (*D* 66; *O* 55). In return he offers his own caricature of

Ardalion, utilizing here a telling metaphor: "Ah, enough about my fool Ardalion! The ultimate dab is laid on his *portrait*. With a last flourish of the brush I have signed it across the corner" (*D* 217, emphasis added; *O* 198). Such images of artistic creation and control proliferate throughout Hermann's discourse. Andrew Field succinctly summarizes Hermann's attitude toward others by stating: "Hermann is striving to establish himself as the primary author of everyone and everything around him while at the same time freeing himself from any possible similar control" (*Life in Art* 236).

Hermann's aversion toward being defined or controlled by others extends from the physical to the metaphysical. He begins the sixth chapter by attempting to prove the "nonexistence of God," and he builds his denial of God on two points. First is the familiar issue of control. He asserts: "if I am not master of my life, not sultan of my own being, then no man's logic and no man's ecstatic fits may force me to find less silly my impossibly silly position: that of God's slave" (*D* 112; *O* 98). Hermann rejects the possibility of God's existence because he refuses to view himself as in the control of a more powerful other. Significantly, the issue of control is linked in this passage to the issue of authorship. Hermann writes: "There is yet another reason why I cannot, nor wish to, believe in God: the fairy tale about him is not really mine, it belongs to strangers, to all men" (*D* 111–12; *O* 97). Hermann not only seeks control over his destiny, he aspires to be the creator of his own mythologies about the mysteries of life. Yet the very urgency with which Hermann tries to deny the authority of another indicates his sense of vulnerability before that other.[12]

Hermann's desire to control the other shows up most clearly in his treatment of Felix. Although he states in his discussion of God that it is impossible to accept the notion "that a serious Jah, all wise and almighty, could employ his time in such inane fashion as playing with manikins" (*D* 111; *O* 97), this is precisely what he does with Felix. Asserting his own *ia* ("I") in place of the Biblical Jah, Hermann directs his victim's every move in the moments before the murder, even ordering him to model his clothes like a living mannequin (see *D* 180–81; *O*

163–64). Indeed, he later admits his amazement over Felix's submissiveness, which he terms "ridiculous, brainless, automatous" (*D* 187; *O* 168–69). Of course, the ultimate act of control over someone else's life is to terminate it, and this too Hermann does with equanimity.

Yet even though he manipulates Felix like "a god gone mad" (Rosenfield "*Despair* and the Lust for Immortality" 74), Hermann does not describe his role in metaphysical terms. Rather, he views himself as an artist and specifically as an author. Having announced his desire to discuss "crime as an art" (*D* 131; *O* 116–17), he underscores his perception of himself as an artist by using several metaphors drawn from the realm of art when he describes the murder scene. He compares his examination of Felix's dead body with the action of "an author reading his work over a thousand times, probing and testing every syllable" (*D* 181; *O* 164), and he states: "I longed, to the point of pain, for that masterpiece of mine (finished and signed on the ninth of March in a gloomy wood) to be appreciated by men" (*D* 188; *O* 170). Again Hermann bares here his need for external approval.

While Hermann's quest for recognition as a creative artist has been discussed repeatedly by Nabokov scholars since the 1930s (see Weidle, "On Sirin" 54 and Khodasevich, "On Sirin" 99–100), these discussions have overlooked the seminal process of self-transformation and self-divestment which this quest entails. To liberate their authorial potential, Nabokov's characters seek to shed that aspect of their identity that functions as a character. Hermann's treatment of Felix manifests this very impulse, even though he himself may not be fully conscious of the underlying dynamic. He first projects certain attributes of his everyday identity onto Felix, and he then tries to eliminate the character surrogate he has created out of the man, thereby unleashing his own authorial center.

The entire identification and projection process consists of several discrete steps. These include: a predilection for dissociating oneself from one's external image; the projection of this dissociated image onto an external other; the transference of attributes of one's identity onto the targeted other; and the elimination of the recipient of the transference. Each of these elements appears in Hermann's story.

The first element – a capacity for dissociation – is illustrated most vividly in a passage which Nabokov includes in his revised English version of the novel but which, he writes, had been omitted in more "timid" times (*D* 8). The passage describes the pleasure Hermann derived from the sensation that he could both make love to his wife and simultaneously watch his lovemaking from a spatially detached vantage point. This voyeuristic habit of self-observation represents a striking progression of the condition which afflicted the narrator of *The Eye*. In the opening passages of that text the narrator had lamented the fact that he was always exposed and wide-eyed and that he did not stop watching himself even in his sleep (*E* 17; *S* 8). For him, this kind of self-consciousness was a source of distress. For Hermann, in contrast, this experience provides exquisite enjoyment.[13] Hermann's pleasure testifies to a high degree of narcissism in his self-absorption, and this narcissism plays a crucial role in his relationship to Felix too. Although Hermann's experiments with self-observation are punctured abruptly by Lydia one evening, he soon develops "a new and wonderful obsession" (*D* 39) – Felix Wohlfahrt.

Hermann describes his discovery of Felix and their amazing resemblance in a series of slow, measured revelations. He first sees the man lying motionless on a hillside, his face covered by a cap. This inert figure offers a neutral surface onto which he can imprint his own features. The very inertness of the form adds to its appeal for Hermann. As he notes later, Felix in repose offered "the flawlessly pure image of my corpse." He continues: "what is death, if not a face at peace – its artistic perfection? Life only marred my double" (*D* 25; *O* 17). We shall return to the element of death in Hermann's conceptualization of Felix shortly, but for the moment it is sufficient to note that signs of life, autonomous and independent, threaten the illusion of identity that Hermann seeks.

Hermann does not immediately inform the reader that he perceives a physical similarity. He does so only through a dogged process of manipulating Felix to allude to the similarity first; then he crows that it was Felix and not he who first noted the resemblance (see *D* 22; *O* 15). This process highlights Hermann's dependence on the other for external validation, and at the same time it raises the suspicion that the similarity itself is an unrealized (and unrealizable) illusion – a desire, not a fact.[14] Indeed, Hermann's perception of his own features on Felix illustrates the extent of his narcissistic delusion, a delusion that may surpass even that of the original Narcissus. Whereas Narcissus stared at a reflection of himself, mistakenly believing that he was looking at another, Hermann stares at another, but sees only a reflection of himself, not realizing that this is just a specular self-projection. The other exists only as a mirror for Hermann. Hermann's lack of perspicacity here offers a variation on Julia Kristeva's comment about the Narcissus myth: "he who loves a reflection without knowing that it is his own does not, in fact, know who he is" (Kristeva *Tales of Love* 107).

Having discovered an external mirror for his own physical features, Hermann displays a complex and contradictory attitude toward this ostensible double. On the one hand, his commentary on his obsession with his double displays overtly sexual overtones and imagery. After leaving Felix for the first time, he writes: "Suddenly I felt limp, dizzy, dead-tired, as after some long and disgusting orgy" (*D* 24; *O* 16). When he departs after their second meeting, during which they have spent the night together in a hotel room, he compares himself to an adolescent, who, "after yielding once again to a solitary and shameful vice, says to himself . . . 'That's finished for good; from this time forth, life shall be pure'" (*D* 107; *O* 95). Finally, stung by the thought that Felix could have tried to visit him in Berlin, he confesses: "my passion for my double was surging anew" (*D* 124; *O* 111).

Nabokov lays on this patina of eroticism largely for comic purposes. Hermann himself speculates that French readers will "discern mirages of sodomy in my partiality for a vagabond" (*D* 169; *O* 151).[15] Hermann's obsession with Felix is, in fact, a form of *self*-obsession; even when Felix is not present, Hermann's comments about himself continually drift into the erotic. At one point he states that his own company was "intolerable, since it excited me too much and to no purpose" (*D* 114; *O* 100). Hermann's intoxication with himself, and with Felix as an external mirror, displays the "vertigo" that stems from narcissistic love, a love "with no object other than a mirage" (Kristeva 104). The notes of erotic infatuation which appear here serve a function analogous to the association raised in *The Defense* between eros and Luzhin's interest in chess. In both novels, Nabokov introduces erotic imagery to signal the inherent danger of uncontrolled, obsessive passion.

The serious undercurrents running beneath the comic surface of Hermann's self-involvement emerge when one perceives that the element of self-*love* found in Hermann's obsession with Felix carries an unsettling degree of self-*loathing* as well. Hermann's sexual imagery contains several negative epithets: "disgusting orgy," "solitary and shameful vice." It is perhaps this element of self-loathing that fuels his ultimate design for his double. He transfers onto Felix all those attributes of his everyday life with which he is dissatisfied, and he attempts to purge himself of those attributes by killing the surrogate who now bears them.

Thus he not only gives his own clothes – the uniform of a failing businessman – to Felix at the time of the murder, he also intends the victim to be the focal point for a series of planted clues about his life. He tells Orlovius that Lydia has a fickle heart and has become interested in another man (*D* 143; *O* 126). Although he claims to the reader that this scenario is invented, the reader recognizes in it a core of truth. By endowing his intended victim with the identity of cuckolded husband, Hermann can perhaps purge himself of that attribute as well. His murder of Felix, then, has the air of a ritual purification.

One recognizes here a sinister evolution of the narrator's impulse in "Terra Incognita." Wishing to free his positive alter ego Gregson from the restrictions of his negative alter ego Cook, the narrator declared that Cook "had to die" (*RB* 121; *S* 119). Cook, however, was merely a figment of the narrator's imagination. Felix, in contrast, is a "real" person in Hermann's world, although Hermann's perception of him is illusionary.

Hermann's attitude toward Felix also represents an interesting development over the narrator's view of Smurov in *The Eye* when one evaluates the two relationships in light of Rank's speculative comments on the role of the double in human society. Whereas the narrator seemed to celebrate Smurov's longevity ("I . . . do not exist. Smurov, however, will live on for a long time" *E* 113; *S* 86), Hermann terminates the life of his supposed double. Rank observed: "Originally, the double was an identical self (shadow, reflection), promising survival in the *future*; later, the double retained together with the individual's life his personal *past*; ultimately, he became an opposing self, appearing in the form of evil which represents the perishable and mortal part of the personality repudiated by the social self" (*Beyond Psychology* 81–82). Although the last portion of Rank's statement involves a psychological generalization which may not be relevant to *Despair*, his perception of a shift in society's view of the double is engaging. As suggested above, Hermann invests his "double" with the attributes of his past and then repudiates them in the person of the bearer.

The murder of Felix carries multilayered significance. In terms of Hermann's everyday life, the murder represents a desperate attempt to leave behind a set of stifling roles as failed businessman and cuckolded husband. Yet while this presumed liberation has practical consequences in Hermann's life, it also has important implications in the aesthetic realm. Since he views Felix as his physical surrogate and treats him as a literary character, Hermann may hope that his destruction of Felix will eradicate his own status as a literary character and provide him with new life as a literary creator.[16] Having discussed Hermann's efforts to transform Felix into a kind of fictive alter ego, we can now look more closely at Hermann's success (or lack of it) in the second dimension of fundamental bifurcation: his aspiration to become an author in the medium of *life*. His difficulties here are immediately apparent.

Like the narrator of *The Eye*, Hermann discovers that the attempt to eradicate the unpleasant realities of his life through a kind of self-destructive act (a "pseudocide"?) is unsuccessful. The former was dismayed to find that he remained vulnerable to the opinions of others in his world, while Hermann is dismayed to find that he has not succeeded in escaping the external image he presents to the outside world. Thus he confesses to a new antipathy toward mirrors after the murder (see *D* 187; *O* 169 and *D* 31; *O* 23). Mirrors provide a singularly apt object of torment for Hermann. First of all, they represent a fitting form of revenge for the consummate narcissist. The man who was erotically obsessed with his mirror image in the form of Felix now finds himself trapped within a hell of reflecting mirrors. More importantly, though, mirrors point to an attribute of physical reality Hermann has tried to ignore – the uniqueness of an individual face. It is up to his rival, the artist Ardalion, to point out that every face is unique (*D* 50; *O* 41) and that no two men in the world are alike, no matter how well one disguises them (*D* 215; *O* 196).[17]

Hermann's blindness to the uniqueness of the other has ethical as well as aesthetic implications. Dismissing the autonomy of the other to pursue his own artistic ends, Hermann assumes that the aesthetic control authors wield over their creations in fiction may override the ethical responsibilities of one individual toward another in the plane of life. Nabokov himself was fond of asserting the absolute control that he wielded over his characters, calling them "galley slaves" (*SO* 95, see also *SO* 69). Yet the power he exercises over his characters cannot be transferred toward the external world. Ellen Pifer notes: "Nabokov's insistence on authorial dictatorship is an unusual stance for a novelist; but it is not meant to undermine the liberty of real people or the essential humanity of literary characters" ("On Human Freedom" 55). Just as it is a crime for one human being to murder another for the sake of art, so too is it a crime for one character to murder another for the same purpose.

Hermann's perverse conceptualization of the artist's relationship to the world around him nullifies his attempt to transform himself into an artist in life.[18] However, he tries to redeem his failure to attain authorial status in the unconventional medium of life with a new effort to gain this status in a more conventional medium – that of verbal art. As he admits, he has begun his written chronicle in an effort to explain to the world the full depth of his "masterpiece" (*D* 205; *O* 187).[19]

It is here, though, that Nabokov extracts the fullest measure of revenge on his would-be author hero. While the mirrors which Hermann encounters after his murder of Felix signal his subjection to the *physical* reality of the *diegetic* world, the words of his narrative form a mirror revealing his subjugation to the *verbal* reality of the *extradiegetic* world. The discourse with which he hopes to demonstrate his powers as author serves instead to expose his status as character.

Hermann's discourse

One of the most striking features of Hermann's discourse is the degree to which it reflects the aspirations he exhibits in his life. He declares, for example, that he possesses "exquisite" control not only over himself, but over his style of writing too (*D* 90; *O* 76). In his verbal art, as in his life, Hermann wishes to display absolute control, and once again he proves inadequate to the task. Before his murder of Felix, Hermann had tried to control the opinions of those around him. Now, in his narrative, he strives to control the opinions of the invisible other – his reader. One finds numerous passages in which he seeks to shape the reader's response by currying favor with the reader, whom he calls "fair-minded" (*D* 216; *O* 197) and "attentive" (*D* 217; *O* 197) and whom, he says "I pet and pamper like a devoted nurse" (*D* 80; *O* 68). Yet this attitude of seeming respect for the reader serves only to cloak his underlying feelings. Like the narrator of *The Eye*, he both longs for his readers' approval and resents them because of his very need.[20] This complex surfaces early in the narrative when he writes: "How I long to convince you! And I will, I will convince you!" This "longing" immediately turns into an angry snarl: "I will force you all, you rogues, to believe" (*D* 26; *O* 18). Only in moments of rare lucidity does he admit his true intentions toward the reader, such as when he writes: "An author's fondest dream is to turn the reader into a spectator" (*D* 26; *O* 19). Here we see that Hermann seeks to transform the reader into a passive creature devoid of autonomous will like Felix. Hermann's discourse reflects the anxiety of influence Mikhail Bakhtin finds in the narrator's monologue in Dostoevsky's *Notes from the Underground*: "His word about the world is both openly and furtively polemical ... He senses in everything above all the *will of the other person*, the will which predefines him" (*Problems* 198).

To control his reader, of course, Hermann must be able to control his pen, and although he asserts that his self-control is "perfect" (*D* 39; *O* 29), it is here that his lack of control stands out most clearly. He fills his narrative with acknowledgments that he has made mistakes in his use of stylistic devices (*D* 55; *O* 45), verb tenses (*SD* 32; *O* 24), and other aspects of his discourse (see *D* 98, 190; *O* 85, 172). Hermann's lack of control over his own narrative also proves glaring in his handling of chronology. He periodically interrupts the chronological flow of his tale with the insertion of proleptic detail. Describing the first visit he made in summer to the woods where he would later murder Felix, he mentions a "bare birch tree" and then immediately catches himself. He wonders why he included the epithet "bare," since it was not yet winter; winter was still a long time away (*D* 46; *O* 36). Shortly thereafter he again makes a slip, now including a description of snow in his scene. Once more he reprimands himself: "What nonsense! How could there be snow in June?" (*D* 47; *O* 37).

What may be occurring here is Hermann's failure to control his "impatient memory" (*D* 47; *O* 37), a failure analogous to his inability to control his "passion" for his double. Yet the insertion of such proleptic images has deeper significance: it points to the profoundly self-reflexive nature of Hermann's narrative as a whole. Just as the narrator continually turns his gaze onto himself, so too does his narrative fold in on itself. The occurrences of proleptic and analeptic passages in Hermann's narrative have a different function than the instances of repetition and recurrence occurring in a novel such as *The Defense*. Whereas the latter promote an appreciation of the resonant complexity structured into the text by the *auctor*, Hermann's chronological gaffs point to his inability to sort out the different moments in his life. Rereading Hermann's narrative, the reader does not learn anything new about the cosmic order of Hermann's invented world, but rather becomes more convinced of the man's shortcomings.

Thus, the formal structure displayed by Hermann's narrative is circular, not spiral, and testifies to the personal validity of his observation on "our eternal subjection to the circle in which we are all imprisoned!" (*D* 73; *O* 61). When he rereads his manuscript in hopes of "freeing" himself from his doubts about the perfection of his crime (*D* 210; *O* 191), he finds not a release, but a grim confirmation of his own blundering carelessness. He now discovers Felix wielding that implement which will lead to Hermann's capture but which Hermann had overlooked in his eagerness to commit murder – a walking stick which bears its owner's name (*D* 212; *O* 193). (Readers of "Lips to Lips" will recognize that the ultimate owner of the stick is not Felix, but the authentic *auctor*.) In effect, then, Hermann's manuscript serves as one more mirror which holds up to him the sobering image of a reality he had sought to escape through aesthetic transformation.[21] Hermann cannot even control the formal structure of his manuscript. Determined to write a ten-chapter work, he finds himself forced to add an eleventh chapter (see *D* 207; *O* 188), and he is subsequently dismayed to find that his tale has "degenerated" into a diary, which he feels is the "lowest" form of literature (*D* 218; *O* 199).

On nearly every level of his artistic endeavor, Hermann proves wanting, critically impaired by his inability to maintain his cherished goal of absolute control. Yet Hermann's lack of control points to an essential fact of his being that he dare not even consider. Hermann wishes to be viewed as a writer of genius, and he compares himself favorably to the great crime writers of the past. Evoking such figures as Doyle, Dostoevsky, Leblanc, and Wallace, he declares that in comparison with him they are nothing more than "fools" (*D* 132; *O* 117).[22] Despite his pretensions, however, Hermann's recurring problems with control underscore the fact that his true affinities lie not with the great *creators* of the past, but with their literary creations – their fictional characters. As critics have noted, Nabokov weaves into *Despair* a network of allusions to earlier literary works which reinforce Hermann's status as character, not creator (see Connolly, "The Function of Literary Allusion," Carroll, "The Cartesian Nightmare" 83–95, and Schroeter, "Detective Stories" 28–29).

Hermann does not wish to acknowledge his affinity with other literary creations. Sensing a resemblance to Dostoevsky's character Raskolnikov (whom he calls "Rascalnikov"), he immediately backs away, protesting: "No, that's wrong. Canceled" (*D* 199; *O* 181). Yet he does drop a hint that he senses his fictional nature. Discussing narrative technique at the beginning of chapter 3, he slyly points out that "the first person is as fictitious as all the rest" (*D* 53; *O* 43). Even here, however, Hermann is far from revealing an understanding of his authentic status. On the contrary, he seems to be celebrating the potential fluidity of identity inherent in the use of the first-person pronoun, a "shifter" whose specific referent can be defined only in relation to the given message (Jakobson "Shifters" 131–32). He assumes that it is he who controls the first-person pronoun, not acknowledging the possibility that this pronoun might serve the purposes of a higher other.[23]

Aside from his diatribe against the existence of God, the only time that Hermann admits to his dependence on an external other comes when he addresses his "first reader," "the well-known author of psychological novels" to whom he plans to send his manuscript (*D* 90; *O* 77–78). Wondering what this writer will feel when he reads the manuscript, he speculates on the possibility that the writer may try to appropriate the manuscript as his own creation, thereby leaving Hermann "out in the cold" (*D* 91; *O* 78). It is fitting that Hermann feels this anxiety, because he had earlier demonstrated just such an attitude of appropriation when he took over Felix's identity for himself.

Hermann's anxiety about his "first reader" represents a distinct variant of the distress felt by several of Nabokov's earlier characters when they became aware of their vulnerability before a more powerful other.[24] Yet unlike a figure such as Luzhin, who cracked under the pressure he felt emanating from this intangible other, Hermann tries to reassure himself that he can resist the influence of the other by taking "proper measures" in advance. Blind Hermann, alas, does not realize that the invisible other has already wrested control of the manuscript and is speaking through Hermann's very words.[25]

Indeed, the authentic creator of *Despair* has embedded several markers of his own sovereignty into his character's discourse. *Despair* is one of the finest examples of the dual-voiced discourse in Nabokov's entire *œuvre*. Although Hermann's text is identical in *form* to the authentic *auctor*'s text, it remains radically different in its intentions and implications. The evidence of Nabokov's authorial control over the text is particularly striking in the Russian version, but it is interesting to observe how the writer transforms the original markers of control into different, but equally compelling signposts in his English translation.

The reader of the Russian text can identify several sites where traces of the author's watermark shine through Hermann's words. One occurs in chapter 2, when Hermann describes Ardalion's art and provides an example of his still life painting: "malinovoi siren'iu v *nabokoi v*aze" (*O* 32, emphasis added. A literal translation would be "raspberry-colored lilacs in a leaning vase," while Nabokov's English version reads: "phallic tulips in a leaning vase" *D* 42.).[26] A second example occurs in chapter 4, when Hermann describes his path to his second meeting with Felix. He writes: "Svernuv s bul'vara *na bokov*uiu ulitsu" (*O* 66, emphasis added; the English version reads: "I turned into a side street" *D* 79). In both of these cases Nabokov has encoded a variation of his name into the very building blocks of his unsuspecting character's manuscript.

Lest the skeptical reader doubt that Nabokov has intentionally inserted these sequences of letters into Hermann's text as a means of suggesting his controlling presence, one should note that an equivalent (though not identical!) mode of patterning occurs in Nabokov's English version at the very same points in the narrative as the encoded names mentioned above. The method of authorial patterning which Nabokov inserts into his English text works as follows: near each point where the encoded name appears in the Russian text, the writer includes in the English text an item of descriptive detail that also appears elsewhere in the text, and this recurrence carries a special resonance which escapes the ostensible narrator's attention. For example, in the case of Ardalion's still-life painting, Nabokov changes the type of flower depicted by the painter from "raspberry-colored lilacs" in his Russian version to "phallic tulips" in his revised English version. Nabokov's insertion of a sexual element here is not incidental, for just a few pages earlier, when describing the chaotic contents of Lydia's dresser, Hermann notes "bits of silk, her passport, *a wilted tulip*" (*D* 35, emphasis added). This "wilted tulip" was not included in the original Russian text, and its appearance here is a humorous signal that Ardalion and Lydia are having an affair, a fact that Hermann either cannot or will not acknowledge. The recurring tulip imagery, then, serves as a marker of authorial patterning which replaces the embedding of Nabokov's name in the Russian text.

The second example of this kind of authorial patterning occurs in Hermann's description of the route he took to meet Felix for the second time. His account includes the following detail: "On a ridiculously curved flowerbed there grew the filthiest flowers in the world; Michaelmas daisies" (*D* 78). Similar flowers appear in the Russian text: "tsveli samye gnusnye v mire tsvety – astry" (*O* 66). However, Hermann does not seem aware that he has mentioned daisies earlier in his manuscript, in a telling remark not found in the Russian original. Commenting on Lydia's superstitiousness, he states: "A field of daisies foretold meeting again one's first lover" (*D* 32; compare *O* 24). This revelation about the meaning of daisies combines with Hermann's observation of Michaelmas daisies just before his second meeting with Felix to suggest that the meeting is akin to a reunion of lovers. Yet while Hermann himself has described his relationship with Felix in quasi-erotic imagery, he does not notice that a master pattern-maker has bedecked his reunion with Felix with fatidic flowers.[27]

Although Hermann is not entirely cognizant of the fact that his destiny is in the hands of a more powerful other, he does sense that his attempts at authorship have not provided him with the feeling of freedom and autonomy which he has sought. Near the end of his narrative he expresses his anxieties more openly. In his refuge in Pignan he describes the effect of nightfall: "As soon as night fell and the shadows of branches ... came sweeping across my room, a sterile and hideous confusion filled my vast vacant soul" (*D* 193; *O* 175). This image of the void recalls the condition which overtakes the narrator of *The Eye* at the end of that novel. Like his predecessor, Hermann finds himself to be "all alone in a treacherous world of reflections" (*D* 193; *O* 175). His murder of Felix and his futile attempt to change his identity have cut himself off from others, but they have not freed him from himself.

Earlier in the novel Hermann had described a recurring nightmare in which he would enter "a perfectly empty, newly whitewashed room." The experience was "so terrible" that he could never "hold out" (*D* 56; *O* 46). This room provides a stark image of the emptiness of Hermann's soul at the end of the novel, and Nabokov added a significant element to the dream in the revised English version. Hermann writes that on one occasion he discovered a chair in the middle of the room, as if someone intended to climb up and fix a bit of drapery. He continues: "since I knew *whom* I would find there next time stretching up with a hammer and a mouthful of nails, I spat them out and never opened that door again" (*D* 56–57). This dream provides Hermann with a chilling glimpse into his own future – solitary confinement in a bare cell of his own making.[28]

At the end of his narrative he finds himself in a room like that of his nightmare. Hunted by the police, he feels trapped in this icy room. He writes: "All is dark, all is dreadful, and I do not see any special reason for my lingering in the dark, vainly invented world" (*D* 220; *O* 200). The phrase "vainly invented world" rings with a double resonance here. It not only applies to the physical cosmos in which Hermann lives, it also applies to the verbal labyrinth he has constructed through his discourse, that "crooked mirror" which reflects his "eyeless" face and his vacant soul.

Despite his despair, however, he makes one last attempt at

escaping the circle closing in around him. Having failed to
create a work of art in the physical world, and then having
failed to redeem that attempt in the medium of a written
narrative, he resorts to one final artistic medium – that of the
film industry. In the last paragraph of the revised version of
Despair Hermann throws open his window and makes a speech
to the crowd below, claiming that he is filming a movie about
an arch-criminal who needs to make an escape from the police.
Just as he tried to control Felix and the reader earlier, so too he
now tries to control the spectators for this film scene: "French
crowd! I want you to make a free passage . . . from door to car.
Remove its driver! Start the motor! Hold those policemen,
knock them down, sit on them" (*D* 222). Once again Hermann
tries to escape his present dilemma by manipulating the roles of
creator and the created. In this case, he seeks to become both
director and actor in a hackneyed film script.

Hermann's last attempt to forge an escape route for himself
will, of course, fail. His hapless fate contrasts with that of
Cincinnatus at the end of *Invitation to a Beheading*. Whereas
Hermann remains trapped in his room, hounded by the police
and public, Cincinnatus marshals his creative resources and
walks away from the prison world which collapses behind him.
One of the crucial differences between Hermann's fate and
Cincinnatus's is the protagonists' use of the act of writing as a
tool for self-discovery and growth. Hermann's self-reflexive
narrative effectively constructs an enclosed hall of reflecting
mirrors, but Cincinnatus's verbal explorations take him out of
his narrow world and lead him toward a realm populated with
kindred spirits. Still, the world of beings toward whom Cincinnatus strides remains forever offstage in *Invitation to a Beheading*.
It is only in Nabokov's last Russian-language novel, *The Gift*,
that the author displays both the triumphant emergence of
authorial potential *and* the achievement of a vital relationship
between the artist and the other.

CHAPTER 6

The struggle for autonomy

During the mid 1930s Nabokov's work reaches ever greater degrees of complexity. The author shifts his focus from the subjective quality of personal vision to a probing investigation of the artifice which lies at the core of the fictional world itself. The creative activities of Nabokov's protagonists and the relationships they establish with others in the diegetic world reflect the activities and relationships of the creative entities in the extradiegetic world. As a result, the self–other relationship takes on new implications and meanings: ambiguity and multivalency emerge as central characteristics in Nabokov's fiction. Works such as "The Leonardo" ("Korolek") and *Invitation to a Beheading* (*Priglashenie na kazn'*) display Nabokov's increasing readiness to challenge the conventions of realist fiction, and they stimulate the reader to a new understanding of the nature of the fictional construct.

"THE LEONARDO"

The short story "The Leonardo," published in July 1933, manifests the growing ambiguity built into Nabokov's works in the mid-1930s. The writer's unusual treatment of the self–other relationship on both the diegetic and extradiegetic levels foreshadows his subsequent achievements in *Invitation to a Beheading* and *The Gift*. While the story's plot foregrounds a struggle between a pair of contrasting character types in the diegetic world, the tensions depicted in that relationship find an echo in the narrator's relationship to his characters and to creativity in the extradiegetic world.

The plot of the work is simple. A man named Romantovski moves into a boarding house where he becomes the target of the intrusive attention of two German brothers, Anton and Gustav. Enraged by Romantovski's penchant for solitude, the brothers contrive a pretext to beat him up; during this assault, they kill him. They are subsequently surprised to learn that he was a counterfeiter and had spent time in jail. While the story itself exposes the tyranny of philistine prejudice, the unusual approach taken by the narrator to the narrated events suggests that the depicted struggle has broader implications.

The narrative frame of the story establishes a contradictory picture of the narrator's relationship to the depicted events. On the one hand, his description of the assemblage of the setting indicates that he has some command over how the scene is arranged. He begins: "The objects *that are being summoned* assemble, draw near from different spots" (*RB* 11, emphasis added; *VF* 57). He then urges these objects along – "Hurry up, please" – and he notes that a poplar tree "takes its stand *where told*" (*RB* 11, emphasis added; *VF* 57). On the other hand, his concluding remarks on the dissolution of the assembled scenery indicate a certain lack of control over the created world: "Alas, the objects I had assembled wander away . . . Everything floats away. Harmony and meaning vanish. The world irks me again with its variegated void" (*RB* 24; *VF* 72).

His relationship to the characters he depicts is also freighted with contradiction. At times, he appears to have unrestricted access to his hero Romantovski's thoughts, and presents these thoughts through a free direct discourse mode. When the brothers seem to swell up into oppressive giants in Romantovski's room, the narrator conveys Romantovski's mental reaction using free direct discourse: "I don't know why they push against me; I implore you, do leave me alone. I'm not touching you, so don't you touch me either" (*RB* 16; *VF* 62). On the other hand, at the conclusion of the story he professes surprise when Anton informs Gustav that Romantovski was a counterfeiter. Mentally addressing Romantovski, he states: "I believed, let me confess, that you were a remarkable poet (*RB* 23; *VF* 71). It seems paradoxical that one who could reproduce verbatim a character's thoughts would later be surprised to learn the character's occupation.

What is one to make of this? Perhaps Nabokov wished to suggest something of the difficulties involved in the process of artistic perception and transcription in general. The spectatorial element of the narrator's relationship to the events he narrates recalls Nabokov's description of his own experience of creative insight.

I do think that in my case it is true that the entire book, before it is written, seems to be ready ideally in some other, now transparent, now dimming, dimension, and my job is to take down as much of it as I can make out and as precisely as I am humanly able to. (*SO* 69)

Two elements of Nabokov's description here accord well with the narrator's approach to his subject matter in "The Leonardo": first, the shifting substantiality of the other dimension itself (which is "now transparent, now dimming"), and second, the suggestion that it may not be easy to "make out" and "take down" the entire vision.

In the narrator of "The Leonardo," then, Nabokov creates a figure who occupies an intermediary position between the powerful *auctor* whose presence can be felt in such works as *The Defense* and "Lips to Lips" and those figures with more limited powers of perception and control who narrate *The Eye* and *Despair*. The narrator may even represent a kind of neophyte or novice author, one who has not yet mastered his capacities of creative control (unlike Nabokov himself who claimed that "every character follows the course *I imagine for him*" *SO* 69 [emphasis added]). Nabokov would return to the theme of authorial apprenticeship in *Invitation to a Beheading*, "Torpid Smoke," and *The Gift*; and the dream-like quality of the narrator's experience here also resurfaces in those works.

Yet if the narrator of "The Leonardo" is not entirely in control of the events he describes, what *is* his relationship to the characters and their fate? To answer this, one must look more closely at the relationship between Romantovski and the brothers Anton and Gustav. On the surface their relationship is one of opposition. Whereas Romantovski represents a principle of autonomous individuality, the brothers take a strong stand in support of communal union, even to the point of imposing their conformist viewpoint onto the other by force (thereby working toward Hermann's utopia of "identical brawny fellows" *D* 30; *O* 22). Such broad contrasts have appeared elsewhere in Nabokov's fiction (compare "Terra Incognita" and "An Affair of Honor"), and as one finds in those works, Nabokov's manipulation of names suggests that the pair of contrasting characters may be combined to form a composite human personality. Anton and Gustav have no surname, while Romantovski lacks a first name. The contrast between Romantovski and the two brothers, then, represents not only a contrast between two sets of separate individuals but a potential conflict within the human psyche itself.

Significantly, the narrator himself is implicated in this potential conflict. That is, while his ostensible sympathies lie with Romantovski ("My poor Romantovski!" *RB* 23; *VF* 71–72), his discourse reproduces the inner world of the *brothers* as faithfully as it does Romantovski's inner world. Along with Romantovski's mental pleas for tranquility – "I implore you, do leave me alone" – one finds expressions of the brothers' inner visions, and these two are presented in the free direct discourse mode: "Now this is the way we'll arrange the world: every man shall sweat, every man shall eat" and "Repeat: the world shall be sweaty and well-fed. Idlers, parasites, and musicians are not admitted" (*RB* 12, 13; *VF* 58, 59). Indeed, the narrator utilizes the free direct discourse mode to convey the brothers' impressions more frequently than he does Romantovski's. Finally, at the end of the tale he displays a link to the brothers' position when he confesses: "I who believed *with them* that you were indeed someone exceptional" (*RB* 23, emphasis added; *VF* 71).

What is the ultimate significance of this? The narrator's treatment of the struggle between Romantovski and the brothers suggests that this struggle has not only *social* implications, but *aesthetic* ones as well.[1] The narrator's attitude toward the events he describes exhibits something of the brothers' voyeuristic, predatory attitude toward Romantovski. Both his initial description of the assemblage of the setting and his final description of its dissolution are charged with notes of impatience and aggressivity. At the outset, he urges the assemblage – "Hurry up, please" (*RB* 11; *VF* 57), and at the conclusion he confesses that he is "irked" when he no longer has any object to entertain him. He also reveals a predilection for order that echoes the brothers' urge to "arrange the world": "Here comes the ovate little poplar, all punctuated with April greenery, and *takes its stand where told* (*RB* 11, emphasis added; *VF* 57).

The conflict between Romantovski and the brothers may thus represent an externalized model of a latent conflict within the narrator himself – a conflict between an acceptance of the uniqueness of the artistic vision and a desire to master, control, and dissect it. Embedded in Romantovski's name is the Russian word for "novel" (*roman*). His demise at the hands of the brothers may therefore reflect the fate of a character or a literary work which falls prey to the overzealous scrutiny of another, either the would-be creator-controller or the reader who comes to the work with a desire to extract every shred of meaning from it.

Romantovski's murder may serve as a warning against the dangers of overdeterminism in one's "readings" of the other – in life and art alike. In this, it directly anticipates the novel *Invitation to a Beheading*, which also features the oppression of an individual by the intrusive gaze of others and which highlights the aesthetic as well as social implications of such oppression. Cincinnatus is clearly Romantovski's successor: he exhibits the same kind of ethereal quality found in Romantovski,[2] and he consequently becomes the target of a ferocious rage by those who want to dissect and define him.[3]

Both "The Leonardo" and *Invitation* illustrate the threat which arises from the desire to know and to control those others who come into one's sphere of attention, whether they be people one encounters in life, or characters one encounters in fiction. In life and in art, one's meeting with another must allow for the inherent uniqueness and autonomy of the other. Indeed, the very ambiguity with which Nabokov surrounds his narrator here (who is he? where do his visions come from?) may indicate the authentic *auctor*'s own recognition of the value of open-ended creative portraits.

Within the diegetic plane of "The Leonardo," however, the forces of totalitarian definition succeed in destroying the enigmatic individual in their midst. As in "Terra Incognita" the destruction of the creative figure at the story's core signals the dissolution of the story's setting and the cessation of the narrator's creative activity. In *Invitation to a Beheading*, on the other hand, the "death" of the protagonist has a different effect. Cincinnatus's execution is also his liberation, and the dissolution of the setting in which he has existed results not in a "variegated void" but unbars the way for him to ascend into a new realm of creativity and artistic engagement.

INVITATION TO A BEHEADING

Together with *The Gift*, *Invitation to a Beheading* represents the crowning achievement of nearly a decade of artistic growth for Vladimir Nabokov.[4] The two novels form a metafictional diptych illustrating the quest of two individuals to actualize their latent authorial potential and to transcend their status as literary characters. In *Invitation to a Beheading* this quest carries several levels of meaning. The very multi-dimensionality of the novel works to oppose any single interpretation which would itself represent a kind of totalitarian gesture of reductionism. On the contrary, the novel celebrates the dazzling freedom and fluidity of the human imagination.[5]

The protagonist of the novel, one Cincinnatus C., finds himself trapped in a world of bizarre, theatrically garbed beings who have judged him guilty of a capital offense and have sentenced him to execution by beheading. The formal charge leveled against Cincinnatus is "gnostical turpitude" (*IB* 72; *PK* 80), but his fundamental crime rests in the fact that he is inherently different from those around him: he is the one among them who possesses a creative imagination and soul. The issue of Cincinnatus's difference provides the context for Nabokov's exploration of the self–other relationship in the novel. It confronts Cincinnatus with the crucial question: what can or should he do about his difference from others?

Throughout his life Cincinnatus has been hounded by the conformist pressures of the surrounding society. As the novel opens, he has been reduced to a state very much like that of a literary character. He is controlled, manipulated, and defined by others who, though not authentic authors themselves, are eager to serve as stage directors for Cincinnatus while they busy themselves with their own roles as prison guard, warden, lawyer, and so on. In an astute essay on the novel Dale Peterson explicates Cincinnatus's status as a character in relationship to the reader and author standing outside the novel ("Nabokov's *Invitation*" 830–31). It is important to note, however, that Cincinnatus fulfills such a function in relation to those *within* his world as well.

The opening scene underscores Cincinnatus's passive, dependent status through the very grammar of the passage. In the Russian original, Cincinnatus is the object, direct or indirect, of a series of transitive verbs, while in the English version, the translator uses the passive voice to indicate Cincinnatus's subordination to actions performed on him: "the death sentence was announced to Cincinnatus C. in a whisper"; "Cincinnatus was taken back to the fortress"; "he had to be supported" (*IB* 11; *PK* 25).[6] Similarly, Cincinnatus is often depicted as the object of instructions read to him by others. After the death sentence is announced to him, he becomes the audience for numerous speeches by the warden, his lawyer, and later the executioner. His cell contains a list of rules outlining activities which prisoners are forbidden to pursue, and his jailers strive to regulate his every move, even controlling the light switch in his cell. A last sign of the society's attempt to control and delimit Cincinnatus is the fact that they have created a finalizing label for his crime, giving it the formal designation of "gnostical turpitude."

Upon first reading, Cincinnatus might seem to be the helpless victim of cruel persecution by others. Yet while he is truly a victim, a contributing factor in his imprisonment is his

own acceptance of the limitations imposed upon him. Ellen
Pifer writes that Cincinnatus's confinement "depends on his
own acquiescence in the role of prisoner" (*Nabokov and the Novel*
54). Pifer's observation is sound, but it should be broadened:
his confinement depends on his acquiescence in the role of
character itself. For his own salvation Cincinnatus needs to
develop a new relationship to the external world, to change the
way he views himself and his relations with those around him.[7]
It is imperative that he nurture the powers of autonomous
vision within himself, and not allow himself to remain entirely
dependent on the beings around him for his self-definition.

Although Cincinnatus appears essentially passive in relation
to the world around him, he does have some responsibility for
permitting the deceptions of the world to operate unchecked,
and at times he admits this to himself. For example, when he
hears the sounds of digging beyond his cell wall, he speculates
on the validity of these sounds as a sign of rescue: "I am quite
willing to admit that they are also a deception but right now *I
believe in them so much that I infect them with truth* (*IB* 138, emphasis
added; *PK* 139). Later, the narrator comments on Cincinnatus's tendency to sustain the illusions around him, stating that
he "inspired the meaningless with meaning, and the lifeless
with life" (*IB* 155; *PK* 155).[8] At that very moment the narrator
notes that Cincinnatus "*permitted* the spotlighted figures of all
his usual visitors to appear ... and *by evoking them* – not
believing in them, perhaps, but still evoking them – Cincinnatus *allowed them the right to exist, supported them, nourished them with
himself*" (*IB* 155–56, emphasis added; *PK* 155–56).

In his relations to those around him, Cincinnatus operates
much like the credulous reader who views literary characters as
authentic human beings. One recalls that Hermann stated that
an "author's fondest dream" is "to turn the reader into a
spectator." Hermann then defined his view of the relationship
between readers and characters: "The pale organisms of literary heroes feeding under the author's supervision swell gradually with the reader's lifeblood;" on this food they may
thrive, "sometimes for centuries" (*D* 26; *O* 19). Like Her-

mann's dream reader, Cincinnatus nourishes the pale organisms of his jailers with his own lifeblood – his imagination. Significantly, Nabokov uses the same verb for "nourished" in the Russian original of *Invitation to a Beheading* that he does for "feeding" in the Russian version of *Despair – pitat'* (compare *PK* 156 – "pital ikh soboi", *O* 19 – "pitaias' pod rukovodstvom avtora").

Nabokov underscores the error Cincinnatus makes in granting the sham creatures around him the semblance of authentic life during the scene in which Cincinnatus reads the novel *Quercus*. The title figure of the novel is also its central hero – a huge oak tree that serves as the focalizer for the author who interweaves activity occurring in the oak's environs with scientific descriptions of the oak itself. This novel, whose main "idea" is considered "the acme of modern thought," is viewed by Cincinnatus's society as "unquestionably the best that his age had produced" (*IB* 122, 123; *PK* 124, 125). To judge from Nabokov's own antipathy to the "modish message" (*SO* 66) and the tendency to celebrate works for their "great ideas" (*SO* 41), such accolades cast the actual merit of this novel into doubt. In fact, as Robert Alter argues, such a work may represent the quintessential "naturalistic novel," a kind of "photographic realism" that is mindless, pointless, and devoid of humanity ("Nabokov and the Art of Politics" 54).[9]

Cincinnatus feels tremendous "melancholy" and "distress" as he reads this novel, and he asks himself why this "deceitful and dead" material should matter to him, since he himself is preparing to die (*IB* 123; *PK* 126). Yet he desperately longs to escape his impending execution, and when he cries out aloud "Will no one save me?" he receives an intriguing response: "From the dense shadows above there fell and bounced on the blanket a large dummy acorn, twice as large as life, splendidly painted a glossy buff, and fitting its cork cup as snugly as an egg" (*IB* 126; *PK* 128). While Cincinnatus's reaction to this event is not recorded, some of the novel's commentators have asserted that the fallen acorn is "a message promising help" from Nabokov the novelist (Toker, *Nabokov* 138).[10] Such a reading, however, may repeat the very mistake that Cincinnatus has made in regard to his entire environment: it invests the lifeless with life, the deceitful with the mantle of authenticity.

Several features of the acorn point to its duplicitous quality. First of all, it is a "dummy" acorn (in Russian, "butaforskii zholud'"). Whether one follows the Russian or the English version, the epithet should signal its suspicious nature. The Russian word *butaforiia* literally means "stage property," "dummies" (as in commercial mannequins), and "sham." The narrator uses this very word (*butaforiia*) in reference to the "stage properties" which adorn the grotesque "photohoroscope" Pierre has made for Emmie (*IB* 170; *PK* 168).[11] If one follows the English translation, one can only conclude that the "dummy" acorn belongs to the same realm as the other theatrical props and "dummies" which surround Cincinnatus, such as the artificial spider perched in a corner of his cell (the artificial spider in turn contrasts with the fabulous moth which escapes the jailer's grasp near the end of the novel). As Cincinnatus writes to Marthe: "we are surrounded by dummies ... you are a dummy yourself" (*IB* 142; *PK* 143). Cincinnatus needs to resist the temptation to credit such dummies with authentic life.

A second feature of the acorn that renders it of dubious value to Cincinnatus is that it comes from an oak. Not only is the oak the hero of the greatest novel Cincinnatus's society has produced, it is also the material out of which the execution platform has been made (see *IB* 219; *PK* 213). It is not surprising that the society which regards Cincinnatus as a threat because of his ineluctable originality would seek to behead him on a platform made of the material celebrated in its greatest novel. The spirit of original art is to be sacrificed on the altar of pseudo-art.

The dummy acorn, then, provides an emblem not of release out of the world in which Cincinnatus is imprisoned, but rather of his continued subjugation to it. Indeed, immediately after the dummy acorn drops onto his bed, he hears for the first time the faint sounds of the tapping that he later "infects with truth" as the harbinger of escape. To his dismay, of course, the long-awaited breakthrough of the tunnel into his cell does not provide him with a means of escape; rather it opens a new route of access into his cell for his executioner Pierre. For Cincinnatus to follow the plots laid down for him in this banal world means for him to acquiesce in his own annihilation.

What Cincinnatus must do instead is to spurn society's preordained role for him and to develop within himself that part of his personality he has allowed to atrophy – his authorial potential. Thus far in his life he has permitted his own imagination to be shaped by the customary blandishments of his world. Such a derivative imagination cannot assist him in breaking out of his dilemma; rather it works to keep him locked within it. This is illustrated during Cincinnatus's fantasy of escape in the first chapter. He walks out of the prison and into the city where he and Marthe had lived. Reaching the door of his house, he pushes it open, but instead of entering his house, he enters his lighted cell! He turns around, but he is already locked in again (*IB* 20; *PK* 33). Cincinnatus's own mind manufactures the mortar holding the walls of his prison cell together. As long as he continues to believe that he can find happiness within the confines of his world, he will remain a prisoner of it.[12]

As his escapist fantasies suggest, the fortress in which Cincinnatus dwells is as much a prisonhouse of the imagination as it is a structure of stone and iron. He must turn away from the seductive illusions of the external world and look within himself to stoke the fires of authentic creative vision. To attain the status of an independent artist in Nabokov's fictional world, Cincinnatus must pursue a dual course: he must stimulate his latent authorial potential, and he must cast off that aspect of himself which functions as a character. Both elements appear in *Invitation to a Beheading*.

Cincinnatus's development of his authorial potential finds its central focus in the process of writing. One of his first actions upon his imprisonment is to pick up "a beautifully sharpened pencil, as long as the life of any man except Cincinnatus" (*IB* 12; *PK* 26). With this pencil he begins to write: "In spite of everything I am comparatively. After all I had premonitions, had premonitions of this finale" (*IB* 12–13; *PK* 26). Cincinnatus's first inscription is a garbled one, and he suspends the activity almost immediately for he senses the eye of his jailer glaring at him through the peephole. Feeling a chill on the back of his head, he crosses out what he had written (*IB* 13; *PK* 26). This gesture of negation anticipates Cincinnatus's final pencil stroke at the end of the novel, but the two gestures have fundamentally different import, as shall be noted later. Here, Cincinnatus reveals himself to be too sensitive to the gaze of the other, and he allows himself to be intimidated into stifling his own nascent creativity.[13]

The initial description of Cincinnatus's pencil deserves attention. The phrase "as long as the life of any man except Cincinnatus" stands out for its unexpected evocation of Cincinnatus's impending fate, and like so much else in this novel, it carries a double meaning. On the surface it refers to the fact that Cincinnatus, unlike the other figures in his world, faces a premature end to his life. On a deeper level, however, it hints at Cincinnatus's unique personality: he will utilize that very pencil to capitalize on his uniqueness and to transform his life. As the pencil grows shorter through Cincinnatus's use of it, Cincinnatus himself grows stronger and more substantial. In exhausting the pencil's life, he is extending his own.[14]

In his first attempt at writing Cincinnatus reveals the incoherence of deep fear. A similar inarticulateness appears in his first oral utterance as well. The first words he speaks in the novel are "Kind. You. Very" (*IB* 15; *PK* 29). Over the course of the novel, however, Cincinnatus gradually becomes more articulate, refining his thoughts and searching out the proper means of self-expression. This change appears already in Cincinnatus's second attempt at writing. He starts off with fragmentary phrases as he tries to record his racing thoughts: "'But then perhaps' (Cincinnatus began to write rapidly on a sheet of ruled paper) 'I am misinterpreting . . . Attributing to the epoch . . . This wealth . . . Torrents . . .'" (*IB* 51; *PK* 61). Slowly, his writing becomes more organized: "But how can these ruminations help my anguish? Oh, my anguish – what shall I do with you, with myself? How dare they conceal from me . . . " (*IB* 51; *PK* 61). Finally, when he hits upon a purpose for his writing, his voice becomes more confident and even eloquent: "On the other hand, were I to know, I could perform . . . a short work . . . a record of verified thoughts . . . Some day someone would read it and would suddenly feel just as if he had awakened for the first time in a strange country. What I mean to say is that I would make him suddenly burst into tears of joy, his eyes would melt, and, after he experiences this, the world will seem to him cleaner, fresher" (*IB* 51–52; *PK* 62).

Two elements within this passage merit attention. First, Cincinnatus reveals an awareness of the desirability of having a responsive audience for his written work. Communication with another has been an essential component of Nabokov's artistic vision since such early sketches as "A Guide to Berlin." Cincinnatus imagines the existence of another, and his very creation of a hypothetical other provides the necessary outlet for his emerging artistry. Secondly, although his diction and imagery are still simple here, he is beginning to find his own voice. Over the course of his written chronicle his lapses into fragmented syntax are increasingly counterbalanced by formulations rich in suggestive imagery. One notes, for example, how eloquently he expresses his concern for articulate communication in the extended entry in chapter 8: "Or will nothing come of what I am trying to tell, its only vestiges being the corpses of strangled words, like hanged men . . . evening silhouettes of gammas and gerunds, gallow crows" (*IB* 90; *PK* 96).[15]

Cincinnatus's image of execution obviously resonates with his anticipation of his own fate. Yet this very image also points to a salient feature of his creative endeavor. His image of the gallows offers a different image of execution than the one planned for him by his society. This difference itself underscores the ultimate function of Cincinnatus's work: in creating his written record, he is constructing a world of words that will overturn the fiction of the society which currently imprisons him. Just as Nabokov constructs his metaliterary text to counter the conventional texts of literary realism, so too

Cincinnatus constructs his visionary discourse to counter the oppression of the banal formulas disseminated by his jailers.

Cincinnatus must overcome one overwhelming temptation as he struggles to develop his authorial potential. Raised in a society that discourages original creativity, he must be wary of his tendency to fall back upon the time-worn formulas of previous traditions. This temptation is evident in his fantasy that the prison director's daughter Emmie will help him to escape. When she first enters his cell, he muses: "If only you were grown up . . . if your soul had a slight touch of my patina, you would, as in poetic antiquity, feed a potion to the turnkey, on a night that is murky" (*IB* 47; *PK* 57). Later, he takes up this fantasy again: "I wondered, *to the rhythm of an ancient poem –* could she not give the guards a drugged potion, could she not rescue me? If only she would remain the child she is, but at the same time mature and understand – and then it would be feasible: her burning cheeks, a black windy night, salvation, salvation . . ." (*IB* 53, emphasis added; *PK* 63). In addition to viewing an inappropriate other as his potential savior, Cincinnatus relies upon plots found in the literature of the past – in this case, Lermontov's "The Neighbor Girl" ("Sosedka"; see Shapiro, "Russkie literaturnye alliuzii" 370) – to provide a blueprint for his own future. Rather than looking within himself for fresh sources of inspiration, he retraces the literary tracks of previous poets, thus repeating the plagiarism of such earlier Nabokov protagonists as Anton Petrovich in "An Affair of Honor" or Smurov in *The Eye*.[16]

Inevitably, such musings do not promote original creativity and consequent release, but rather keep Cincinnatus mired in a morass of repetition, imitation, and continued confinement. Cincinnatus discovers this for himself when he meets Emmie outside the prison walls. Believing that she will lead him away from the prison, he meekly follows her back into the fortress (*IB* 165–166; *PK* 165). What has entrapped him here is not Emmie, but his own delusions. As long as he continues to believe that salvation can be found within the confines of his world, he is doomed never to find a way out of it.

His written work, however, stimulates him to keep prospecting for the sources of original vision, and the imagery he utilizes indicates that he is headed in the right direction. At one point he tries to define his perception of a radiant dimension lying beyond the confines of his physical realm: "*there* shines the mirror that now and then sends a chance reflection here" (*IB* 94; *PK* 100). Cincinnatus's introduction of the mirror image here suggests that he has gained intimations of the wellsprings of authentic creative consciousness. From his early prose sketch, "A Guide to Berlin," to a novel such as *Bend Sinister*, where he writes of "the mind behind the mirror" (*BS* 233) Nabokov utilizes mirror imagery to evoke the refracting properties of the artistic imagination.

Not only does Cincinnatus himself glimpse the reflection of such a mirror, but the narrator later describes him in such a way as to highlight the figure's affinity with the wondrous properties of mirrors and their reflections: "It seemed as though at any moment . . . Cincinnatus would step in such a way as to slip naturally and effortlessly through some chink of the air into its unknown coulisses to disappear there with the same easy smoothness with which the flashing reflection of a rotated mirror moves across every object in the room and suddenly vanishes, as if beyond the air, in some new depth of ether" (*IB* 121; *PK* 124). As Cincinnatus nurtures his creative energies, he evinces more and more the scintillating qualities of such dynamic mirrors.[17]

Aiding Cincinnatus in the maturation of his artistic proclivities is his appreciation for the craft of poetry. As he nears the end of his written record, he writes: "Envious of poets. How wonderful it must be to speed along a page and, right from the page, where only a shadow continues to run, to take off into the blue" (*IB* 194; *PK* 190). Cincinnatus's metaphor of poets using their lines to catapult themselves into the heavens neatly expresses the effect of his own burgeoning talent. Moreover, his image of the shadow running along the page uncannily anticipates the execution scene in which Cincinnatus himself will later participate. Cincinnatus is in effect writing the scenario for his own execution, an event that will serve to liberate him from the confines of the present text and to direct him toward a new realm beyond its horizons.

Cincinnatus's final written gesture confirms that his artistic maturation process has reached its goal. The very last word that he writes is "death" (*IB* 206; *PK* 201), but he immediately crosses the word out to search for a more precise term for his inner vision. He never finishes the note, for Pierre and his henchmen unexpectedly enter the cell to take Cincinnatus to his execution. At first Cincinnatus asks for more time – "To finish writing something" – but then he pauses, "straining his thoughts, and suddenly understood that everything had in fact been written already" (*IB* 209; *PK* 204). Cincinnatus experiences here a moment of crucial insight, and his epiphany has multiple significance.

First of all, he realizes that he does not need to find one specific word to finish his thought, for the written sign he has left on the page conveys the full richness of his vision. In crossing out the word "death" Cincinnatus expresses his own intuition that for him (as for Tolstoy's Ivan Ilyich) there will be no death, at least as it is conventionally understood. Cincinnatus's gesture here creates a miniature *nonnon* mirror of words. In negating "death," which is itself a negation of life, Cincinnatus reproduces the workings of that fabulous mirror: "minus by minus equaled plus, everything was restored, everything was fine" (*IB* 135; *PK* 137). A similar result emerges when one compares Cincinnatus's gesture here with his first attempt to create a written text. Then, he crossed out his disordered notes because he was afraid of the reaction of the spying "other," his jailer Rodion. Now, he crosses the word out not because he fears another's reaction, but because he is striving to meet his own aesthetic standards.[18] Taken together, these two incidents of negation combine to make a positive result: the two scenes prove that Cincinnatus has made enormous strides in finding within himself a center of independent judgment and value. It is significant too that Cincinnatus achieves his negation of death with his pencil. This implement points to the capacity of the literary process itself to cope with death in uncommon ways. Skillfully applied, verbal art can transform that which is transient into something beyond the reach of annihilation and oblivion.

Finally, Cincinnatus's realization that "everything had in fact been written already" indicates that he has learned an important truth about genuine art. In works of authentic art, not everything must or even should be spelled out to the last degree. Cincinnatus has been imprisoned in a world in which "everything had a name" (*IB* 26; *PK* 38). To counter the pressures of this world of "unabashed nominalism" (*The Novels* Clancy 67) one must create art which is allusive, suggestive, multidimensional. Cincinnatus's acceptance of a certain degree of indefiniteness reflects his creator's rejection of art (and critical interpretations of art) that reduce the work to simplistic, one-dimensional formulas.[19]

Cincinnatus has successfully nurtured within himself the shoots of authentic artistry. To ascend to the status of autonomous author, however, he must still relinquish that aspect of himself which functions as a character. Nabokov depicts this process of divestment in *Invitation to a Beheading* through the image of a double. In several passages the narrator indicates the outlines of a latent bifurcation within Cincinnatus. The clearest statement of this occurs in chapter 2: "Therefore Cincinnatus did not crumple the motley newspapers, did not hurl them, as his double did (the double, the gangrel, that accompanies each of us – you, and me, and him over there – doing what we would like to do at that very moment, but cannot . . .). Cincinnatus very calmly laid the papers aside and finished his chocolate" (*IB* 25; *PK* 37).

Over the course of the narrative it becomes clear that one element within Cincinnatus regards the external world with trepidation, while the other displays an essential calmness and self-control. This division becomes especially clear on the eve of the execution when Cincinnatus is writing about his dread of dying. The narrative states: "Cincinnatus got up, made a running start and smashed headlong into the wall – the real Cincinnatus, however, remained sitting at the table . . . and continued to write, a little less rapidly" (*IB* 193; *PK* 189). This episode offers an illuminating observation on the relationship between the two Cincinnatuses. The "real" Cincinnatus (the one who embodies his authorial potential) remains calm in the face of death and pursues his artistic activity at a controlled pace, while the other Cincinnatus (the one who represents his character dimension) becomes caught up in the role prescribed for him by the others in his environment.[20] It is this second aspect of Cincinnatus to which the narrator refers when he states that "fear was dragging him" into the "false logic of things" and "into a system that was perilous to him" (*IB* 213; *PK* 207–8). Contrasting with that aspect is the other, authorial Cincinnatus, and it is he who insists on mounting the execution block and lying down there "By myself" (*IB* 218; *PK* 213; see also *IB* 221; *PK* 216). By the end of the novel the authorial Cincinnatus has nearly completed his process of marshalling his inner resources. He now needs only to banish the more timorous character aspect of himself. This he does during the execution scene.

The execution scene has occasioned much discussion from Nabokov's readers. Some readers affirm that Cincinnatus is not beheaded (see Pifer, *Nabokov and the Novel* 63–65, and Houk, "The Spider and the Moth" 39), while others conclude that he is (see Johnson, *Worlds* 167, and Rowe, *Nabokov's Spectral Dimension* 79); a third group finds a fundamental ambiguity in the scene (see Lee, *Vladimir Nabokov* 79, Peterson, "Nabokov's Invitation" 833, and Toker, *Nabokov* 137). The description of the scene, however, provides its own indications, and thus deserves examination:

"I am not doing anything yet," said M'sieur Pierre with an extraneous note of gasping effort, and the shadow of his swing was already running along the boards, when Cincinnatus began counting loudly and firmly: one Cincinnatus was counting, but the other Cincinnatus had already stopped heeding the sound of the unnecessary count which was fading away in the distance; and, with a clarity he had never experienced before – at first almost painful, so suddenly did it come, but then suffusing him with joy, he reflected: why am I here? Why am I lying like this? And, having asked himself these simple questions, he answered them by getting up and looking around.

All around there was a strange confusion. Through the headsman's still swinging hips the railing showed. On the steps the pale librarian sat doubled up, vomiting. (*IB* 222; *PK* 217)

Nabokov's description encourages a most peculiar interpretation – that the execution both *does* and *does not* take place. Bolstering the view that a beheading has taken place is the librarian's reaction; it seems plausible that he is responding to the sight of an actual decapitation rather than to the mere anticipation of it. On the other hand, the narrative states that Cincinnatus manages to get up, look around, and even to walk away. What this description depicts, then, is the execution of one dimension of Cincinnatus's personality and the simultaneous liberation of the other. While the *character* aspect of Cincinnatus's personality is destroyed, his *authorial* dimension is set free, much to the consternation of those around him.

This liberated persona now moves off "in that direction where, to judge by the voices, stood beings akin to him" (*IB* 223; *PK* 218). Dale Peterson speculates that Cincinnatus seems about to join "whatever posterity literary characters enjoy, or possibly, to blend into the company of us readers" (833). However, it is not a group of characters or even readers that Cincinnatus is heading to join. Only one attribute of these beings is given – their voices – and this attribute may point to the essential status of these beings: they may represent tellers of tales, verbal creators.[21] Having cultivated his own resources of autonomous authorial potential, Cincinnatus is now ready to enter the company of authentic authors.[22]

Of course, Cincinnatus's transformation from character to author cannot be depicted literally within the text of the novel, since from the reader's perspective, Cincinnatus remains a literary character as long as he is portrayed within the boundaries of the text. Nabokov was perhaps sensitive to this problem, for he raises it again when he depicts the maturation of authorial potential in *The Gift*. There he utilizes a different strategy to evoke the power and magnitude that the transformation from character to author might entail.[23]

Although the trajectory of Cincinnatus's liberation is clear, one major question about his relationship to the world which imprisoned him remains to be asked. The narrative clearly indicates that Cincinnatus "allowed" the phantoms around him to exist, but it does not assert that Cincinnatus himself is the original source of the vision. Who then *is* the original source? Is it Cincinnatus, or someone else? One way to deal with the epistemological quandary raised in the novel would be to view the text as the verbal record of an elaborate dream. Images of sleep, dreams, and awakening run throughout the novel (see in particular *IB* 36; *PK* 47), and although they are predominantly associated with Cincinnatus, one must not rush to label him the primary dreamer. Nabokov's handling of the dream scenario is complex, and while it may be reasonable to view Cincinnatus as the individual figure within the diegetic plane who represents most closely the fears and aspirations of the dreamer, one must be wary of confusing the *character* of Cincinnatus with that *auctorial* entity responsible for generating the images of the dream. For clarity's sake it may be preferable to regard Cincinnatus as the main representative of the dreamer *within* the world of the dream, and to envision the dreamer as a figure who stands outside or above that world.

The resulting scheme, then, would be as follows. *Invitation to a Beheading* represents the verbal account of a dream experienced by an artist figure who is beset by anxieties about the potential suppression of his creative energies.[24] This figure envisions himself within the dream world primarily in the character of Cincinnatus. Within dreams, as Kimberly Devlin has put it, "the self sometimes becomes its own spectacle, an object of its own theatrical viewing" ("'See ourselves as others see us'" 882).[25] As for the other characters in the novel, they represent incarnations of the dreamer's anxieties about potential threats to his creativity, as well as unsettling traits which the dreamer may fear within himself. The narrative voice which recounts the events of the novel represents the consciousness of the dreamer as it observes and registers the experiences of the various figures within the dream. The scene of Cincinnatus's execution represents the dreamer waking up from his nightmare. The entire scheme can be visualized as a series of nested bifurcations as outlined in the following diagram:

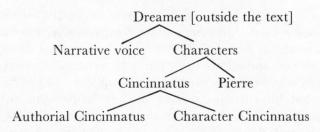

One can elucidate this scheme through closer examination, beginning with the narrative voice.

The narrative voice represents the consciousness of the dreamer as it is manifest on the level of discourse. The narrative voice not only recounts the events of the dream, it glides in and out of the minds of the central characters, using either a free direct [FDD] or free indirect discourse [FID] mode. It is predominantly associated with Cincinnatus's consciousness, but at times it reproduces the inner workings of other characters as well. The narrative voice even conveys the impressions of the moth which the jailer brings into Cincinnatus's cell: "But to me your daytime is dark, why did you disturb my slumber?" (*IB* 204; *PK* 199). The reference to "slumber" is of course suggestive. The moth, which serves as an emblem of Cincinnatus's coming metamorphosis and escape, may be a charmed emissary from the slumbering dreamer to the prisoner temporarily trapped in the created world of the dream.

The interrelationship between the perspective of the narrator and the figure of Cincinnatus is particularly intimate. Cincinnatus appears in every scene, and it is sometimes difficult to distinguish whether a given passage represents the perspective of Cincinnatus or that of an extradiegetic narrator.[26] This intimate link is understandable if one regards Cincinnatus as the central representative or mask of the dreamer *within* the dream – that is, on the level of the story which the dreamer envisions. The figure of Cincinnatus bears the dreamer's deepest anxieties and aspirations. Although Cincinnatus contains within himself the clear spark of artistic originality, his imprisonment may indicate the dreamer's fear of being unable to express his artistic visions in compelling forms and of having his talent suppressed by an unsympathetic world. If Cincinnatus does serve as the dreamer's main representative, this would explain why he feels as though it is he who nourishes the beings around him and allows them the right to exist. It would also explain why he feels a need to "wake up" (see *IB* 36; *PK* 47) and that his current "waking life" is "semi-sleep, an evil drowsiness into which penetrate in grotesque disguise the sounds and sights of the real world, flowing beyond the periphery of the mind" (*IB* 92; *PK* 97).

Yet while Cincinnatus serves as the dreamer's main representative within the diegetic world, the other characters may also represent certain unsavory aspects of the dreamer's personality as well.[27] This seems particularly likely with the figure of Pierre, for within the world of the novel he functions as a kind of perverse double for Cincinnatus.[28] Both characters are thirty years old, and their initials are near mirror images of one another in Cyrillic: П (Р) Ц (С). The initials would become identical mirror reflections if one were to chop off the extra appendage on the letter Ц, which is precisely what Pierre seeks to do with Cincinnatus's head.

The type of structure Nabokov has created here corresponds to that in "Terra Incognita." Like Gregson and Cook, Pierre and Cincinnatus represent two potential tendencies within the central dreamer's psyche. While Cincinnatus displays a genuine impulse toward unfettered creativity, Pierre manifests that element within the dreamer which longs for absolute control over the created world. Nabokov's statement that he was "the perfect dictator" in the private world of his novel (*SO* 69) may find a parodic reflection in the figure of Pierre who strives for just such control over Cincinnatus.[29]

As in "Terra Incognita," the two fictive representatives of the central dreamer's consciousness oppose each other in a mortal struggle for dominance. Unlike the earlier work, however, the positive figure emerges victorious in *Invitation to a Beheading*, and thus the dissolution of the created world does not plunge the central consciousness back into "the furnished rooms of nonexistence" (*RB* 127–28; *S* 127). On the contrary, as Cincinnatus strides off to join the beings akin to him, the dreamer awakens from his grotesque nightmare to enter the realm of the liberated imagination.[30]

The premise that the final scene represents the dreamer's awakening from a nightmare gains support when one looks at Nabokov's remarks about sleep and waking in his own life. In *Speak, Memory* he writes: "Sleep is the most moronic fraternity in the world, with the heaviest dues and the crudest rituals. It is a mental torture I find debasing" (*SM* 108). The images of "moronic fraternity" "crudest rituals" and "mental torture" all apply well to Cincinnatus's experiences in the world depicted in *Invitation to a Beheading*.[31] The most convincing evidence, however, is provided by his subsequent comment: "I loathe Somnus, that black-masked headsman binding me to the block" (*SM* 109). One will recall that a statue of "Captain Somnus" occupies a prominent position in Cincinnatus's town (*IB* 74; *PK* 81), and that on the way to the execution site Cincinnatus glimpses the statue in ruins: "All that remained of the statue of Captain Somnus was the legs up to the hips, surrounded by roses – it too must have been struck by lightning" (*IB* 218; *PK* 212). The reign of Captain Somnus is over; the reign of creative lucidity is set to begin.

The end of the novel depicts Cincinnatus picking himself up from the rubble of the world disintegrating around him and heading off toward a new realm of kindred spirits. This image of the transcendence of mortality resonates with a remark Nabokov makes in *Speak, Memory* about dreams, waking, and intimations of immortality. He writes: "It is certainly not then – not in dreams – but when one is wide awake, at moments of robust joy and achievement . . . that mortality has a chance to peer beyond its own limits, from the mast, from the past and its castle tower. And although nothing much *can be seen* through the mist, there is somehow the blissful feeling that one is looking *in the right direction*" (*SM* 50, emphasis added). Cincinnatus, at the moment of his awakening, strides off in a direction where he can only hear voices but not as yet see anything. Nonetheless, having left behind that part of himself which is subject to coercion, oppression, and the threat of execution, he seems ready to enter a transcendent realm much like that outlined in Nabokov's joyful vision.

In *Invitation to a Beheading* Nabokov depicts for the first time the successful outcome of a character's struggle to throw off the yoke of subordination and to actualize the powerful authorial potential lying within the self. The conclusion of the novel is meant to evoke the process of imminent ascension into the ranks of the unfettered artist. In *Invitation to a Beheading* such an ascension can occur only beyond the horizons of the text. In *The Gift*, however, Nabokov returns again to the subject of authorial aspirations, depicting the transformation of character to author with stunning subtlety and grace. According to Nabokov, *Invitation to a Beheading* was written in a fortnight (*SO* 68). The very swiftness and concentration of its composition undoubtedly contributes to the wondrous allusiveness and magic of its pages. Written over a much longer period, *The Gift* records in precise detail the larger dimensions of the quest to actualize one's creative potential, and it serves as a fitting complement to the inspired vision created in *Invitation to a Beheading*.

CHAPTER 7

The transforming rays of creative consciousness

"RECRUITING"

The brief sketch "Recruiting" ("Nabor"), which was written and published in the summer of 1935, provides a provocative examination of a central issue for Nabokov in the mid-1930s: the relationship of the artistic consciousness to the subject of its creative apprehension. In probing the issue here, Nabokov touches upon one of its most protean facets – the treatment of one's own self as other. The architectonics of the work recalls Chekhov. Nabokov initially orients his focus in one direction, but then shifts the focus over the course of the narrative to end up in quite a different place. The sketch begins with a description of the inner impressions of a certain "Vasiliy Ivanovich," an elderly émigré who has just attended the funeral of a friend and then sits in a park to reflect upon the past. The narrative mode which prevails in the opening section suggests that the narrator is of the omniscient, extrinsic type. At intervals, however, one detects signs of the presence of an intrinsic narrator, and about two-thirds of the way into the sketch, the work abruptly changes course, leaving Vasiliy Ivanovich to concentrate on a different set of subjects – an autobiographic intrinsic narrator, his relationship with the figure of Vasiliy Ivanovich, and his relationship to his own representative within the narrated world.

To the reader's surprise, the narrator reveals that this Vasiliy Ivanovich is a total stranger about whom the narrator knows nothing, not even his real name. Vasiliy Ivanovich's story turns out to be a fabrication made up by the narrator as part of the germination process for a novel he is writing. With this revelation, the reader realizes that the main concern of the sketch is *not* Vasiliy Ivanovich and his experiences, but rather the process by which a creative individual fashions a fictional construct out of the material at hand.

This is not to say that the information provided about Vasiliy Ivanovich is insignificant. The narrative provides a moving evocation of the character's (hypothetical) concern with illness, old age, and the isolation he had experienced after the death of his sister. Of particular interest is a sudden swell of joy that overtakes the character as he sits on the park bench (*TD* 107; *VF* 123). This unexpected surge of joy manifests a Nabokovian impulse to find an emotional counter to the specters of death and pain which ultimately consume all.

More important, however, is the source of this joy. In Nabokov's English version, the narrator discloses that it is he who has "infected" the stranger "with the blazing *creative* happiness that sends a chill over an *artist's* skin" (*TD* 109, emphasis added; compare *VF* 125). This process of "infection" represents a vital progression in the theme of emotional communication which traces back to such early sketches as "Grace." Solitude can devastate the human soul, and empathic communication offers a salutary outlet. In "Grace," it was an artist locked in a state of solipsistic grief who received a vision of human kinship and compassion. Here, it is the artist figure himself who wishes to share his sensations with another so that he might lighten the other's perceived isolation and sorrow. This impulse displays an integral feature of the artist figure's emotional orientation: he is not exclusively parasitic (like Axel Rex), but rather is outer-directed as well. The narrator's predilection for projecting personal impressions onto an out-sider recalls Hermann Karlovich's wild propensities in *Despair*, but one should note a key difference. The narrator's impulse here seems more benign and less intrusive than Hermann's. He does not manipulate or interfere with the other, but uses his creative visions to fuel his verbal art.

Behind the narrator's unusual relationship to the unknown other looms an even more intriguing relationship – to himself.

The narrator's introduction of his persona into the text represents an important development beyond the kind of self-portraiture depicted in *The Eye*. In that novel the narrator's portrayal of the Smurov persona is confused and chaotic: he oscillates between attempts to maintain the illusion that Smurov was an individual separate from himself and an involuntary surrender to emotional identification with Smurov's travails. Here, in contrast, the narrator reveals a more self-assured, controlled attitude toward self-representation. He evinces an awareness that the self-portrait he provides in his narrative is itself a fictional construct. As Michael Boyd observes in connection with *Look at the Harlequins!*, when the author enters the fictional plane, "he too is fictionalized" (*The Reflexive Novel* 161). This conscious appreciation of the fictionality of self-depiction deserves closer inspection.

The narrator's introduction of himself into the narrative occurs in several discrete stages. As noted above, the opening of the sketch suggests that the narrative is generated by an omniscient, maximally effaced, extrinsic narrator. More than a page into the work, however, the reader encounters an indication that some type of intrinsic narrator may be involved: "In the impersonal Berlin crush of the tram, there was another old refugee ... a non-practising lawyer, who was also returning from the cemetery and was also of little use to anyone *except me*" (*TD* 104, emphasis added: *VF* 120). At this point, the figure denoted by the first-person pronoun "me" is still an unknown quantity. In the third stage, the narrator provides an externalized view of himself, but he does so in an unusual manner, not informing the reader that the figure he describes is meant to represent himself until *after* the figure is introduced. He notes: "A man with the local Russian newspaper sat down on the same ... bench. It is difficult for me to describe this man; then again, it would be useless, since a self-portrait is seldom successful, because of a certain tension that always remains in the expression of the eyes – the hypnotic spell of the indispensable mirror" (*TD* 107–8; *VF* 124). Here he depicts himself as if from the outside, as a "he."[1] Finally, the narrator seems to enter the scene directly, using a first-person pronoun to identify his presence in the body of the man who sat down on the bench alongside Vasiliy Ivanovich. He muses: "Why did I decide that the man next to whom *I had sat down* was named Vasiliy Ivanovich?" (*TD* 108, emphasis added; *VF* 124).

Why does Nabokov utilize such a disparate set of narrative perspectives in this sketch? Perhaps he wished to have his narrator demonstrate his mastery of narrative technique in much the same way as Sebastian Knight did with "methods of composition" in his first novel *The Prismatic Bezel*: "It is as if a painter said: look, here I'm going to show you not the painting of a landscape, but the painting of different ways of painting a certain landscape, and I trust their harmonious fusion will disclose the landscape as I intend you to see it" (*SK* 95). Nabokov's narrator in "Recruiting" glides easily through an entire range of techniques for representing point of view and narratorial presence; he may be "recruiting" these techniques for service in other texts, other fictions.

Of particular interest in *this* sketch, however, is the narrator's approach toward the representation of himself in the narrated world. Having introduced himself into the narrated scene with the first-person pronoun, the narrator again retreats from this degree of involvement at the end of the sketch, and he concludes his narrative with the externalized, detached perspective with which he had introduced the man with the Russian newspaper: "My representative, the man with the Russian newspaper, was now alone on the bench and, as he had moved over into the shade where V. I. had just been sitting, the same cool linden pattern that had annointed his predecessor now rippled across his forehead" (*TD* 110; *VF* 126).

The narrator's act of withdrawal and the terminology he uses here are highly significant. Calling the man with the Russian newspaper "my representative," the narrator signals his recognition that the image of himself which he depicts within the diegetic plane of his narrative is merely a stand-in, a created surrogate who is not to be regarded as identical to the entity who generates the discourse itself.[2] Indeed, in having his "representative" move over into the precise location in the shade which had just been occupied by Vasiliy Ivanovich, the narrator underscores an affinity between the figure of V. I. and his own representative: both figures are, from an extradiegetic perspective, fictional creations with the same ontological status as literary characters.[3] Whatever identity the man designated as Vasiliy Ivanovich and the man carrying the newspaper had *before* their depiction by the narrator, once they have been apprehended by the creative eye and set down in a literary text, they are transformed into fictional beings in the storyteller's universe.[4]

The narrator's perception that the image of himself which he introduces into his text is actually a fictional representative manifests a crucial breakthrough in the treatment of self as other in Nabokov. Previous Nabokov protagonists had experienced wild swings of emotion as they reacted to their uncontrolled sensation of dissociation and self-replication. In "Recruiting," by contrast, the narrator's understanding that any representation of oneself in one's discourse transforms one into a fictional character has powerful ramifications. Utilizing this understanding, a disciplined creator can successfully activate the seminal bifurcation of identity in Nabokov's work. It can liberate its authorial potential by creating a fictional representative of itself and then transferring onto that representative its essential character functions. As Nabokov's subsequent novel *The Gift* indicates, this can be achieved with triumphant results quite different from those found in the misshapen strivings of Hermann in *Despair* and the narrator in *The Eye*.

"Recruiting" also anticipates *The Gift* in its manipulation of the relationship between the narrating subject which uses a first-person pronoun ("I") and the diegetic representative of the subject, which is seen as a separate entity, a "he." Although the two are linked, the narrator himself insists upon observing a distinction between the two when he refers to the man with the newspaper as "my representative." The grammatical distinction between "I" and "he" thus points to a deeper ontological distinction. Nabokov creates a structure similar to that observed in *Invitation to a Beheading*. In that novel, the dreamer standing outside the text was represented within the text by a binary set of delegates: the narrative voice on the level of discourse and the characters (primarily Cincinnatus) on the level of story. Here, one can posit the existence of an authorial consciousness standing outside the text who is represented within the text by the first-person narrative voice on the level of discourse and by the figure of the man with the newspaper on the level of story. In *The Gift* Nabokov will utilize the distinction between the narrating consciousness on the level of discourse and the narrated character on the level of story to set the stage for the magnificent transformation which occurs at the conclusion of the novel.

With "Recruiting" Nabokov raises the established theme of the fictionality of the created world to a new level of intricacy. The narrator's treatment of his representation of himself in his text paves the way toward a mature understanding of the relationship between observation, projection, and (self-)creation that becomes an indispensable ingredient for the transformation of evanescent experience into the timeless realm of art.

"TORPID SMOKE"

Like "Recruiting," "Torpid Smoke" ("Tiazhelyi dym") was published in 1935, and it too provides an exploratory treatment of techniques utilized in *The Gift*. Among its salient links to the novel are its focus on the experiences of a young writer and its use of unexpected shifts between intrinsic and extrinsic narrative perspectives. The protagonist here, however, is, at nineteen, several years younger than Fyodor Godunov-Cherdyntsev. He still lives with his family, and he writes "puerile" poetry (*RB* 33; compare *VF* 83 – the verses are called "nichtozhnye" ["insignificant"]). Fyodor, in contrast, lives alone, and has already published one book of verse when the novel begins. These disparities help account for the ultimate difference between the story and the novel. An examination of "Torpid Smoke" casts into relief Nabokov's accomplishment in *The Gift*.

The work has the appearance of a slight sketch, but as often occurs in Nabokov, the material presented on the surface of the narrative hints at deeper complexities lying below. Two issues merit special attention. First is Grisha's strained relationship with the others in his world, here seen in the figures of his sister and his father. Second is a certain vagueness in Grisha's own sense of self-identity. Lacking a clear, coherent relationship to himself, he also fails to sustain harmonious relationships with others.

The latter issue arises initially in Grisha's dealings with his sister. The sketch opens with Grisha lying in a darkened room. His sister and her boyfriend are in the next room, and he gathers from "the mysterious pauses" that the two are kissing. The sister's relationship with her friend contrasts with Grisha's present isolation, and Nabokov underscores the latent disjuncture between the two siblings through the spatial setting he introduces at the outset. She is in a parlor which is "separated from his room" by sliding doors (*RB* 28; *VF* 76). When she opens the door to ask him for cigarettes, she does not enter his space, but only thrusts her head into the room. Their verbal interchange exposes a strain in communication. Her first utterance is a request couched in an imperative: "Grisha dear . . . be an angel, do get some cigarettes from Father." Significantly, "He did not respond." Again she utilizes the imperative: "Get them for me, Grishenka." This time he does answer her, but in the negative. Finally, she urges him with a third imperative: "Hurry, hurry . . . come on, Grisha dear!" He now assents to her request, but he too uses an imperative: "All right, lay off" (*RB* 30; *VF* 79). Despite some tenderness in her tone (perhaps a ploy to stir him to action?), the two siblings engage not in a cordial conversation, but rather in a sparring exchange of exhortations and commands. This unwillingness or inability to accommodate the other's desire or to achieve empathy with the other's position becomes even more glaring in Grisha's subsequent encounter – his meeting with his father.

Before Grisha approaches his father, however, he first turns to his bookshelf. This detour might seem unusual, but Grisha hopes that he has some cigarettes stashed between his books. It is telling that Grisha seeks to avoid dealing with his father by turning first to the place where his favorite authors (including Sirin) are represented: he looks in the direction of literature, not life, to fulfill a need expressed by another. When it finally does occur, the dreaded meeting of father and son is even colder than that between brother and sister. His father's discourse is limited to three questions – "What is it?" "Cigarettes?" and "Is he gone?" – while Grisha's discourse is limited to a single word: "No" (*RB* 32; *VF* 81). The father's meager attempt to engage his son in some kind of dialogue is cut off by the latter's intransigent silence.

Yet it is after this cool interchange (or lack thereof) that Grisha experiences a remarkable epiphany:

With terrifying clarity, as if my soul were lit up by a noiseless explosion, I glimpsed a future recollection; it dawned upon me that exactly as I recalled such images of the past as the way my dead mother had of making a weepy face and clutching her temples when mealtime squabbles became too loud, so one day I would have to recall, with merciless, irreparable sharpness, the hurt look of my father's shoulders as he leaned over that torn map, morose, wearing his warm indoor jacket powdered with ashes and dandruff... (*RB* 33; *VF* 82)

Grisha, whose thoughts are now presented as if from the perspective of an autobiographic intrinsic narrator, articulates his recognition that at some point in the future he will recall the pain which he has inflicted on his father. This revelatory moment indicates that Grisha possesses a significant capacity for self-observation and self-understanding. He comprehends the strains in his relationship with his father, even as he continues to engage in the very behavior that he knows causes his father pain.

How does he respond to this moment of insight? As he had earlier turned toward his books to look for the missing cigarettes, so too he now retreats from the pain of life into the realm of artistic creation. The passage cited above ends with the phrase: "and all this mingled creatively with the recent vision of blue smoke clinging to dead leaves on a wet roof" (*RB* 33; *VF* 82). Grisha immerses himself in the creation of a new poem, and the narrative concludes: "at this moment I trust the ravishing promises of the still breathing, still revolving verse, my face is wet with tears, my heart is bursting with happiness, and I know that this happiness is the greatest thing existing on earth" (*RB* 33; *VF* 83). The pain of his encounter with his father momentarily gives way to his intoxication with his own creative impulse.

Grisha's vulnerability to potential pain in his interactions with his family leads him to erect palpable barriers between himself and the others. The separation he structures into his relationship with his family also finds an interesting counter-part in his relationship to himself. This relationship to self exhibits two distinctive features. First, in the scene which opens the sketch, Grisha lies in a dimly lit room and engages in a series of optical and sensory hallucinations. Gazing across the room, he transforms the physical reality around him, and he feels himself transformed as well: "everything traversed his inner being, and that sense of fluidity became transfigured into something like second sight" (*RB* 28; *VF* 76).

As the narrative describes this sensation of "second sight" further, it becomes clear that Grisha has a remarkable ability to envision several external settings simultaneously. Fyodor extols this very capacity in *The Gift* (see the commentary on "multi-level thinking" in chapter 3: *G* 175; *Dr* 183), and Nabokov's work amply indicates the importance of such a capacity within the creative artist. Yet a disquieting note surfaces here. The narrative continues: "To move was, however, incredibly diffi-cult; difficult, because the very form of his being had now lost all distinctive marks, all fixed boundaries" (*RB* 29; *VF* 77). Again, a sense of fluidity can be a virtue for Nabokov's creative artists, but Grisha's sensation of losing his formal boundaries here may indicate an unformed or uncontrolled impulse to-ward dissolution. Successful artists in Nabokov's work must be able to recognize and respect the essential coordinates of their own identity.[5]

Grisha's tendency toward dissociation soon finds realization. As he moves toward the dining room where his father is sitting, he suddenly experiences a disjuncture from his physical form: "this time the renewed vibration within him possessed such power, and especially, was so much more vivid than all external perceptions, that he did not immediately identify as his proper confines and countenance the stoop-shouldered youth ... who glided soundlessly by in the mirror" (*RB* 32; *VF* 80–81). This passage, with its incorporation of the rift between the viewing consciousness and the viewed image in the mirror, recalls the opening passages of "Terror," where the narrator records his sense of alienation from the image staring back at him in the mirror after periods of intense concentration at his desk.

What makes "Torpid Smoke" so interesting, however, is that Nabokov utilizes this dissociation experience as the basis for a distinctive manipulation of narrative point of view throughout the sketch. Although the work begins by describing Grisha from the outside, using an extrinsic, third-person narrative perspective, it concludes with Grisha himself expressing his inner impressions directly, as if he were an autobiographic intrinsic narrator. Between these two points the narrative shifts from one mode to the other several times, an unusual alternation that warrants further scrutiny.

A casual examination of the text might suggest that the intrinsic mode is utilized whenever the most cherished part of Grisha's personality – his artistic inclinations – is evoked. At other times, such as when he is depicted moving through the apartment or lying on his couch, the extrinsic, third-person mode occurs. Such a division would broadly correspond to the central duality depicted in Nabokov's mature work – the dichotomy between that aspect of the self which carries creative potential and that aspect of the self which functions as a character.

Yet even without performing an exhaustive analysis of the sketch, one realizes that this distinction only applies in a rough way to the shifting narrational modes of "Torpid Smoke." While the initial shift into the intrinsic, first-person mode occurs during an account of how the forces of inspiration tease Grisha early in the day, two later references to the "gentle, mysterious shock" of inspiration depict this experience from an external perspective, with Grisha denoted by the pronoun "he." For example: "Here ... *he* again stepped into a zone of mist, and this time, the renewed vibration within *him* possessed such power ..." (*RB* 31–32, emphasis added; *VF* 80–81).[6]

Although it is largely true that the passages which utilize the first-person narrative mode are connected with the world of Grisha's inner feelings, the shifts into this mode are not always consistent or predictable. This is a telling point: such lack of consistency underscores the basic lack of definition tainting Grisha's relationship with others and particularly with himself. When he first emerges from the trance described in the opening passages of the sketch and "restores" his "corporeal image," the narrative states: "He perceived himself (the pince-nez, the thin, dark mustache, the bad skin on his forehead) *with that utter revulsion he always experienced* on coming back to his body out of the languorous mist" (*RB* 29, emphasis added; *VF* 78). Grisha's revulsion here has something in common with the discomfort felt by the narrator of *The Eye* when he saw his reflection in a mirror after he was beaten by his mistress's husband. Grisha is apparently uncomfortable with his physical form, and he has difficulty mediating between the imperatives of the two essential poles of his being – the physical and the cerebral.

Grisha's troubled relationship to himself and to others anticipates issues of central significance in *The Gift*. Like Grisha, Fyodor Godunov-Cherdyntsev is an aspiring writer, and one of the basic concerns facing him in his literary apprenticeship is the problem of finding the proper relationship between his creative consciousness and the other who serves as the subject of creative apprehension. *The Gift* affirms a principle which was raised in "Recruiting" but which is not fully realized in "Torpid Smoke": to achieve success as a creator, one must learn the proper boundaries between oneself and the subject of one's creation, whether that subject be an external other, or one's own self. The creative personality must learn how to mediate the conflicting impulses between engagement and detachment from the other so as to arrive at the ideal range for creative transformation.

While Fyodor comes to recognize the essential parameters of this problem by the end of *The Gift*, Grisha is depicted at an earlier stage in the process of discovery. Nonetheless, the sketch suggests that Grisha, too, may one day attain the needed balance. One notes that Grisha's glimpse of a future recollection about his father's pain is connected with the tickling sensation of creative inspiration which has been teasing him all day. Perhaps he will learn how to cope with his troubled relationships with his family and to redeem those relationships through his art. For the moment, though, he remains caught up in a swirl of undifferentiated feelings about himself and the others in his family; the poetry of this moment is consequently "puerile" and "perishable" (*RB* 33; *VF* 83). Even so, the reader's understanding of Grisha's difficulties in life and art paves the way for a heightened appreciation of the later triumphs of Fyodor Godunov-Cherdyntsev in *The Gift*.

THE GIFT

In *Invitation to a Beheading* Nabokov portrays the gradual maturation of authorial potential within the imprisoned character Cincinnatus. The conclusion of that novel depicts the newly-liberated authorial Cincinnatus casting off that part of his identity which had been restricted to its character status and heading in a direction where kindred beings – perhaps fellow authors – stand. Yet Nabokov never shows the reader what the specific properties of that other realm are, and the Cincinnatus who walks toward that realm remains a character from the reader's point of view. Nabokov evokes the transfiguration of character into author in allegorical, not literal terms. With *The Gift*, however, Nabokov attempts to provide a more literal (or metaliteral) rendering of such a transformation, and the key to deciphering this design lies in a close evaluation of the author's intricate handling of narrative point of view. Following soon on the heels of "Recruiting" and "Torpid Smoke," *The Gift* is the most metaliterary of all of Nabokov's Russian-language novels, the one which draws attention to the dynamics of its own genesis most consistently. Nabokov's novel bears out Boris Pasternak's observation: "the world's best works of art, while telling of the most diverse things, are in fact speaking of their own birth" ("Okhrannaia gramota" 229; pt. 2, ch. 7).

Written in the mid-1930s and published serially in 1937–38

(with the exception of chapter 4, which was suppressed by the editors of *Sovremennye zapiski*), the novel can best be described as a *Künstlerroman* which traces the growth and maturation of a young émigré writer living in Berlin – Fyodor Godunov-Cherdyntsev – over a three-year period in the late 1920s. Significantly, this growth process is not only illustrated on the level of story, in terms of the character's increasing understanding of the proper tools for his creative work; it finds reflection on the level of discourse as well, where it can be observed in a striking manipulation of narrative modes. Throughout the novel the narrative perspective alternates between an intrinsic, first-person point of view and an extrinsic, third-person point of view, a strategy that has generated a certain amount of critical commentary (and confusion).[7]

The complexity of Nabokov's narrative design manifests itself in the opening pages of the novel. In the first paragraph, which provides a description of time and place, readers may assume that they are dealing with an autobiographic intrinsic narrator, because three parenthetical asides in the chain of neutral descriptive detail contain evidence of an intrinsic narrating center of consciousness: "in keeping with the honesty peculiar to *our* literature," "in which *I* too shall dwell," and "in *my* suitcase there are more manuscripts than shirts" (*G* 15, emphasis added in the first two quotations; *Dr* 9). The next paragraph, however, shifts to an extrinsic, third-person point of view: "Some day, *he* thought, I must use such a scene to start a good, thick old-fashioned novel. The fleeting thought was touched with a careless irony; an irony, however, that was quite unnecessary, because somebody within him, on his behalf, independently from him, had absorbed all this, recorded it, and filed it away" (*G* 16, emphasis added; *Dr* 10). At the end of the third paragraph, the narrative switches once more into the first person, this time apparently providing a glimpse into the newly-introduced character's inner thoughts (using the free direct discourse mode): "God, how I hate all this – the things in the shop windows . . ." (*G* 17; *Dr* 11). As this pattern continues for another page, the reader gradually concludes that the first-person autobiographic voice must be linked with the character of Fyodor Godunov-Cherdyntsev. Although the text of *The Gift* is primarily conducted in the third-person narrative mode, large segments are conducted in the first-person by a speaker identified with Fyodor himself.[8]

Upon closer inspection, however, one perceives that the first-person narrative voice does not simply function as a reflector of the character's impressions at a given moment. At times, particularly toward the end of the novel, the first-person voice appears detached from the character of Fyodor and displays a consciousness of the fictive nature of the ongoing discourse that Fyodor himself is not expressly shown to possess.

Thus, although the narrating "I" on the extradiegetic level has a clear and intimate connection with the character Fyodor on the diegetic level, one can argue that the identity is not precisely congruent, and that the relationship between the two is subject to an important process of evolution over the course of the novel. While this evolution will be the focus of the following analysis of *The Gift*, a preliminary statement of the relationship might be useful. Broadly speaking, one can correlate the two modes of narrative presentation with the general distinction between the authorial and the character components of the self seen earlier in Nabokov's work. While the third-person narrative mode which depicts Fyodor from the outside clearly underscores the *character* dimensions of the figure, the passages conveying a first-person perspective may point to the figure's *authorial* dimensions. In essence, then, the bifurcation in Fyodor's representation into entities designated by the pronouns "he" and "I" may reflect the fundamental bifurcation of identity treated elsewhere in Nabokov's work.[9]

It is important to note, however, that this underlying distinction is not manifest in a uniform way throughout the novel. Since the novel itself illustrates a process of artistic growth, one might expect that the relationship between the first- and third-person narrative modes would undergo an evolutionary process as well. As the figure of the writer Fyodor matures and develops over the course of the novel, so too does the relationship between these two modes. One can compare chapter 1, where the shifts between first-person and third-person narrative modes are numerous (and at times, almost chaotic), to chapter 5, where the shifts continue, but in a more coherent and controlled pattern.

The increasing coherence demonstrated on the level of narrative modes mirrors a significant development taking place within the protagonist's consciousness. By the time the novel ends, the authorial component within Fyodor has matured to the point where it can break away from the character component and attain the status of authentic author. According to this view, the final lines of the novel mark the point at which the *authorial* element within the figure of Fyodor leaves behind the *character* element and begins its ascent to a higher state of authorial omniscience and control. The situation obtaining at the end of *The Gift* is analogous, then, to the ending of *Invitation to a Beheading*. Just as the authorial component of Cincinnatus leaves behind the character component and strides off toward a realm populated by other beings with "voices," so too does the authorial component of Fyodor leave behind his character component. Yet this authorial component does not merely head *in the direction of* the authorial realm – it actually becomes the generating source of the text which we read. This is a spectacular tour de force, and will be discussed in more detail at the end of the chapter.

The story line of *The Gift* concentrates on Fyodor's discovery of the glories and difficulties of creative vision. Yet this process of discovery does not simply involve the development of Fyodor's technical skills or expressive virtuosity. Rather, the writer's growth centers on a specific problem in the novel – the development of one's artistic capacities in response to the inevitability of death and loss in life. The number of deaths which occur or are mentioned in the novel is striking. *The Gift* depicts Fyodor's quest to find an adequate way to deal with this persistent phenomenon through his art.

Fyodor's most important discoveries about aesthetics occur in passages which are marked by a distinctive manipulation of the first-person and third-person narrative modes. While most episodes containing a shift from the prevailing extrinsic third-person mode into the first-person mode are quite brief and simply provide immediacy to the description of Fyodor's experiences (using a form of free direct discourse), there are several important passages where such a shift is extended, and it is at these moments that seminal lessons about artistic expression are absorbed by the developing authorial component within Fyodor. One such passage occurs in each of the first three chapters, and each of these passages follows a fixed pattern.

The pattern is as follows. In each case, the segment of extended first-person narration arises out of the prevailing stream of third-person narration and depicts Fyodor pondering his efforts as an aspiring writer. In every case, the shift immediately follows the character's encounter with a written text. When the shift occurs, the ensuing passage of first-person narration portrays a two-fold experience. Fyodor both recalls a specific period earlier in his life and undertakes a critical evaluation of his artistic accomplishments. A brief look at this pattern in execution should clarify the matter.

The relevant segment in chapter 1 occurs when Fyodor imagines a favorable review of his first book of poetry. The text which signals a shift from the third-person to the first-person mode is the opening poem of the tome – "The Lost Ball." Immediately after this poem is quoted, the narrative shift transpires: "Why doesn't the epithet 'quivering' quite satisfy *me*?" (*G* 22, emphasis added; *Dr* 17). The passage then presents Fyodor's recollections of childhood and his evaluation of his attempts to convey these childhood memories in verse. With the exception of a few fleeting shifts into the first-person *plural* (which are meant to suggest the commentary of the imagined reviewer), the entire passage is conducted in the first-person singular narrative mode.

The analogous segment in chapter 2 arises during a description of the research Fyodor undertakes for a proposed biography of his father, a famous explorer who never returned from his final expedition. The initial preparations are conveyed from the extrinsic, third-person perspective, but as Fyodor's absorption with his task increases, the narrative mode shifts. As in chapter 1, the shift occurs directly following the insertion of a literary text. After quoting from a published memoir about Fyodor's grandfather, the narrative continues: "Suhoshchokov errs in depicting *my* grandfather as an empty-headed rake" (*G* 113, emphasis added; *Dr* 115). The segment goes on to describe Fyodor's recollection of his relationship with his father and his critical evaluation of the literary task now confronting him.

The third segment in the series occurs in chapter 3. The chapter begins in the third-person narrative mode, but shifts into the first-person after the now characteristic insertion of a literary text, in this case an aunt's French translation of a poem by Apukhtin. Fyodor then recalls his first attempts at writing poetry and engages in a retrospective critique of the merits and shortcomings of that work.

The parallels linking these three segments are substantial. In each case, the shift from third-person to first-person narrative mode is marked by the insertion of a specific literary text foregrounding the issue of preservation and transmission of experience in verbal art: a poem about childhood, a memoir about the past, and a translation of a poem from one language to another. Significantly, the ensuing segments of first-person narrative depict activities very much in the spirit of the inserted texts which precede them: in each instance, the writer recalls a significant moment from his past and evaluates the effectiveness of his literary work in preserving and transmitting the recorded experience.

What is more, the *content* of Fyodor's recollections manifests a distinctive pattern too. Each of the successive passages of recollection deals with a later period in the writer's life. The first set of recollections depicts his early childhood. The next set involves his memories of his relationship with his father in the years leading up to the father's departure in June 1916. The final set revolves around his adolescent attempts to write poetry, an experience connected with his first love, whom, he recalls, he met "in June 1916" (*G* 161; *Dr* 168). This sequence of recollections neatly echoes the central theme of growth in the novel as a whole.

Fyodor's urge to grow as an artist lies behind his willingness to examine his work critically during these segments of first-person narration. Indeed, the effect of these passages is to suggest that the authorial component of the Fyodor figure is actively at work, learning vital lessons about his capacity to animate in art the cherished experiences of his life. Thus, while the experiential aspect of the figure recalls his *life*, the authorial aspect of the figure hones its *artistic propensities*. A brief examination of the lessons Fyodor learns over the first part of the novel will delineate his central growth process.

Analyzing the poetry about his childhood, the poet laments that he is beginning to forget connections between objects that still remain vivid in his memory, and that therefore he condemns these objects to extinction. He continues: "What, then, compels me to compose poems about my childhood if in spite of everything my words go wide of the mark, or else slay both the pard and the hart with the exploding bullet of an 'accurate' epithet?" (*G* 30–31; *Dr* 25). We shall return to the specific imagery used here by Fyodor in due course, but for the moment it is sufficient to note that Fyodor's question foregrounds an issue of fundamental import in *The Gift* – the potential of art to retain and renew prior experiences in life. The poet worries that his poems on childhood somehow lack life. Though they are finely chiselled miniatures, he wonders whether they ever rise above the genre of "album poetry." To endow the lifeless with life – this will be one of Fyodor's future missions.

Ironically, in his attempt to write a biography of his father, Fyodor goes too far in the opposite direction. As he engages in his mental recreation of his father's journeys, he not only imagines how his father might have experienced his travels, he begins to project *his own* impressions onto his father's figure. He thus loses that critical measure of detachment which the writer requires when giving completion to the inner life of another, and he in effect displaces the other with a projection of his own interiority.

The process through which this occurs in chapter 2 is compelling. Having revealed in chapter 1 a penchant for envisioning the inner lives of others,[10] Fyodor continues to display this capacity for imaginative projection in chapter 2. His initial descriptions of his father's expedition establish his perspective as an *external* observer: "After that I see the caravan", "this is the way I see it", and so on (*G* 128; *Dr* 132). As the passage continues, however, the writer cloaks his disembodied perspective in a more immediate, physical form. Referring to some mounted riders in his father's retinue, he includes among them "that representative of mine whom I sent in the wake of my father throughout my boyhood" (*G* 130; *Dr* 134). This figure recalls the image used by the narrator of "Recruiting," who referred to the "man with the local Russian newspaper" as "my representative" (*TD* 110; *VF* 126).

Having introduced a physical representative of himself into the scene that he creates in his mind, Fyodor increases the strength of his personal projection. A few paragraphs later he is not merely represented by an externalized alter ego; rather, he now seems to have joined the expedition himself. He thus utilizes the first-person plural pronoun: "*our* caravan moved east ... *We* saw ..." (*G* 131, emphasis added; *Dr* 136). This, however, is merely a prelude to the most dramatic shift of all. Three pages later, the writer locates himself next to his father: "*he and I* would take Elwes' Swallowtail" (*G* 134, emphasis added; *Dr* 139). Placed in such proximity with the subject of his reverie, the writer obliterates the last traces of the separation between himself and his father. When the pronoun "I" is next used, it is no longer clear that it refers to a figure who is *accompanying* the great explorer; subsequent usages suggest that the figure denoted by the pronoun "I" has *become* the explorer himself (for example "In Tatsien-Lu shaven-headed lamas roamed about the crooked, narrow streets spreading the rumor that I was catching children in order to brew their eyes into a potion for the belly of my Kodak" *G* 134–35; *Dr* 139).[11] A profound metamorphosis has taken place. The creative consciousness of the writer has usurped the identity of the subject of his narration; Fyodor has taken over his father's place.

Having finished his account of this imaginary journey, Fyodor himself acknowledges his predilection for projection and its inherent dangers. He writes to his mother: "If you like I'll admit it: I myself am a mere seeker of verbal adventures ... I have realized, you see, the impossibility of having the imagery of his travels germinate *without contaminating them with a kind of secondary poetization*, which keeps departing further and further from that real poetry with which the live experience of these . . . naturalists endowed their research" (*G* 151, emphasis added; *Dr* 157).[12]

Fyodor here articulates a critical perception – the possibility that a literary creator may become so caught up in his creative process that he loses all detachment, projecting his own personality onto the subject of his creation to the point where the latter disappears altogether.[13] Fyodor's experience complements Bakhtin's theory that aesthetic contemplation involves a two-stage process: in the first stage the artist puts himself in the place of the subject he contemplates, and in the second he withdraws and returns to his own position. Fyodor's biography of his father reveals a failure to follow through on the second stage of this process. Fyodor commits here the antithesis of the shortcoming he detected in his poetry collection. Whereas the latter seemed devoid of its creator's personality and vitality, the former displays too much of those qualities. The most satisfying art occupies a middle ground, and Fyodor's quest for the correct balance needs further refinement.

Something close to the proper synthesis arises in Fyodor's biography of Chernyshevski, which makes up chapter 4 of *The Gift*. The intervening chapter forms the hub of the five-chapter novel, and the "real hub" of *this* chapter, as Nabokov himself defines it, is Fyodor's "love poem dedicated to Zina" (*G* 10). Nabokov's comment underscores an element in Fyodor's life that had been sorely lacking in the lives of most of Nabokov's earlier would-be artist–heroes – a vital relationship to another in the surrounding world. Anna Maria Salehar has pointed out that Zina's full name – Zinaida ("daughter of Zeus") – and her relationship to Mnemosyne suggest that she is one of the Muses ("Nabokov's *Gift*" 76–77); this is the function she fulfills for Fyodor (see also Johnson, *Worlds* 97–99). Inspired by deep emotion for another, Fyodor creates a poem that neither overwhelms the subject with personal projection nor suffers from sterile formalism. He constructs this poem out of vibrant imagery that resonates with all that is precious in his life, and particularly with emblems of his father and of creativity.[14]

This encounter marks a turning point for Fyodor. He now gathers his creative forces for a new literary endeavor – his biography of Nikolay Chernyshevski. The Chernyshevski piece reveals Fyodor's emerging mastery of the proper relationship between the creative consciousness and the subject of literary apprehension. Many of Fyodor's earlier problems – his failure to animate his poems with pulsing life, or the contrasting tendency to project too much of his own emotional world onto the subject of his prose – are significantly tempered in this work. Although still showing signs of immaturity, the finished text manifests a marked degree of artistic growth within Fyodor.

Fyodor's treatment of Chernyshevski has aroused a certain amount of controversy. The editors of *Sovremennye zapiski* would not publish this chapter when they serialized the novel, and since that time, the debate has continued. While many readers find Fyodor's portrait of Chernyshevski to be a refreshing corrective to the stiff icon revered by numerous nineteenth and twentieth-century Russian critics (see Field, *Life in Art* 25 and Couturier, *Nabokov* 26), David Rampton devotes considerable space to an analysis of this representation, finding it one-sided and injudicious in its handling of original sources (*A Critical Study of the Novels* 65–87).

This debate over the accuracy or verisimilitude of the portrait, however, nearly misses the point. As Fyodor states, his purpose here is "Firing practice" (*G* 208; *Dr* 221 – "Uprazhnenie v strel'be"), an image that merits closer examination. Although a simplistic interpretation of the image might suggest that Fyodor aims to "kill" Chernyshevski, the image itself has more complex associations. One should recall that Fyodor used a related metaphor to describe the shortcomings of his first book of poetry: "What, then, compels me to compose poems about my childhood if . . . my words go wide of the mark, or else slay both the pard and the hart with the exploding bullet of an 'accurate' epithet?" (*G* 30–31; *Dr* 25). When one explores *The*

Gift for the possible source for such imagery, one is led back, as is so often the case, to the pervasive influence of Fyodor's father on the son. Fyodor makes several references to his father's habit of exercising his marksmanship skills, both on his travels ("in camp he practiced shooting" *G* 125; *Dr* 129 – "uprazhnialsia v strel'be." Compare "Uprazhnenie v strel'be" above.) and at home: "and then Father had taken the pistol, swiftly and dexterously ramming bullets into the clip, and knocked out a smooth *K* with seven shots" (*G* 91; *Dr* 90).[15] The latter scene, Fyodor notes, occurs next to an "old acquaintance," a birch tree with a double trunk – "a birch-lyre" (*G* 90; *Dr* 90). This last image directly connects the theme of marksmanship with art. In his biography of Chernyshevski Fyodor sets out to achieve in literary form that which his father has mastered in the physical realm: he wishes to hone his skills to the point where he can carve his personal monogram on his work with precision, accuracy, and grace.

Before evaluating the specific characteristics of Fyodor's handling of the other in the Chernyshevski chapter, it might be useful to discuss Fyodor's choice of this figure as the subject for his work. The obvious explanation for the choice is that Chernyshevski's views on art and literature are antithetical to those of Fyodor's ultimate creator, Nabokov. The writer may have wished to expose the theoretical shortcomings of a figure who had exercised such a powerful influence on succeeding generations of Russian critics. Yet while numerous commentators have articulated the differences between Nabokov's and Chernyshevski's views on art (see Davydov, "*The Gift*", Karlinsky, "Vladimir Nabokov's Novel *Dar*" 287–88, and Rampton 70–84), the peculiar set of parallels which Nabokov creates between his hero Fyodor and his target Chernyshevski has escaped attention.[16] These parallels extend beyond the general fact that both figures are writers of fiction who at one time became interested in problems of prosody (see *G* 253–54 and 163–64; *Dr* 270–71 and 170–71). Recalling Fyodor's penchant for imagining himself in others' minds and for creating fictitious alter egos, the reader will note Chernyshevski's claim that his diary is the draft of a novel: "I place myself and others in various positions and develop them quite fancifully ... One 'I' speaks of the possibility of arrest, another 'I' is beaten with a stick in front of his fiancée" (*G* 243; *Dr* 259). Chernyshevski's crude gestures in the direction of creative projection contrast starkly with Fyodor's intricate and nuanced imaginative skills.

The most interesting connection between Fyodor and Chernyshevski, though, is the fact that they share a birthday. Chernyshevski was born on July 12, 1828 (*G* 312; *Dr* 334) and Fyodor was born on July 12, 1900 (*G* 24; *Dr* 19). Repeating Fyodor's own observation that a "coincidence of anniversaries, a card index of dates" is "how fate sorts them in anticipation of the researcher's needs" (*G* 232; *Dr* 247), and keeping in mind that "fate" in Nabokov's fiction often serves as an authorial agent, one may ask why Nabokov endowed his hero with the same birthday as his target. The link he draws between the two could reflect another example of predilection for creating pairs of characters in which one character functions as the negative double or shadow of the other. Such pairs include Cincinnatus and Pierre, Gregson and Cook, and later, Humbert Humbert and Clare Quilty. Fyodor's literary mastery over Chernyshevski's life may represent a kind of ritual exorcism in which the artistic hero expunges through the figure of his double any negative propensies he may possess or fear, thereby freeing himself to grow and mature as a genuine artist.[17]

The predominant tone that Fyodor adopts toward Chernyshevski in his biography is satirical, but his tone softens somewhat after Chernyshevski has been sent into exile. This change in attitude may arise from personal considerations: confronted with the image of Chernyshevski separated by vast spaces from his family, Fyodor may be reminded of his own father's fate.[18] Despite any compassion this state of exile may have evoked, however, one element of Chernyshevski's life would have surely captured Fyodor's interest – the relationship between Chernyshevski and his son Sasha. Sasha, a mentally unbalanced mathematician and poet, was viewed by his father as a shiftless parasite, and their life together was "a joint hell" (*G* 310; *Dr* 332). This is a far cry from the "paradisal" air which Fyodor imagines would inform a meeting with his own father (see *G* 367; *Dr* 398). The Chernyshevski–Sasha relationship thus provides a tragic shadow for the Konstantin–Fyodor relationship.[19]

Given the element of personal interest which Fyodor may have in Chernyshevski's life story, his handling of the narrative subject merits special attention. In his unfinished biography of his father Fyodor succumbed to the lure of "secondary poetization," and substituted himself for the subject of his narrative. In *this* biography, however, the temptation finds a different resolution. Fyodor does not lose himself in a projection of Chernyshevski's position; he remains a detached chronicler of the subject's life.

The most distinctive feature of Fyodor's treatment of Chernyshevski as other is the way he transforms the historical figure into something of a literary character. Fyodor works this transformation in two ways: first, by portraying Chernyshevski in images that have reminded readers of Gogol's fiction,[20] and second, by enmeshing the figure in a controlling web of stylistic artifice.[21] What is Fyodor's aim here? He is not simply making fun of Chernyshevski. Having set out to create a work that would traverse the narrow ridge between the "brink of parody" and "an abyss of seriousness" (*G* 212; *Dr* 225), Fyodor endows the transformation of Chernyshevski the *man* into Chernyshevski the *character* with serious import. Such a transformation works an ironic revenge on a critic who argued that works of art were inferior to life. The biography points out several places in Chernyshevski's career where the critic upheld the superiority of life over art (see *G* 249 and 234–35; *Dr* 266 and 250–51). Now, however, this denigrator of pure art has himself been transformed into a literary character and imprisoned in a verbal edifice that is unabashedly "literary" and "artistic." "Facts" become "themes" and other historical figures become new "characters" in the hero's story. This reversal recalls the situation in *Despair* where Hermann Karlovich's pretensions to the status of controlling creator were undermined by the very text which he claims to have created; Chernyshevski's own words come back to haunt him in Fyodor's text.

For the figure of Chernyshevski the image of imprisonment resonates with both physical and metaphorical meaning. Having been freed from imprisonment in the Peter-Paul Fortress and in Siberia, he is now imprisoned in a work of art. The very structure of Fyodor's Chernyshevski biography, which begins with the last six lines of a sonnet and concludes with the first octave of the same sonnet, forms a seamless circle holding Chernyshevski fast within its confines.[22] Chernyshevski's imprisonment in Fyodor's text recalls Cincinnatus's imprisonment in the fictional world depicted in *Invitation to a Beheading*, and it subtly raises the issue of Fyodor's own relationship to the text in which *he* is situated, an issue that will come to the fore at the conclusion of the novel. For the moment, one can say that Fyodor's transformation of the nineteenth-century author Chernyshevski into a twentieth-century literary character facilitates a transformation of Fyodor himself, but in the opposite direction. Through his re-creation of Chernyshevski as a literary character, Fyodor prepares the way to re-create himself as a literary author as well. Fyodor's distinctive handling of the sacred figure of Chernyshevski indicates the ripening of his literary talent. Although he does not entirely avoid the tendency to overshadow his subject with the force of his own personality, his "firing practice" has improved his accuracy immeasurably.[23]

The rewards of his labor emerge in chapter 5. Fyodor's understanding of the seminal distinction between the creative consciousness (self) and the object of creative perception (other) has found concrete application. His resulting artistic maturity is illustrated in several ways. One can contrast Fyodor's imaginary conversation with Koncheev in this chapter, for example, with a corresponding conversation in chapter 1. The imaginary conversation here is not marred by lapses in the illusion that these are two separate entities. His creation Koncheev does not suddenly reveal insights accessible only to his creator Fyodor (such as the fact that Fyodor's new shoes "pinch unbearably" *G* 84; *Dr* 83). Indeed, the narrative into which this conversation is set indicates the clarity of the separation when it uses such identifying phrases as "said Koncheev" and "said Fyodor" (see *G* 350–54; *Dr* 378–83).

Throughout the last chapter, the general flow of narrative discourse evinces a more stable treatment of the alternations between the extrinsic, third-person and the intrinsic, first-person narrative modes. In comparison to chapter 1, the transitions into the first-person mode are less frequent, and the shifts that do occur generally have a specific, clearly discernible purpose. Their primary function is to articulate Fyodor's emotions or thoughts at a given moment, using the free direct discourse technique (for example "I'll risk it" *G* 337; *Dr* 364).

What is more, in the sole passage of extended first-person narration occurring in the chapter – an account of Fyodor's excursions into the Grunewald – the reader may detect an increased tone of self-assurance or assertiveness on the part of the narrating voice. It declares, for example, "Give me your hand, dear reader, and let's go into the forest together" (*G* 343; *Dr* 370). No longer is the first-person voice preoccupied with its activities in the past; the time evoked in this segment is essentially contemporaneous with the main time frame of the ongoing story. Nor does it dwell on the inadequacies of Fyodor's literary creations. On the contrary, the first-person voice tends now to conceptualize its creative activity in terms of the *future*: "Where shall I put all these gifts with which the summer morning rewards me – and only me? Save them up for future books?" (*G* 340; *Dr* 368). What is most striking, however, is a growing sense that the first-person voice may be detached from its external representative, the character "Fyodor."

This new potential is raised during a crucial scene that takes place on an excursion into the Grunewald. The Grunewald episode brings to a culmination a number of themes that have been building up throughout the novel. The most important of these is the presence of death and the concomitant urge to find a means of preventing the loss of the beloved other to the oblivion of time. The twenty-page description of the Grunewald outing offers a delicate yet brilliant verbal fugue in which reminders of death are interwoven with counterbalancing images of life and vitality. Within this one episode such emblems of death as a black hearse (*G* 340; *Dr* 367), a reminder of Alexander Chernyshevski's cremation (*G* 341; *Dr* 368), traces of a plane crash (*G* 343; *Dr* 371), and a reminder of Yasha Chernyshevski's suicide (*G* 345; *Dr* 373), alternate with images of vibrant life in the world of nature, especially the play of sunlight on living beings such as an Angle Wing butterfly (*G* 344; *Dr* 372).

Significantly, this interplay of images of death and life leads Fyodor into a series of meditative reflections in which philosophical speculation takes on aesthetic implications. In the passage quoted above, Fyodor raises the question of what he can do about the evanescent phenomena of life: "Where shall I put all these gifts . . . ?" (*G* 340; *Dr* 368). Critical here is his sense that there *does* exist a plane of meaning beyond the surface plane of everyday experience. Ruminating on his desire to understand what is concealed behind the external play of life, he concludes that there really *is* "something" there (*G* 340; *Dr* 368).

Armed with this sense of "something" beyond the surface of life, Fyodor is primed for a dramatic epiphanic experience. This experience will unlock the potent bifurcation of identity evoked within Fyodor's developing artistic sensibility by exposing him to another realm – the realm of the unfettered imagination. The epiphanic moment transpires after the writer, now represented by the first-person narrative voice, penetrates deep into the Grunewald, which he perceives as a "primeval paradise."[24] He takes off his clothes, thereby divesting himself of the external shell of his identity.[25] In this primal state he undergoes his revelatory experience:

The sun bore down. The sun licked me all over with its big, smooth tongue. I gradually felt that I was becoming moltenly transparent, that I was permeated with flame and existed only insofar as it did. As a book is translated into an exotic idiom, so was I translated into sun. The scrawny, chilly, hiemal Fyodor Godunov-Cherdyntsev was now as remote from me as if I had exiled him to the Yakutsk province. He was a pallid copy of me, whereas this aestival one was his magnified bronze replica. My personal I, the one that wrote books, the one that

loved words, colors, mental fireworks, Russia, chocolate and Zina –
had somehow disintegrated and dissolved; after being made transparent by the strength of the light, it was now assimilated to the
shimmering of the summer forest with its satiny pine needles and
heavenly-green leaves ... (*G* 345–46; *Dr* 373–74)

This passage depicts a decisive experience for that innermost
part of Fyodor's consciousness associated with his authorial
propensities, and Nabokov constructs the passage out of imagery that carries complex associations developed earlier in the
text. For example, the force of the sun which now serves as an
agent of transformation and fusion has a powerful resonance
that traces back to chapter 1. There Fyodor (or more precisely,
the first-person voice representing his authorial consciousness)
describes how he studied the figures of Yasha, Olya, and
Rudolf as he considered turning their story into a literary work:
"I use a different method to study each of the three individuals
... until, at the last minute, the *rays of a sun* that is my own and
yet is incomprehensible to me, strikes them and equalizes them
in the same *burst of light*" (*G* 54, emphasis added; *Dr* 50). The
sun image used by Fyodor here stands for the workings of
creative consciousness itself.

In the Grunewald scene, then, the "sun" which begins to
transform (or "translate") the narrating entity into itself may
be an emblem of a higher authorial consciousness – that which
is responsible for creating the character Fyodor. If so, the
experience depicted here represents a moment of enlighten-
ment in which Fyodor's developing authorial component gains
insight into the true nature of authorial power. This insight in
turn may encourage the authorial component to actualize its
latent capacities and to break away from its character counter-
part, denoted here as a remote figure, "scrawny, chilly,
hiemal."

Despite this burgeoning sensation of dissolution and translation, however, the process does not result in total disintegration, and the narrative suddenly switches back into the
third-person mode: "One might dissolve completely that way.
Fyodor raised himself and sat up" (*G* 346; *Dr* 374). This
transition is intriguing. Although the innermost element of the

Fyodor figure is drawn toward fusion with a higher state of consciousness, the abrupt withdrawal may indicate that the character himself has a further evolution to undergo. Indeed, the ensuing narrative indicates that the character still has to come to terms with the loss of his father. The narrative indicates this in lines that culminate with the specter of death in an emphatic position at the end of the paragraph: "here it was most difficult of all to believe that despite the freedom, despite the greenery and the happy, sun-shot dark shade, his father was nonetheless *dead*" (*G* 347, emphasis added; *Dr* 375).[26]

Fyodor had gone into the forest world weighed down by an awareness of the tenuous balance between life and death and by a vague desire to do something with his aspirations towards the infinite (see *G* 341; *Dr* 369), but he did not know what he could do. Now, however, after the innermost part of his being has come into contact with a higher creative force, he emerges with a sharper sense of purpose. Reviewing the experience of Alexander Chernyshevski's illness and his family's grief, Fyodor is at first seized by a desire not to allow this to get lost somewhere in his soul. On the contrary, he wishes to apply it to himself and to his own "truth" so that it can "sprout up" in a new way. He concludes: "There is a way – the only way" (*G* 349; *Dr* 378). Fyodor's experience in the Grunewald has revealed to him the path of the creative consciousness – the path of art – as "the way" to transform and preserve the past.

A subsequent corroboration of Fyodor's new insight into the powers of transforming consciousness occurs near the end of the novel, when his yearning for reunion with his father finds fulfillment – not in the physical plane, nor in a meeting of ghost and man – but in the plane of creative consciousness itself. The reunion takes place in a dream which is constructed out of highly charged images like those appearing in the Grunewald epiphany, and indeed, there is an important parallel between this scene and the earlier one. Here, the experiential or "character" element of Fyodor undergoes an epiphany equivalent to that which affected his authorial component in the Grunewald, and one notes a similar progression from emblems of death into images of light and warmth.

The content of the dream involves a mysterious summons to Fyodor's old apartment, the room where he had worked on his unfinished biography of his father, thereby growing spiritually closer to his father in the realm of art. After some moments of fearful anticipation (recalling Cincinnatus's anxiety before the execution), the reunion occurs and he embraces his father: "in the collective sensation of woolen jacket, big hands and the tender prickle of trimmed moustaches there swelled an ecstatically happy, living, enormous, paradisal warmth in which his icy heart melted and dissolved" (G 367; Dr 398). One notes here the combination of images – paradisal warmth, melting and dissolution – that figured so prominently in the Grunewald scene.

The climax of this dream testifies to the successful process of maturation that has occurred within Fyodor. In his early creative endeavors he had been subject to lapses of control, unable to sustain the proper degree of separation between his creating consciousness and the subject of its creative apprehension. As a result, his creations were either stiff and lifeless, or contaminated with too much personal content. Through his contact with Zina, his work on the Chernyshevski biography, and his epiphanic experience in the Grunewald, he has come to understand the essential scope of the creative consciousness. He now understands its capacity to apprehend elements of real life and to transform them into a fresh realm of imagination impervious to the forces of the everyday world. In his dream of reunion he conjures up an image of his father that is neither lifeless nor overshadowed by the strength of his own personality. He has found the appropriate balance between engagement and separation in his conceptualization of the other.[27]

Having come to this understanding, Fyodor now believes that he is ready to author a real novel. As he tells Zina: "You know, I'm black as a gypsy from the Grunewald sun. Something is beginning to take shape – I think I'll write a classical novel, with 'types,' love, fate, conversations ..." (G 361; Dr 392). Yet despite Fyodor's self-assurance, the authentic *auctor*'s own handling of Fyodor at this point underscores the fact that

Fyodor is still a *character*, and will remain one as long as he is the subject of the actual *auctor*'s literary portrayal.

The *auctor* emphasizes Fyodor's character status through the celebrated "keys" episode.[28] At the end of the novel Fyodor is flushed with anticipation at the thought of spending the night with Zina in the apartment which her parents have just left. He, however, has had his keys stolen by an unseen thief (a handy authorial agent?) in the Grunewald, and he mistakenly believes that Zina is carrying her keys with her. The reader, however, knows that Zina is no longer in possession of her keys, and has learned this fact through a unique scene in the novel. That scene – Zina's last conversation with her parents – is the *only* moment in the novel involving an interaction between two characters which is not witnessed by Fyodor himself.

The incident is of crucial importance for two reasons. First, in setting up a situation where Fyodor erroneously believes that he will soon experience a delicious romantic interlude with Zina, the narrative underscores Fyodor's true ignorance of his destiny, and contrasts his ignorance as a *character* with the authentic *auctor*'s powers of omniscience and control. Secondly, it is during this scene that the narrating entity assumes a position of absolute autonomous omniscience for the first time in the novel and displays an ability to record events without depending on Fyodor's presence as focalizer. This striking movement toward the establishment of an independent, detached narrative center paves the way for the sudden separation of the first-person narrative voice from the character of Fyodor at the end of the novel.

Indeed, it is at this point that the authorial component which has been developing within Fyodor is ready to break away from the external shell of the character. This decoupling occurs at the very end of the novel when the narrative voice moves away from the figure of Fyodor walking with Zina and suddenly exclaims:

Good-by, my book! Like mortal eyes, imagined ones must close some day. Onegin from his knees will rise – but his creator strolls away. And yet the ear cannot right now part with the music and allow the tale to fade; the chords of fate itself continue to vibrate; and no obstruction for the sage exists where I have put The End: the shadows of my world extend beyond the skyline of the page, blue as tomorrow's morning haze – nor does this terminate the phrase. (*G* 378; *Dr* 411)

In alluding to *Eugene Onegin* here (even reflecting its stanzaic structure), Nabokov draws attention to a crucial distinction between the figure of the narrator – the author's representative on the extradiegetic level – and the figure of the main character – the subject of the narrative on the diegetic level. This crucial distinction applies to the end of *The Gift* as well. Although these two entities – the narrating voice and Fyodor – have been closely linked throughout the preceding narrative, they now separate.

The concluding passage of *The Gift*, then, corresponds to the conclusion of *Invitation to a Beheading*, where the authorial Cincinnatus walks away from his character counterpart and sets off to join others with authorial power. Yet while the reader of *Invitation to a Beheading* never sees Cincinnatus join those kindred beings, Nabokov indicates at the end of *The Gift* just what such a transformation from character to author might entail. While the *character* Fyodor remains frozen within the text as a created entity subject to the control of a powerful creator, the *authorial* component within Fyodor ascends to the higher realm of creative power itself. Indeed, the authorial component within Fyodor now becomes a creative entity capable of generating the text in which the character Fyodor exists. This is a remarkable transformation, and it is more complex than might first appear.

Those critics who say that Fyodor is the author of the novel which features his growth have some justification for their view, but their interpretation obscures an important element in Nabokov's design. His handling of narrative point of view underscores the fact that the character called "Fyodor" can not actually author the text in which he appears. The keys episode is inserted specifically to demonstrate that this character does not possess the omniscience of the authorial consciousness which has created him. What the ending of Nabokov's novel is intended to evoke is nothing less than a full-scale metaphysical (and metaliterary) transformation – the ascension of a mature authorial potential onto the plane of creative consciousness itself. The authorial consciousness responsible for the discourse of the novel, then, is that entity which the authorial potential within Fyodor becomes when it is liberated from its character shell. Catapulted into this higher realm, the authorial component within Fyodor becomes an entity vastly more powerful and knowledgeable than the diegetic character was shown to be.[29]

The metamorphosis which Fyodor's authorial potential undergoes is so dramatic that the liberated consciousness becomes nearly inaccessible to the reader's gaze. That is, it appears only to the reader through oblique manifestations, much like that otherworldly mirror which, to use Cincinnatus's image, "now and then sends a chance reflection here" (*IB* 94; *PK* 100). One such reflection occurs in chapter 1, during a segment of third-person narration that describes Fyodor walking along his neighborhood streets: "Here at last is the square where we dined and the tall brick church and the still quite transparent poplar" (*G* 65; *Dr* 62). This momentary break into the first-person mode cannot express the impressions of the character Fyodor at that moment, because the comment about the square "where we dined" refers to an event that has not yet been experienced by the character (it occurs only after he meets Zina). The proleptic comment, then, can only reflect the consciousness of the entity generating the text, a figure who knows more than his representative Fyodor and who regards Fyodor's experiences with some warmth as well as with irony.[30]

The Gift represents the culmination of several years of exploration for Nabokov, and the complex relationship he sets up between the entities of character, narrator, and authorial consciousness reflects the fruits of his experimentation. In this novel one perceives an echo of the structure created in *Invitation to a Beheading*, where the dreamer responsible for the events of the novel is represented within the text by the narrative voice on the level of discourse and by Cincinnatus on the level of story. Here, the authorial consciousness responsible for the production of the novel is also represented within the text on two levels – by Fyodor on the level of story and by the narrating voice on the level of discourse.

The handling of the figure of Fyodor by the authorial consciousness in *The Gift* also reflects the understanding displayed in "Recruiting" that any narration about oneself turns one into a character. Due to this principle, the structural design of this novel can be said to resemble a Möbius strip: the story line of the novel depicts the evolution and liberation of an independent authorial potential within the figure of Fyodor, but once that authorial potential is liberated and can begin to tell the story of its growth and maturation, it of necessity treats the narrated self as a literary character; that is, it creates the character Fyodor to be its diegetic representative within the text.[31]

The wondrous moment of metamorphosis depicted at the end of *The Gift* not only signals the successful completion of Fyodor's maturation as an artist, it also points to the novelist's appreciation of the capacity of aesthetic transformation to deal with the problem of transience and loss in life. Over the course of the novel Fyodor learns how to apprehend the evanescent material of life and to give it new permanence in the timeless medium of art. The character's discoveries on the diegetic level then receive emblematic validation on the extradiegetic level when his inner authorial potential is transformed and ascends to the involute abode of art itself.

A crucial element in this process is a proper understanding of one's relationship to others and to oneself. In approaching others as the subject of literary treatment, a writer must be familiar with both the powers and perils of creative projection. Such a writer must know how to breathe life into the created entity without overwhelming it with excessive subjectivity. Successfully applied, however, the beam of creative vision can give new life both to the created entity (as a fictional character) and to the creating entity (as an authentic author). *The Gift* illustrates this process in an especially rich and resonant form.

With *Invitation to a Beheading* and *The Gift*, Nabokov demonstrates that he had reached the high point of his development as a writer of fiction in Russian. When he subsequently shifted into English, he developed additional concerns, but his fundamental interest in the relationship between the creative consciousness and the subjects it apprehends never diminished. Having explored in his late Russian works the essential fluidity of the boundaries between various levels of fictional "reality," Nabokov went on to write a series of novels that became increasingly self-reflexive and complex. All his subsequent artist–heroes would confront the issues faced by Fyodor, and the processes through which they learn to sort out the complex interrelationships between themselves, their projections, and the actual "others" who serve as the targets for their projections find ever more intriguing manifestations.

AFTERWORD

The course of Nabokov's fiction grows more complex after the completion of *The Gift*. "Ultima Thule" and "Solus Rex" – the fragments of a novel which Nabokov began in 1940 but never finished – hint at a new construct in which the familiar problem of the need to preserve or recover precious beings lost in time is recast in settings of bold fantasy.[32] Moreover, when Nabokov began to write in English, he introduced an entirely new type of "other" into his fiction – the medium of language itself. Nabokov's penchant for verbal play, where the shadow of other words lurks within the sound texture of the given word, becomes even more prominent in his English prose than it was in his Russian work. Nonetheless, one can recognize the continued vitality of Nabokov's fundamental thematic dichotomies in the writer's English fiction. Although the body of this fiction is too large to analyze here, one can make a few preliminary comments on the way some of the relationships and structures identified in the Russian-language fiction resonate in Nabokov's later prose. I do not wish to claim that the ideas presented below represent a definitive reading of Nabokov's English-language fiction; I merely wish to indicate how the patterns discerned in Nabokov's Russian-language fiction may inform his subsequent work as well.

The first novel that Nabokov wrote in English, *The Real Life of Sebastian Knight* (written in 1938–39 and published in 1941) takes as its point of departure the final position presented in *The Gift*. At the end of *The Gift* Nabokov leaves the reader with a vision of the authorial element within Fyodor ascending to the ranks of authentic *auctor*. From this realm, he can represent himself within the text in two forms: as a narrating entity denoted by the shifter "I" and as the subject of the narrative identified in the text as "Fyodor." An appreciation of this structure helps to illuminate certain aspects of *The Real Life of Sebastian Knight* as well. In discussing the relationship between the novel's narrator "V." and the subject of V.'s narration – the life of V.'s half-brother Sebastian Knight – critics have pointed out a strange overlap between the people V. encounters in his quest for information on Sebastian's life and characters who appear in one or another of Sebastian's novels (this is especially obvious in the case of Sebastian's character – "Mr. Siller" – and the man who wondrously helps V. – a "Mr. Silbermann").[33] To explain this kind of overlap, some critics are tempted to label either V. or Sebastian as the creator of the other brother, or to see V. as a narrator guided by Sebastian's spirit.[34] The effect Nabokov achieves in this novel is somewhat like that depicted in M. C. Escher's famous lithograph "Drawing Hands," in which two hands are depicted in the process of creating each other.

One gains an additional perspective, however, when one considers *The Real Life of Sebastian Knight* in light of the pattern laid down in *The Gift*. As the narrating voice represented by the shifter "I" and the subject of the narration "Fyodor" are both textual representatives of a higher authorial force, so too in *The Real Life of Sebastian Knight* both the narrator "V." and the subject "Sebastian Knight" may be paired representatives of a higher authorial force. Returning to the Escher work mentioned above, we could depict the presence of this higher entity by turning the two-dimensional sketch into a three-dimensional construct and adding a third hand whose pen creates both the hands represented in the original lithograph. This third hand, of course, belongs to Vladimir Nabokov, and his creation of a scheme in which V.'s and Sebastian's life and art interpenetrate each other places the reader in a hall of mirrors in which the creative primacy of one character over the other is difficult to ascertain.

Nevertheless, the clear relationship which Nabokov establishes between Sebastian's fiction and the biographical quest experienced by V. encourages one to surmise that the authorial entity responsible for the events and design of the novel is closer to Sebastian than to V. Such would be the case if Sebastian's spirit guides V.'s quest and V.'s pen from beyond the grave.[35] It is possible that Nabokov is working in this novel with a variation of the pattern found in *The Gift*. As the authorial element in Fyodor has ascended to the ranks of authentic *auctor* and is able to depict himself as a character in a biographical novel (indeed, the depiction of the self as a character is a necessary element of auctorial status), so too, perhaps, the authorial element within Sebastian Knight, having attained *its* full potential, now seeks to depict "Sebastian Knight" as a character in a biographical novel. Unlike the situation in *The Gift*, however, the pattern prevailing here contains an added degree of complexity: the authorial entity in this novel has created or is operating through an intermediary mask to describe Sebastian's life – the mask of the narrator V. *The Real Life of Sebastian Knight* thus becomes the last novel envisioned by Sebastian but never completed by him, a "fictitious biography" (*SK* 40).[36]

The design created by Nabokov in *The Real Life of Sebastian Knight* may arise out of that which underpins *The Gift*, but it evinces a clear development beyond the earlier novel. In *The Gift*, the two textual representatives of the authorial entity – the narrating "I" and the subject "Fyodor" – are nearly congruent; the pronoun "I" often refers to the interior processes of Fyodor himself. Here, however, the two textual representatives – the narrator V. and the subject Sebastian – are depicted as two distinct entities. They are, according to V., half-brothers. Still, this relationship is itself suggestive. Two halves make a whole, and as Sebastian's works affirm, the only real number is one (see *SK* 105). It is not until the end of his chronicle, however, that V. gains an intimation of the true nature of his relationship to Sebastian. Then he writes: "I am Sebastian, or Sebastian is I, *or perhaps we both are someone whom neither of us knows*" (*SK* 205, emphasis added). In my view, the final section of V.'s statement points directly to the underlying relationship between the narrator V., the subject Sebastian, and the authorial entity who has created them both.

A second question remains, however: why would the authorial entity choose such a structure to tell the story of Sebastian's life? What advantage would be gained by recounting Sebastian's life through the secondary filter of the narrator V.? There are, of course, several reasons for this. First of all, the creation of V. and of his quest to uncover Sebastian's "real" life (which then becomes a quest for self-knowledge and identity for V. himself) allows the *auctor* to explore issues of consciousness, identity, and biographical "truth" or plausibility in ways that are especially rich and complex. Moreover, the introduction of V. as an intermediary allows the authorial entity to approach the seminal experiences of Sebastian's life obliquely, from new perspectives, and at a remove. Having V. retrace the steps of Sebastian's life, but in a manner that is sometimes touched with irony (and even farce), the author can suggest to the sensitive reader the salient dimensions of Sebastian's experience, but he does not run the risk of slipping into moments of awkward or excessive emotionality. A passage from the novel illuminates this method of biographical exposition: "Two modes of his life question each other and the answer is his life itself, and that is the nearest one ever can approach a human truth" (*SK* 137). This statement points to a core element of Nabokov's mature fiction. He often juxtaposes two different approaches to the central experiences of life, thereby stimulating the reader to arrive at an unarticulated synthesis that may be closer to the human truth than any single articulation could attain.

Indeed, for some readers of *Pale Fire*, this is precisely what Nabokov seems to be doing in that novel. As Julia Bader has suggested in the *Crystal Land*, Shade's poem and Kinbote's commentary together provide a contrapuntal exploration of death and creativity in which the divergence between Shade's contemplative meditations and Kinbote's grandiose fantasies conceals an underlying communality of concern. Readers may debate the issue of whether either Shade or Kinbote can be seen as the creator of the other (Page Stegner offers Kinbote as primary creator, while Field supports Shade for this role. See *Escape into Aesthetics* 130, and *Life in Art* 300 and 305.), but again, one could argue that both figures are the creation of yet a third entity (D. Barton Johnson views Professor Botkin as "the source from which all else flows" within the world of the novel. See *Worlds in Regression* 72.).[37]

In any case, the relationship between the narratorial entity (Kinbote) and the ostensible subject of the narration (Shade) represents a variation on the pattern appearing earlier in Nabokov's career, but at the same time, it moves beyond the design found in a work such as *The Real Life of Sebastian Knight*. While V. and Sebastian are depicted as autonomous figures in the novel, they are still linked through a common father. Kinbote and Shade, in contrast, have few direct connections, and knew each other for only a relatively short period of time.[38] As a result, the contrapuntal structure created by the thematic interlacements of their texts exhibits an especially "plexed artistry" (*PF* 63). Furthermore, while V.'s account of his own experiences threatens to overwhelm his account of Sebastian's life in *The Real Life of Sebastian Knight*, this threat of displacement becomes even more palpable in *Pale Fire*. Kinbote's commentary not only supplants the record of Shade's experience with a fantastic account of Zemblan intrigue and royal exile, he intimates in the final lines of his commentary that this story itself may be an invention and that he may assume other disguises in the future. By demonstrating this predilection for continual self-invention, Kinbote follows the pattern of previous authorial aspirants in Nabokov's work. One stage on the road to becoming an authentic *auctor* involves the creation of a literary character out of oneself. Kinbote's creation of the saga of King Charles manifests this impulse, and his own language at the end of *Pale Fire* suggests that he views himself in such

terms. There he speaks of his personal intention not to follow
the example of "two other *characters* in this work" (*PF* 300,
emphasis added).

The impulse of the narrator to overshadow and replace the
subject of his narration also appears (in a more muted way) in
Pnin. Here too, however, a familiar pattern takes on a new
form. As the narrator of the text intrudes more noticeably into
the narrative itself (becoming especially obtrusive in the final
chapter), he unwittingly comes closer to assuming the role of a
diegetic character in the narrative (as opposed to maintaining
the detached stance of an extradiegetic author). Ironically,
although he seeks to retain control over Pnin (who has thus far
been the subject of his narrative) by becoming his actual boss at
Waindell College, he ends up replacing Pnin in the main
setting of the novel – the Waindell campus – while Pnin himself
manages to escape into a radiant vista where there is simply no
telling what "miracle" might happen.[39] Pnin's departure echoes Cincinnatus's escape at the end of *Invitation to a Beheading*,
and his transcendence may have been eased by the subtle
assistance of two authorial agents – Victor Wind and the spirit
of Pnin's dead love, Mira Belochkin.[40] As in many works by
Nabokov, the authentic *auctor* punishes a would-be author's
aspiration for control of others by underscoring the aspirant's
actual status as a created character. As Jack Cockerell's
penchant for imitating Pnin has the effect of making *him* the
victim of his joke instead of his intended target, so too does the
narrator of Pnin's life find himself replacing Pnin as the object
of narrative scrutiny. Instead of preserving his status as omniscient narrator–controller, he ends up as a diegetic character
condemned to act out a role in a story plotted according to
another's design.[41]

Patterns of doubling, substitution, and quests to retain for
oneself the power and status of authentic *auctor* surface in
Nabokov's other English-language novels. These problems
stand in the foreground of a work such as *Look at the Harlequins!*,
in which the narrator Vadim Vadimovich is troubled by his
sense that behind him stands another, more powerful authorial
figure,[42] and they emerge in a rich form in *Lolita*, where

Humbert Humbert's struggle to demonstrate the capacities of a genuine artist intimately involves issues of self and other on both the aesthetic and personal planes. The ruinous form of imaginative activity manifest when Humbert "solipsizes" Lolita (*L* 62) and possesses her as his own "creation" with no life of her own (*L* 64) must be repudiated to facilitate the emergence of an authentic (and morally sensitive) creative impulse which will enable Humbert to immortalize Dolores Haze in the refuge of verbal art. This again involves the recognition and separation of that aspect of the self which bears the attributes of a literary character, and we see this process at work in two dimensions. It appears in the *language* of Humbert's discourse (for example, in the frequent third-person references to "Humbert Humbert" and the creation of several alternate identities such as "Humbert the Hoarse" [*L* 50], "Humbert the Humble" [*L* 57], and "Humbert the Cubus" [*L* 73]), and in the *subject* of his discourse, the identification by the narrating Humbert of the sins and failings of his younger self. As some readers have noted (see, for example, Tammi 278–86), an awareness of the distinction between the narrating entity (the Humbert Humbert – or "I" – who writes the text) and the narrated entity (the diegetic character Humbert Humbert who participates in the narrated events) is crucial to understanding Nabokov's intentions in the novel.[43] The two entities are not identical. Indeed, the narrating entity recalls and revives the delusive assumptions of his younger self in an attempt to reject and to atone for them.[44]

The narrator's treatment of his former self as character finds secondary reflection in his approach to the figure of Clare Quilty as well. Although Quilty's aura can be discerned in many parts of Humbert's narrative, the figure's *active* presence in Humbert's life seems almost to be generated by Humbert's unfettered creative urges in a manner analogous to the way in which Kinbote imagines Gradus propelled by the creation of Shade's poem (compare *PF* 78 and 136).[45] Quilty physically materializes before Humbert for the first time at the point where Humbert is about to cross the line from harboring an inner fantasy about possession of Lolita to making this a physical reality at the Enchanted Hunter hotel. He then grows more and more threatening in Humbert's mind until he spirits the child away from Humbert, a move that causes Humbert to begin reevaluating his feelings for his lost love. Once Humbert sees Dolly again, no longer as a fantasy "nymphet," but as a woman who is pregnant with another's child, he acknowledges the full extent of his crime toward her, and he feels compelled to attack those behaviors and attitudes which have so injured the girl (see *L* 285 and 289). Although Humbert's motives for killing Quilty include "outrage and a desire for revenge" (Maddox, *Nabokov's Novels in English* 70), his attitude toward the figure and his treatment of the event suggest that the deed carries some expiatory weight as well. Quilty's aesthetic and sexual propensities mock Humbert's own, and some readers have viewed Quilty as a kind of parody of Humbert (see, for example, Clifton, "Humbert Humbert" 160). Thus, Humbert's murder of this shadow figure may be intended to assist Humbert in casting off his negative proclivities and to promote his emergence as an authentic artist who could then create a moving account of his painful relationship with Dolores Haze.[46] That account, perhaps, is the only kind of reparation that he can offer.[47]

We could fruitfully explore each of these novels in detail, for the relationship of self and other in them (as well as in *Bend Sinister*, *Transparent Things*, and *Ada*) exhibits numerous guises and carries multivalent implications. Such a task, however, must await another forum. The aim here is more modest. We hope that the preceding discussion of Nabokov's Russian-language fiction provides insights and ideas for further investigations of his intricate, multilayered achievement.

Notes

INTRODUCTION

1. Citations from these texts will be drawn primarily from the English translations completed under Nabokov's supervision or with his collaboration. In places where the English-language version differs significantly in terms of content and imagery from the earlier Russian-language version, some commentary acknowledging the difference will generally be included.

2. It may be telling that one of the few lines remembered by Nabokov's students in his Russian class at Wellesley was: "And now we come to the saddest story ever told, 'She is here. He is there'" (quoted in Field, *Life in Part* 248).

3. This distinction finds a broad parallel in Phyllis Greenacre's distinction between the "creative self" and the "social, conventional self" within the artist's personality. (For a brief discussion of this distinction see Layton and Schapiro, *Narcissism* 22.) Certain other aspects of Nabokov's treatment of the self–other relationship resonate with the object relations concepts of such theorists as Margaret Mahler, Otto Kernberg, and Heinz Kohut, but this study will not attempt to interpret Nabokov's work using these theories as an analytic tool. Nabokov's fiction itself offers the appropriate structures for addressing the questions it poses.

4. The most comprehensive examination of Nabokov's metaphysics is provided by Alexandrov (see *Nabokov's Otherworld*). He demonstrates how Nabokov's manipulation of authorial patterning carries distinct metaphysical implications, and he reveals the close interrelationship of metaphysics, ethics, and aesthetics in Nabokov's work. The present study focuses mainly on the latter two elements of the triad.

5. Nabokov gave the dichotomy even broader application when lecturing on Tolstoy. There he declares that within everyone is waged a struggle between introversion (with a concentration on

227

one's inner life and thoughts) and extroversion (interest directed
toward other people and "tangible values" *LRL* 236).

6. Wayne Booth's term for such a figure is "implied author" (*The Rhetoric of Fiction* 73).

CHAPTER 1 THE QUEST FOR THE OTHER

1. The date given in parenthesis is the date of publication provided
   by Michael Juliar's descriptive bibliography. This bibliography
   is the source of all subsequent publication dates, unless otherwise
   noted.

2. A similar premise is articulated in the novel *Pnin*, when Pnin
   writes disparagingly about group psychotherapy and asks why
   people cannot be left alone with their private sorrows. Such
   sorrow may be the only thing they truly possess (*Pn* 52).

3. Characteristically, however, he fails to note upon meeting the
   prostitute that she is fairly pretty; he discovers this only later.
   Again, he seems oblivious to the living individuals he encounters.

4. Even before his wife's death, Chorb may have been a very private
   person. The description of his interaction with the external world
   in his wife's company suggests that his contact with it was
   conditioned by *her* rapture with the world (see *DS* 65; *VCh* 11).

5. Several elements link Chorb's wife with Eurydice. Both women
   were associated with trees: Eurydice was a Dryad, a wood
   nymph; and one of Chorb's happiest memories concerns his wife
   playing with falling leaves. Both women die suddenly: Eurydice
   stepped on a snake and was bitten; Chorb's wife touched a live
   wire and was electrocuted.

6. Brian Boyd discusses a similar attempt to recover the past by
   revisiting a physical location in the novel *Transparent Things*, and
   he points out that the fate of Nabokov's characters stresses the
   disjuncture between the human ability to return to a place in
   space and the inability to return in *time* (*The Russian Years* 311).

7. In broader terms, the play of light and shadow in Nabokov's
   work may be charged with deep emotional and spiritual content.
   See, for example, the handling of light and shadow in "The
   Fight" ("Draka"), which was published just prior to "The
   Return of Chorb" (in September 1925).

8. The image of moving vans is itself distinctive; a moving van also
   appears in the opening paragraph of *The Gift*. Such objects
   belong to a broader image system of moving, construction, and
   renovation that occurs in several of Nabokov's works (other
   examples include the building observed by Ganin at the end of

Mary and the theater being constructed in *King, Queen, Knave*). Such images may point to the transforming activity of the creative consciousness which exists beyond the confines of the text, and are inserted into the narrative as cryptic emblems whose true significance cannot be grasped by the characters who encounter them.

9. The one major exception is an inserted scene in which Klara's mother tells Mark's mother that Klara's old lover has returned and that Klara is again "mad" over him (*DS* 21; *VCh* 151). This scene heightens the reader's suspense over Mark's fate and underscores the distinction between the character Mark and the reader who can piece together Mark's story.

10. Nabokov had prefigured the moment of doubling in several ways earlier in the narrative. The opening scene, for example, depicts Mark walking home drunk and talking to himself, addressing himself as "you" and "Mark": "Well, might as well just plod along, even though you are pretty drunk, Mark, pretty drunk ..." (*DS* 17; *VCh* 147). Later, he sees the double bed, and he tells his mother that he thinks that his employers will "double" (*udvoiat*) his salary when he gets married (*DS* 20; *VCh* 150). This use of the image of doubling in the form of a verb within the character's own discourse may be modelled upon Pushkin's use of a similar device in "The Queen of Spades." In that story, the protagonist Hermann becomes obsessed by the thought of obtaining a winning card combination. His anticipation of increasing his capital "threefold" and "sevenfold" (Pushkin uses the verb forms *utroit* and *usemerit*) prefigures two of the cards he believes will win him a fortune. His conscious use of those numbers perhaps leads to their reappearance on the deeper level of his subconscious. Likewise, Mark's conscious use of the word "to double" perhaps prepares the way for his unconscious sense of doubling later. In both tales the protagonists display a fundamental difficulty in distinguishing fantasy from reality.

11. It is interesting to note that throughout the story, Klara, like Chorb's wife and later the title figure of *Mary*, never appears directly before the reader, but is depicted only in the memories or words of other characters. She may thus be termed a "second-degree" fictional character, one who is created in the thoughts or words of another fictional character.

12. An obvious example from Russian literature is the "sacred lyre" in Pushkin's famous poem "The Poet." One notes, by the way, that the poet in Pushkin's work is described as being "insignificant" in the moments when inspiration is not affecting him; he is

"immersed in the cares of the vain world." This may correspond to the everyday preoccupations of "day-people," Mark included, in Nabokov's story (see *DS* 22; *VCh* 152).

13. Note also the description of Fred's appearance: except for a few wrinkles, "our dwarf would have easily passed for a gentle eight-year old boy" (*RB* 222; *VCh* 166). One finds a small "litter of eights" in this story: eight years separate Fred's fateful meetings with Nora, and thus their child would have been nearly eight at the time of his death. (There are also eight chapters in the English version of the text; Nabokov split what had been Chapter Seven into two segments.)

14. Inside his isolated home too, Fred continues to exhibit child-like behavior: at night he often enters the pantry to get, "like a little boy," some chocolate-coated biscuits (*RB* 242; *VCh* 186).

15. The clothes that Fred puts on to follow Nora to the train station confirm the fact that he succeeds in seeing himself transformed. He dons not his child-disguise, but adult clothing, and therefore sees in the mirror the image of "a stately elderly gentleman" in formal dress (*RB* 250; *VCh* 193).

16. For Fred, such an act of projection proves beneficial: it helps him to perceive himself as an adult. For later Nabokov characters such as Hermann Karlovich in *Despair* or Humbert Humbert in *Lolita*, however, such a process can have pernicious consequences. What distinguishes their endeavor from Fred's is that the figure onto whom Fred projects his features is purely imaginary, whereas Hermann and Humbert project their personal visions onto others, thus obscuring the individual identity of those others.

17. Nora's statement rings with a double resonance: Fred, the biological father of her child, was himself her first "child": that was how she saw him eight years earlier.

18. The two moments of interaction with Fred display a parallel but reverse dynamic. In the first encounter, Nora's sense of maternal compassion for another yields to a desire for the personal satisfaction of spiting her husband. In the second encounter, her personal need to see the image of her dead child is replaced by a spirit of compassion for Fred's innocent joy. Having suffered an enormous loss of her own, she feels no compulsion to put Fred through a similar experience. Incidentally, her refusal to tell Fred of the death of his child can be contrasted to Chorb's refusal to tell the Kellers of the death of their child. Nora's refusal is altruistic; Chorb's is solipsistic.

19. One character in the story whose transformations are of a

different sort is the conjurer Shock. His machinations have occasioned much deliberation. Marina Naumann even speculates that he has supernatural powers (*Blue Evenings* 141). In the most imaginative interpretation of Shock's role Walter Evans argues that it is Shock himself who arranges Fred's sexual encounter with Nora, thus performing an act of "almost divine benevolence" ("The Conjurer" 80). Such an interpretation raises many questions that Evans's analysis does not address, and it may be preferable to see Shock not as a god-like creator, but rather as a lesser demiurge, an early representative of what can be called an "authorial agent" in Nabokov's fiction. Such agents emerge to facilitate the occurrence of central events and then disappear when their work is done. Shock travels to America immediately after bringing Fred and Nora together.

20. For purposes of definition one could apply Dorrit Cohn's term of "self-narrated monologue" (*Transparent Minds* 167) to this text.

21. This passage also indicates a salient characteristic of the writer's artistic outlook: his devotion to the observation and recording of what may seem the most trivial detail. As he explained in "The Lermontov Mirage," to be a good "visionary" one must be a good "observer" (Ler 34).

22. Nabokov later mentions this sensation of apprehending a child's future recollection in his essay "Pushkin, or the Real and the Plausible." There he writes that when one observes a child transfixed by the sight of some event that the child will undoubtedly remember in later years, the observer becomes "time's accomplice," for he sees the child storing away "a future recollection" that already casts it aura over the child (P 42).

23. The narrator's concern over the effects of passing time shows up in his manipulation of chronological elements in the narrative. After opening the sketch in the present tense, he provides scenes from the immediate past (his visit to the zoo), the recent past (snow fell a week after the pipes were unloaded), the middle past (he recalls seeing horse-drawn trams in Petersburg eighteen years ago), and the distant, even legendary past, referring to "sunken Atlantica, which long ago lived through various upheavals" (*DS* 96; *VCh* 99). Then he returns again to the present, thereby freezing all those prior moments in one, unchanging present moment.

24. Why did Nabokov make this change? One possibility is that the introduction of images of wounding into the description of the narrator enhances the specter of physical destruction and loss that is thematized in the sketch as a whole.

25. The relationship of character to narrator is also touched upon here, but it remains very much in the background.

26. See, for example, Toker (*Nabokov* 36). Is it mere chance that Ganin worked at a restaurant named "Pir Goroy" (*M* 9; *Mk* 17)?

27. One can contrast the novel's opening scene, which depicts Ganin stuck with Alfyorov in a dark elevator and thus introduces an aura of stasis and darkness, with the concluding scene of the novel, which depicts Ganin leaving this aura behind: he is portrayed walking through a city flooded with light and embarking on a southbound express train.

28. Similar imagery appears in connection with Ganin even earlier: "The day, like the previous days, dragged sluggishly by in a kind of insipid idleness, devoid even of that dreamy expectancy which can make idleness so enchanting" (*M* 17; *Mk* 30). At this point Ganin's life lacks even that kind of "reverie" (*mechta*) that Klara so cherishes: (the Russian word translated as "dreamy expectancy" is *mechtatel'nost'*). Ganin's admission to Podtyagin that he suffers from insomnia (*M* 8; *Mk* 17) is perfectly understandable from the reader's point of view: Ganin is unable to sleep at night because his entire waking life is itself a form of somnolence.

29. An element of the grotesque tinges Ganin's perception of Lyudmila's physical features. A list of her features which Ganin finds repulsive concludes: "and above all her lips, glossy with purple-red lipstick" (*M* 11; *Mk* 20). The Russian color word is *lilovyi*, which is the same word for the color of the smear left by the obscene graffiti about Ganin and Mary later in the novel (*M* 59 – "ridiculous lilac color"; *Mk* 92) as well as of the smear left by Alfyorov on his clock at the end of the novel (*M* 104 – "smeared a mauve mark"; *Mk* 154).

30. Stephen Jan Parker notes several links between the two women (*Understanding Vladimir Nabokov* 30).

31. The most famous example is Humbert's view of Dolores Haze: when he first glimpses her, he recognizes her as his lost "Riviera love" (*L* 41). This blending of a real figure with an image derived from the past provides a close approximation of that first meeting of Ganin and Mary, where the "living person" is seen as "an uninterrupted continuation of the image which had foreshadowed her." Later Humbert underscores the solipsistic element in his perception when he writes: "What I had madly possessed was not she, *but my own creation, another, fanciful Lolita – perhaps, more real than Lolita*" (*L* 64, emphasis added).

32. Ganin's recognition of his first love in a photograph of Alfyorov's wife has struck some readers as suspicious. Since the narrator

never confirms to the reader that the person in Alfyorov's photograph is actually Ganin's first love, one could argue that Ganin may be projecting such an identity onto the photograph. According to this interpretation, Ganin's projection could stem either from his earlier thought that Alfyorov's wife was surely "frisky" and that it would be a shame not to be unfaithful to a man like him (*M* 16; *Mk* 28), or from a more unconscious recollection of his first love (see Toker, *Nabokov* 43–44). As intriguing as this hypothesis may be, it is unlikely that Nabokov intended to invoke such a plot twist in this early novel. While later works such as *Despair* feature characters whose delusions lead to the projection of illusory identifications onto others, such novels also foreground the theme of subjective vision itself in a way that *Mary* does not, and the characters' very insistence on the veracity of their vision calls attention to its illusory quality. Here, though, no attempt is made to focus on such issues.

33. This is so much so, in fact, that Ganin protests: "Why can't they leave me alone today?" (*M* 66; *Mk* 101). His lament may represent the instinctual protest of a character over the continual scrutiny of his identity by strangers.

34. In his essay "Pushkin, or the Real and the Plausible" Nabokov comments on love of disguise, stating that a fondness for "the mask" is an essential characteristic of the authentic poet (P 40).

35. On the other hand, the Russian version of Ganin's declaration to Podtyagin – "I've started a wonderful affair" (M 43) – contains a tantalizing ambiguity: "U menia nachalsia chudesneishii roman" (*Mk* 68). The word *roman* can mean "novel" as well as "romantic affair."

36. It may be significant, then, that just before Ganin decides not to meet Mary, he "for some reason" recalls how he had gone to say goodbye to Lyudmila (*M* 113; *Mk* 167).

37. It is interesting that Ganin thinks that his four days of thinking about his relationship with Mary were perhaps the happiest days of his life (*M* 114; *Mk* 168). Is it possible that this cerebral activity may have given the dreamer more pleasure than the original experience itself?

38. Trains carry multiple associations in Nabokov's works. While the writer's memoirs often evoke the romantic allure of train travel (for example *SM* 142–46; *SO* 203), his fiction exposes an element of impersonality and detachment inherent in train travel. In *Glory* he writes: "Martin developed a passion for trains, travels ... and the waxworks vividness of local stations flashing by, with *people never to be seen again*" (*Gl* 24, emphasis added; *Pod* 32–33).

One also recalls the fate of the protagonist Luzhin in "A Matter of Chance" ("Sluchainost'" 1924): doomed to an empty life of riding a train back and forth from Berlin to Paris, he commits suicide when a train strikes him.

39. Ganin shares several traits with future Nabokov protagonists. Toker points out, for example, that his solipsistic tendencies link him with Van Veen (*Nabokov* 41); the two are specifically linked through their common ability to walk on their hands. One can also detect affinities with other Nabokov characters. Ganin shares with Hermann Karlovich a penchant for lying about himself as a young man (see *M* 41; *Mk* 65), and he relishes the idea of living under a false identity (see *M* 81; *Mk* 122). He even shares one attribute with the vulgar M'sieur Pierre in *Invitation to a Beheading*: he was able to lift a chair in his teeth (*M* 8; *Mk* 16). Brian Boyd reports that Nabokov himself considered Ganin to be not very likeable (*The Russian Years* 244).

CHAPTER 2 ALTERING THE THEMES OF LIFE

1. The amount of attention the writer lavishes on this foot and its toenail is unusual, and the limb takes on grotesque proportions. One is reminded of Gogol's "The Overcoat," where the first thing that Akaky Akakievich notices about the tailor Petrovich is "his big toe ... with a misshapen nail as thick and strong as the shell of a tortoise" (*The Complete Tales of Nikolai Gogol* 2: 311). It also recalls the narrator's description of Otto's thumbnail in "The Fight." At such moments, the magnifying power of the observer's gaze exposes a profound imbalance in the compressed world of the protagonists' emotions, highlighting a powerful tension searching for release.

2. One can, of course, view this situation allegorically, and give the story a metaphysical cast: the world of the author (i.e. "real" life) itself displays the designs imposed upon it by a higher transcendent.

3. In his introduction to the tale in *Details of a Sunset* Nabokov stresses the element of artifice involved in its generation when he points out that the burnt match dropped in the critic's wine glass at the outset of the story is apparently forgotten by everyone within the tale. The very existence of this match underscores the diegetic writer's ignorance of the true nature of the design in which he has been placed.

4. In the Russian original the third-person pronoun *on* ("he") is occasionally used in this passage. This pronoun, which techni-

cally serves as a marker of the free indirect discourse mode (see
Rimmon-Kenan, *Narrative Fiction* 112), may also hint at the fact
that when Anton Petrovich imagines himself as a duellist he is
creating an externalized fictional alter ego for whom such a third-
person pronoun would be appropriate.

5. In his 1937 essay on Pushkin, Nabokov expressed his disdain for
the operatic reworkings of the poet's work in remarkably harsh
terms. He called the libretto writers "sinister individuals" who
"criminally mutilated" Pushkin's texts (P 39). Nabokov also
mentions Tchaikovsky's "vile" librettos in *Speak, Memory* (*SM*
263).

6. Nabokov's intensification of literary allusions in his English
version of the story is representative of the changes he often
worked on his early fiction. Not only do these changes emphasize
the derivative quality of Anton Petrovich's reveries, they remind
the reader of the artifice involved in a piece of Nabokovian
fiction: Anton Petrovich himself, one realizes, belongs to the
world of literary characters and not the world of living humans.

7. This particular passage is presented in the present tense in the
Russian original, and therefore it is not identical with the general
pattern of the extrinsic narrative which primarily uses the past
tense. On the other hand, the past tense does appear in this
episode in the Russian original in such places as "Spokoino,
sovsem spokoino on vylez iz avtomobilia" (*VCh* 137; "Calmly,
quite calmly, he climbed out of the automobile").

8. In this regard it is worth noting Anton Petrovich's plaint over the
inevitability of his impending duel: "Just five minutes ago there
had still been hope … fate might have intervened, suspended
events, saved him" (*RB* 105; *VCh* 127). Since, as shall be noted
below, an entity called "Fate" figures as an agent of authorial
control in *King, Queen, Knave*, one may detect in Anton's lament
the first hints of the anguish felt by literary characters who may
be dismayed by their creator's designs.

9. M. Tsetlin, writing a review for *Sovremennye zapiski* in 1928,
pointed out this element and gave it a broad sociological interpretation: "The author wished to show us the mechanicalness,
lack of soul, automatism of contemporary people" (*Sovremennye
zapiski* 37: 537). Stripped of the sociological message, similar
views may be found in more recent criticism: Franz and Martha
are "cardboard characters" (Appel, *Dark Cinema* 109); Franz is
an "automaton" and the dummies that stand around Dreyer's
store are "objective correlatives of Franz's state of soul" (Hyde,
America's Russian Novelist 48); "Throughout the novel, Nabokov

emphasises the pasteboard quality of the characters" (Clancy, *The Novels* 28); Nabokov's English translation dehumanizes Martha and "makes her more of a puppet" (Rampton, *A Critical Study of the Novels* 17).

10. Franz's endeavor forms the subject of numerous examples of the nineteenth-century *Bildungsroman*. Rampton cites Julien Sorel and Rastignac as Franz's predecessors (16). Instead of liberation and enrichment, however, Franz finds only enslavement and spiritual poverty.

11. This "complete stranger" within Franz may represent a latent creative potential, but it is telling that his transforming vision works to dehumanize the person he observes.

12. Three variants of the tale are provided in A. N. Afanas'ev's collection of folktales (the tale is listed as number 150 in the five-volume edition of 1913–14, and as numbers 267–69 in the three-volume edition of 1985). One version of the tale may be found in English translation in the volume entitled *Russian Fairy Tales* (119–23). As my colleague Natalie Kononenko pointed out for me, the tale was also illustrated by the artist Ivan Bilibin.

13. The phrase "to Berlin from Eden" does not occur in the Russian version, but one finds in the Russian an additional reference to paradise that does not occur in the English. Describing Franz's impression of Martha moving away from him to lock the door, the narrative states: "Raiskaia teplota na mig skol'znula proch'" (*KDV* 95) – "The paradisal warmth slipped away for a moment."

14. Humbert Humbert describes the motel rooms he shares with Lolita as "a prison cell of paradise" (*L* 147) and states that the skies of his "elected paradise" "were the color of hell-flames" (*L* 168). Carl Proffer asserted that "in Nabokov's world, heaven is always in hell, or hell in heaven" ("A new deck" 307).

15. Note how the narrator describes Franz and Martha's physical relationship at the Dreyers' party: "Thus a chess player playing blind feels his trapped bishop and his opponent's versatile queen move in relentless relation to each other ... though they seemed to move independently they were nonetheless securely bound by the invisible, inexorable lines of that figure" (*KQK* 142–43; *KDV* 141). This image of unyielding interlacement anticipates Luzhin's relationship to his invisible opponent in the second half of *The Defense*.

16. Further links between this novel and Tolstoy's short story emerge when one reads Nabokov's Cornell lecture on the story. He identifies "automatic mechanism" and "automatism" as among

the most important elements in the lives of Tolstoy's characters (LRL 239).

17. Toker writes of Martha that she "enters, as it were, into a presumptuous competition with the novelist himself" (*Nabokov* 53). This formulation may overstate the case somewhat, but it raises a significant point, and the relationship between Martha's authorial aspirations and those of the authentic *auctor* will be discussed in more detail later in the chapter.

18. A further affinity between Martha and Hermann is their desire for their subjects to be immobile. Noting in Franz "the immobility of hypnosis," Martha is "afraid to disturb Franz's immobility, the immobile image of future happiness" (*KQK* 167; *KDV* 163). One can compare this to Hermann's excitement over the "immobility" of Felix's body when he first sees the man asleep (*D* 17; *O* 9). Later he writes: "Life only marred my double" (*D* 25; *O* 17).

19. The corresponding passage in Russian does not explicitly mention Dreyer's *artistic* aspirations, but rather alludes to an undefined "dream" (*mechta*): "On vtaine soznaval, chto kommersant on sluchainyi, nenastoiashchii, i chto, v sushchnosti govoria, on v torgovykh delakh ishchet to-zhe samoe, – to letuchee, obol'stitel'noe, raznotsvetnoe nechto, chto mog by on naiti vo vsiakoi otrasli zhizni ... Stranno, chto vot den'gi est', a mechta ostaetsia mechtoi" (*KDV* 215). A literal translation would read: "He secretly acknowledged that he was a businessman by accident and not a real one, and that he was, in essence, seeking in his business dealings that very thing – that volatile, enticing, variegated something he could have found in any branch of life ... It's strange: here he has money, but the dream remains a dream."

20. Dreyer even resents changes in those he knew in the past. After an unexpected meeting with his former mistress Erica, he laments that he would never again remember Erica as he had remembered her before. This new Erica would always be in the way (*KQK* 176; *KDV* 172). Dreyer's attitude recalls Ganin's decision not to jeopardize his image of Mary by meeting her again in the flesh.

21. A telling moment occurs when Dreyer is walking in the hot sun with the Inventor of the automannequins. He does not listen to his companion's suggestion that they move into the shade. He reasons that if *he* enjoys the sun, others are bound to enjoy it too (*KQK* 205; *KDV* 198). Dreyer's solipsism is not amiable here.

22. As Gene Barabtarlo has pointed out in correspondence with me, there may be other games in play in Nabokov's enlarged cata-

logue of photographic subjects. He detects, for example, a subtle pun on the word "grave" embedded in the sequence "engravers, engravers' widows." If the image of "engravers' widows" echoes one of Martha's desired self-images (see *KQK* 197; *KDV* 191), and "soldiers" alludes to Franz's potential destiny, then Nabokov has inserted all three of his heroes into the frame.

23. The third time that Dreyer feels a sudden rush of melancholy occurs at the dance at the *kursaal*, when he hears someone singing a song featuring the word "Montevideo." This is the name of the hotel where first Franz and later the Inventor (sent by Fate in Franz's wake) had stayed. (In the Russian original, the hotel is called the "Video," compare *KQK* 107; *KDV* 105.) Does the mention of this name alert Dreyer to the invisible touch of a higher controlling power? Barabtarlo suggests that the name "Montevideo" itself hints at an "elevated vantage point."

24. The presence of the creative consciousness may also be detected in the phrase "one is sorry to say." Could this phrase indicate the narrator's feelings of regret that his characters do not welcome the company of his diegetic representative?

25. Franz's reaction also introduces a motif of increasing importance in Nabokov's work: the protagonists' Lacanian hypersensitivity to the "gaze" (*régard*) of the other. Lacan discusses the gaze that surprises one and reduces one to "shame," and he says of this gaze: "the gaze I encounter ... is, not a seen gaze, but a gaze imagined by me in the field of the Other" (*The Four Concepts* 84). Nabokov's protagonists will find themselves increasingly concerned with the power of the other (real or imagined) to observe and judge them.

26. The English version notes: "A delightfully compliant mist veiled the receding beach" (*KQK* 241). This detail, which does not appear in the Russian original (compare *KDV* 228), is suggestive, for mists often accompany flights of creative fancy in Nabokov's work (for example, Ganin's initial fascination with Lyudmila).

27. Phyllis Roth argues that a concern for "absolute artistic control" lies at the core of Nabokov's own work ("Toward the Man" 44–45).

28. The association between Dreyer's near-discovery of Martha's affair and the workings of the forces of "Fate" is enhanced in the Russian version of the novel. When Dreyer meets Franz on his walk in Franz's neighborhood, he exclaims: "'Neozhidannyi sluchai ... Vot ono chto. Sluchai'" (*KDV* 208). A literal translation might read: "'An unexpected chance event ... That's what it is. A chance event.'" The English version reads: "'Well, well,

well, fancy running into you'" (*KQK* 216). The English version helps identify such "chance" with authorial design in a narrative aside that occurs just six pages later: "That little trip to Pomerania Bay was in fact proving to be quite a boon for everybody concerned, including the god of chance (Cazelty or Sluch, or whatever his real name was), once you imagined that god in the role of a novelist or a playwright, as Goldemar had in his most famous work" (*KQK* 224). Dreyer's exclamation – "Sluchai" – directly connects his meeting with Franz to the designs of "Sluch," "the god of chance," who is then momentarily blocked by Enricht.

29. In the Russian version the dummies do not literally fall apart, but Dreyer finds their movements too monotonous and their expressions unpleasant and cloying (*KDV* 246). Their movements gradually decelerate until they come to a complete standstill, unable to move at all.

30. For a discussion of these references see Grayson (*Nabokov Translated*) and Proffer ("A new deck"). One device Nabokov uses to underscore the fictionality of his created world is the inclusion of details which link events in the diegetic world with the encompassing structure of the narrative text itself (for example, one reads in chapter 5: "A paperback novelette on the chest-of-drawers left open *at Chapter Five* skipped several pages" [*KQK* 98, emphasis added; compare *KDV* 97]).

CHAPTER 3 THE EVIL DIFFERENTIATION OF SHADOWS

1. In *Speak, Memory* Nabokov gives a moving account of the sense of dissociation which accompanied his own encounter with a mirror after the creation of his first poem. When he looked into his own eyes in the mirror, he experienced the "shocking" sensation of finding only a few pieces of his "usual self." He states that his reason had to make quite an effort to gather again the scattered pieces of his "evaporated identity" (*SM* 227). A similar moment occurs in the sketch "Torpid Smoke" (*RB* 32; *VF* 81).

2. In the Russian version the narrator refers to his own image using the personal reflexive pronoun *svoi* ("svoe otrazhenie"), rather than the possessive pronoun *moi*. This choice may subtly reflect the degree of detachment from his image that he feels. (See Yokoyama's discussion of the semantic implications of reflexivization in Russian, "Russian Functional Syntax," especially 659–76.)

3. Nabokov's narrator echoes Gogol's narrator more closely in the Russian original. Gogol's hero asks: "Pochemu imenno tituliar-nyi sovetnik?"; the corresponding phrase in Nabokov is "pochemu imenno èto – ia" (*VCh* 197).

4. D. Barton Johnson finds parallels between the narrator's experience of "vastation" and similar moments in Tolstoy's "Memoirs of a Madman" and William James's *The Varieties of Religious Experience* (see Johnson, "Nabokov's 'Terror'").

5. In attempting to explain his sense of alienation the narrator questions the arbitrariness of all human sign-systems when he states: "I looked at houses and they had lost their usual meaning . . . leaving nothing but an absurd shell the same way an absurd sound is left after one has repeated sufficiently long the commonest word without heeding its meaning: house, howss, whowss" (*TD* 119; *VCh* 202). From the narrator's perspective, not only is human language an arbitrary system of signs, but the physical world too is a realm in which the visible "signifiers" refer to unknown or enigmatic "signifieds." (One is reminded of an entry in the journal of a German poet known for his elaborate word play, Christian Morgenstern: "Often a word suddenly strikes me. The total arbitrariness of language, which encompasses our world view – and, consequently, the arbitrariness of the world view – is revealed" [quoted in Kayser, *The Grotesque in Art and Literature* 154].) The narrator's perception in "Terror" is especially striking when one considers that the narrator himself is a fictional creation, a creature produced by a linguistic system of signs.

6. The narrator's affirmation here anticipates the ending of *Pale Fire* when Kinbote acknowledges his recognition of the inevitability of death, envisioning a bigger and more competent Gradus ringing at his door (*PF* 301).

7. Nabokov underscores this problem in his manipulation of Luzhin's name. From the first sentence of the novel the character is referred to merely as "Luzhin," and it is only in the last lines that his first name and patronymic are given. As far as those around him are concerned, Luzhin's external, social role is all that exists. His personal identity remains cloaked.

8. Only at rare moments would Luzhin become aware of his isolation, and Nabokov evokes this with a marvelous image as he describes the impression one has of looking into a hotel corridor and seeing only "shoes, shoes, shoes" while hearing in one's ears "the roar of loneliness" (*Df* 96; *ZL* 105).

9. Like Ganin, Luzhin discovers that the external world has been

transformed into a world of shadows. Although Michael Scammell's translation uses several different words for the Russian word for shadow (*ten'*), Luzhin's dilemma remains clear: "A phantom [*ten'*] went by ... abruptly a black shade [*ten'*] with a white breast began to hover about him ... 'This way,' said the ghost [*ten'*] briskly" (*Df* 140; *ZL* 150–51). Unlike Ganin, however, Luzhin cannot negotiate his way out of this realm.

10. For a discussion of the specific reasons which may have led Nabokov to associate chess with music, see Alexandrov (*Nabokov's Otherworld* 58–59).

11. In kinship terms, Luzhin's aunt is closer to his grandfather (first cousin once removed) than to his mother (second cousin). She may serve as an agent for the grandfather in the same way that the Inventor served Fate in *King, Queen, Knave*. Other agents whom the grandfather may command include Luzhin's manager Valentinov and his geography teacher Valentin Ivanovich (Luzhin witnesses his first chess moves in the latter's class, and a chess victory over the geography teacher is one of the milestones in his early career). The name that links both men – "Valentin" – recalls St. Valentine, the patron of lovers. Their names thus point to the fatal passion for chess which ultimately consumes Luzhin.

12. A mixture of contradictory feelings also informs Luzhin Senior's attitude toward Luzhin Junior's chess skills. Watching his son's games, the elder Luzhin feels "both frightened and overjoyed" when his son wins (*Df* 68; *ZL* 76).

13. In addition to the evidence Boyd adduces (for example, the way she is introduced into the novel, her efforts to bring Luzhin to his father's grave, her view of Luzhin as a musician, etc.), one can also cite her use of Luzhin's surname and second-person plural verb forms and pronouns when addressing him, even after they are married (see *Df* 190; *ZL* 201); this is a form of address used by Luzhin Senior (see *Df* 62; *ZL* 70). Similarly, the difficulty she has in placing Valentinov in her reconstruction of Luzhin's biography (see *Df* 240; *ZL* 251–52) recalls Luzhin Senior's struggle with his planned novel *The Gambit* (*Df* 81; *ZL* 89–90).

14. The Russian version offers a spatial image of separation rather than a temporal one: "uzhe vpolne terpimye, smiagchennye dymkoi *rasstoianiia* obrazy ego roditelei" ("the images of his parents were now completely bearable, softened by the haze of *distance*," emphasis added).

15. Nabokov waxes uncharacteristically warm about this figure in his foreword to the English translation, calling her "my gentle young lady" and "a dear girl in her own right" (*Df* 10).

16. Luzhin Senior's obsession with his mistress led him to be absent from his wife's side at the time of her death. Luzhin Junior's obsession with chess alienates him from his wife too; his suicide may reflect a misguided attempt to avoid repeating the precise pattern of his parents' lives.

17. The climax of this process of discovery is reached in "Ultima Thule" and *Bend Sinister* (see Johnson, *Worlds* 185–223).

18. Later, Luzhin Senior contemplates turning his son into a literary character by writing a novel based on his son's life.

19. For example, his "childish elation" over the pseudo-Russian atmosphere in the apartment of his future in-laws indicates a certain flaw in his vision, an inability to distinguish the phony from the genuine. As the narrative notes, Luzhin had never in his life felt "so cozy and so at ease" (*Df* 120; *ZL* 130).

20. Nabokov himself points to this element in *The Defense* in his foreword to the English translation, utilizing the appropriate image drawn from chess to do so: "toward the end of chapter 4 an unexpected move is made by me in a corner of the board, sixteen years elapse in the course of one paragraph . . ." (*Df* 9).

21. For a broad discussion of Nabokov's conception of consciousness and its treatment in his work, see chapter 5 of Boyd's monograph on *Ada* (see also Stegner, *Escape into Aesthetics* chapter 3).

22. For a discussion of the relationship between the two works, see Connolly, "Vladimir Nabokov's *Defense* and the legacy of Nikolai Gogol."

23. See, *inter alia*, Johnson (*Worlds* 83–92), Purdy ("Solus Rex" 382–84), Toker (*Nabokov* 78–81), and Updike ("Grandmaster Nabokov").

24. Luzhin Senior's activity in particular recalls those authors mentioned by the writer in "The Passenger" who seek to alter the themes of life and to "cut out of Life's untrammeled novels our *neat little tales for the use of schoolchildren*" (*DS* 74, emphasis added; *VCh* 140). Luzhin Senior, of course, is a writer of tales for schoolchildren. The authentic *auctor* shows his own superiority over this second-rate author in chapter 5 when he depicts Luzhin Senior wrestling with the problem of how to deal with the years of war and revolution in the novel he envisions writing about his son. As the narrator puts it, these events hindered Luzhin's memories from tending to "a neat literary plot" (*Df* 78; *ZL* 87). Ironically, the authentic *auctor* manages to convey the necessary information about Luzhin Junior's life through those very lines in which he describes Luzhin Senior's struggle.

25. Linda Hutcheon envisions an even more limited scenario. She

sees the dark and pale squares of the ground below Luzhin as "the black and white of the printed page – all that is left of the hero" (*Narcissistic Narrative* 83).

26. For a more detailed evaluation of Luzhin's place in Nabokov's gallery of visionary heroes, see Connolly, "Delusions or Clairvoyance?"

CHAPTER 4 A FONDNESS FOR THE MASK

1. Preparing for his suicide, the narrator smashes his watch. This perhaps indicates his longing to escape the bounds of *chronos* – the empty passage of mortal time (see Kermode *Sense of an Ending* 47–50) – and to attain a state of being outside of time.

2. For a discussion of the relationship between the two works, see Connolly, "Madness and Doubling: From Dostoevsky's *The Double* to Nabokov's *The Eye*."

3. The narrator states that it is truly "frightening" when that which one had believed to be a dream suddenly starts to "congeal" into reality (*E* 108; *S* 82).

4. The narrator's humiliating encounter with Vanya is overheard by Mukhin, and this presence of a witnessing other may remind the narrator of the humiliating episode which initially prompted his suicide. Thus he returns to the scene of the suicide attempt and seeks verification that he had actually killed himself.

5. The narrator's perception of Smurov's longevity resonates with Otto Rank's observations on the aspiration for immortality he perceived in primitive man's attitude toward shadows and doubles (see *Beyond Psychology* 62–101). Rank's views will be discussed further in the next chapter.

6. In Lacanian terms the narrator has just gone through an intricate set of metamorphoses in his attempt to cope with the gaze of others. At the outset he reveals his extreme sensitivity to the gaze of others. After his humiliation in front of curious spectators he tries to shield his vulnerability (or as Lacan would put it, to "elide" the gaze; *The Four Concepts* 83) by becoming one of the gazers: he attempts to assume control by adopting the role of Smurov's observer. He is not able, however, to retain a sense of separation from that part of himself which is watched by others, and so he makes one last, desperate attempt to eliminate any traces of corporeal substance that would allow him to be scrutinized by others: he seeks to become "nothing but a big, slightly vitreous, somewhat bloodshot, unblinking eye" (*E* 113; *S* 87 – "prosto glazet'").

7. This shift provides a fine example of a Nabokovian spiral (see *SM* 275). That which is treated on the diegetic level and disclosed during a first reading of the text suddenly receives an unexpected twist at the end of the narrative, thereby stimulating the reader to re-read the text once again on a higher level of awareness. Nabokov would tell his students that one cannot *read* a book; rather, one can only *re*-read it (*LL* 3).

8. The narrator's shortcomings in perceptual acuity and in originality are numerous. His failure to observe clearly the flow of life around him leads to his crushed reaction to the news that Vanya loves Mukhin; he (as Smurov) confesses with dismay that he simply didn't know this (*E* 78; *S* 58). Later, when he acknowledges his failure to understand Vanya herself, he uses a revealing visual metaphor: "I really knew nothing about her, *blinded* as I was by that burning loveliness" (*E* 80, emphasis added; *S* 60). The issue of creative originality will be discussed below.

9. At one point the narrator perceives Smurov looking at him with resentment: "At this moment one could have noted in Smurov's face a most violent desire that ... I – the cold, insistent, tireless eye – disappear" (*E* 76; *S* 56). Although Smurov's demeanor can be explained by his desire to be alone (and spontaneous) with Vanya, this moment provides an intriguing reflection of the resentment felt by Nabokov's characters when they sense the presence of their creator or his diegetic representative (as in *King, Queen, Knave*). The uneasy relationship between "Smurov" and the narrator in the company of Vanya accords with an observation made by Rank on doubles: "So it happens that the double, who personifies narcissistic self-love, becomes an unequivocal rival in sexual love" (quoted by Berman [*The Talking Cure* 234] in reference to the relationship between Humbert Humbert and Clare Quilty).

10. Curiously, the contrasting visions of Smurov as bold lover and of Smurov as "sexual lefty" both derive from written works by Roman Bogdanovich – the former from one of his stories, and the latter from a letter which he wrote and which was then stolen by the narrator. *Roman* in Russian means novel, and the patronymic Bogdanovich roughly means "the son of one given by God." This character's presence in the novel is one indication of the degree to which issues of fictionality are foregrounded in the text. (It is also possible, however, that the letter is a fabrication of the narrator himself, for he had speculated that the chances of finding any reference to himself in the first letter he stole were extremely remote. If the letter is his own creation, then he emulates here the

example of the narrator of Gogol's "Diary of a Madman" who steals letters ostensibly written by dogs and who finds in them unflattering references to himself, thus engaging in an oblique form of self-recognition and self-definition.)

11. The confusion between the narrator and Smurov peaks during the episode of the theft of Roman Bogdanovich's letter and the narrator's dream that follows it. As one picks at the thematic thread of thievery in the novel, one finds that the fabric of the narrator's tale is a tangled heap of interwoven strands connecting Smurov, the narrator, and the Khrushchov's maid, all three of whom are suspected of theft.

12. Smurov's description – "I was bleeding to death, alone in a mountain gorge" (*E* 56; *S* 40) – recalls the opening of Lermontov's poem "A Dream" ("Son"), which Nabokov discusses in "The Lermontov Mirage." The subsequent comment (found only in the English version) that the good friend who sheltered him had a young daughter who nursed him tenderly ("but that's another story," Smurov admits) evokes both Pushkin's *A Prisoner of the Caucasus* and "The Stationmaster." Like Anton Petrovich in "An Affair of Honor," the narrator has clearly been influenced by the plots of Romantic literature. For a discussion of other literary allusions in *The Eye*, see Schaeffer, and Johnson ("Eyeing" and "The Books Reflected").

13. Only in rare moments of objectivity does the narrator admit his lack of imagination. Listing a few reckless acts he could commit before his suicide, he concludes that these were about the only things he could come up with; the "imagination of lawlessness," he states, "has a limited range" (*E* 29; *S* 18). Later, when he decides to search Vanya's room, he indicates that he took his inspiration from a banal art form: he relates that he imagined a "sleek movie villain" reading a document he has discovered on someone else's desk (*E* 67; *S* 49).

14. One can compare the narrator's imagined image of Matilda's husband "gnashing his teeth, rolling his eyes, and breathing heavily through the nose" (*E* 17; *S* 8) with the actual figure who shows up to confront the narrator: this figure has "protruding eyes" and "dilated nostrils" (*E* 22; *S* 12). Matilda may also be responsible for giving the narrator (and Smurov) an identity as a poet. The narrator remarks that she would coyly ask him whether he wrote poetry (*E* 18; *S* 9). This attribute later becomes the identity Smurov creates for himself when he enters into a relationship with Vanya's maid: according to the latter, he was a "foreign poet" who had suffered a tragic love affair (*E* 85; *S* 64).

15. Uncle Pasha undergoes an accelerated growth process in the novel. Born like "a robust babe" from a maternal envelope, he seems to age before the narrator's eyes when he appears in the Khrushchov household: "At first sight this Uncle Pasha seemed merely three times her age but one had only to look a little closer and he deteriorated under your very eyes. In point of fact, he was not 50 but 80" (*E* 71–72; *S* 52). Pasha ages thirty years in the span of a single sentence! (Actually, he ages ten more years in the English translation. In the Russian version his age is given as seventy.) Soon he is described as a "jolly corpse in a blue suit," and just a few pages later, his death is announced in a telegram (*E* 102; *S* 78). Both the "birth" and the death of this preeminently fictional being are announced in written documents.

16. W. W. Rowe also sees Uncle Pasha as an aid to the narrator in his quest for Vanya's affections. He argues that the spirit of Uncle Pasha may be present during the narrator's final encounter with Vanya and may encourage the character to confess his love (*Nabokov's Spectral Dimension* 94–95).

17. In addition to the bold manipulation of such figures as Uncle Pasha, one notes the manipulation of minor details, such as the curious monetary exchanges that occur between the narrator's recollection of an incident in which a stranger had asked for ninety pfennigs but had received only twenty (*E* 37; *S* 24) and a subsequent observation that Vanya's family had noticed a multitude of petty losses, including "70 pfennigs in change" (*E* 84; *S* 63. The amount of missing change in the Russian version is a full mark.).

18. Daniel Albright draws a distinction between two different types of fantasy in Nabokov that illuminates the narrator's shortcomings in *The Eye*. Contrasted to "heroic fantasy, which is a continual convergence upon the earth of experience" is "evasive fantasy, which is a continual exclusion of the earth of experience" (*Representation and the Imagination* 85). Both Luzhin's and the narrator's fantasies belong to the second type.

19. Bakhtin is aware of the difficulty inherent in attempting to gain an outside view of oneself. He writes that even when one succeeds in this, the resulting image contains "some kind of special *emptiness, transparency* and a somewhat eerie *loneliness*" (29). Coincidentally, the narrator's Romantic portrait of Smurov shimmers with similar tones: he describes his face as "pale" and "thin," marked with "traces of sorrow and experience," and he further comments on his "enigmatic modesty, that pallor of forehead and slenderness of hand" (*E* 43–44; *S* 29–30).

20. Bakhtin again anticipates such difficulties: "The author does not immediately find a purposeful, creatively principled vision of the hero ... the hero displays many grimaces, haphazard masks, false gestures, and unexpected acts, depending on the chance emotional reactions ... of the author" (8).

21. The first excerpts from *Podvig* appeared in January 1931; it was serialized in *Sovremennye zapiski* later that year; and it was published in book form in November 1932; the first English language edition carries a 1971 copyright date. The publishing history of *Kamera obskura* was more complex. The first excerpts appeared in May 1931; it was serialized in *Sovremennye zapiski* in 1932–33; and it was published as a book in December 1933. The first translation of the novel by Winifred Roy appeared with the title *Camera Obscura* in 1936; Nabokov translated the novel as *Laughter in the Dark* and published it in 1938; minor alterations were made in the 1960s (see Grayson, *Nabokov Translated* 27–28). The discussion of the novel in this chapter will concentrate on Nabokov's English version with commentary about the original where appropriate.

22. Nabokov's use of cinematic imagery has been discussed at length by Stuart (*The Dimensions of Parody* 89–106) and Appel (*Nabokov's Dark Cinema* 258–69). A prime function of this imagery is to underscore the fact that the central characters behave like actors filling conventional cinematic roles.

23. The timing of this invitation is significant: it arrives in the same batch of mail as the letter from Margot exposing his adulterous inclinations. The Dreyers' invitation heralds Albinus's initiation into an adulterous world where he will be destroyed by blind desire.

24. It is noteworthy that Irma's concern for her father's well-being does not reflect an obsession with a single individual: after she realizes that the man on the street is *not* her father, she "felt sorry" for him too (*LD* 160; *KO* 108).

25. The comment that Rex is a "fine artist" with a pencil in hand does not appear in the Russian original. Rex's predecessor Horn is described as a "talantlivyi karikaturist" ("talented caricaturist"; *KO* 97), which seems more appropriate for what the narrator describes.

26. Earlier in the novel Rex is said to view himself as the "partner" of the author of any book he may be discussing (*LD* 182; *KO* 124), and he feels that a place for him has been reserved in "the stage manager's private box" (*LD* 183; *KO* 124). Although the stage manager Rex envisions may resemble Nabokov ("an elusive,

double, triple, self-reflecting magic Proteus of a phantom" *LD* 183; *KO* 124), Rex never becomes more than a minion who can be dismissed when his services are no longer required.

27. Albinus too is depicted in the novel framed by a window and making pantomime gestures; this occurs when he searches for Margot after learning that she has deceived him with Rex (*LD* 223; *KO* 153). This scene also establishes Albinus's puppet-like status, an association that is underscored in the revised novel's final scene: he falls "like a big, soft doll" (*LD* 292; compare *KO* 204). The mutual association of Albinus and Rex with puppets is one of several images linking the two. At one point the narrator states that Rex was Albinus's "shadow" (*LD* 208; *KO* 141). The two figures form a characteristic Nabokovian pair – the predator and the prey – like Berg and Anton Petrovich.

28. When he discussed the novel with Alfred Appel, Jr., Nabokov said that all the characters were "hopeless clichés" except for the novelist: "He's all right" (Appel, *Dark Cinema* 262).

29. The tension is not fully resolved until *Lolita*, when Humbert both acknowledges his culpability for the injury he has done to Dolores Haze and attempts to redeem it by transforming it into a work of timeless art. "Pity" is the password, John Shade declares in *Pale Fire* (*PF* 225), but it takes a rare individual who can both comprehend the woes afflicting another and at the same time retain enough aesthetic detachment to render the other's pain with effectiveness.

30. Leona Toker points out that Nabokov's use of aesthetic detachment as a means of suppressing the reader's sympathy for the characters is a salient feature of the novel as a whole (*Nabokov* 115–18).

31. Elisabeth's ability to sense misfortune occurring many miles away from her echoes the ability ascribed to the woman who becomes Luzhin's wife (see *Df* 105; *ZL* 115). This is one component of the kind of vision that Alexandrov associates with "cosmic synchronization," which he sees as a trait belonging to all of Nabokov's positive characters (*Nabokov's Otherworld* 27).

CHAPTER 5 DIMMING THE BLISS OF NARCISSUS

1. The narrator's longing to be in a remote land represents an evolution of the obsession with an absent other noted in Nabokov's early fiction. In works written around this time (1930–31), it is a distant *land* that can serve as the object of such an obsession. For other examples, see "The Aurelian" ("Pil'gram") and *Glory*.

2. The plot bears a tangible resemblance to the kind of fiction written by H. Rider Haggard. Several of Haggard's works are written as first-person autobiographic narratives and feature three Europeans traveling together. See in particular *King Solomon's Mine*, in which the narrator Quatermain is accompanied by two men named Curtis and Good, and *Queen Sheba's Ring*, in which the narrator Adams is accompanied by two men named Quick and Orme. For a discussion of the relationship of this work to some kindred antecedents, see Connolly, "Vladimir Nabokov and Valerij Brjusov: An Examination of a Literary Heritage."

3. Earlier, Khodasevich had adopted a similar position. In his essay "On Sirin" he writes that the hero of "Terra Incognita" "dies at that instant when he finally plunges completely into the world of the imagination" from the world of reality (98). Khodasevich, however, accepts without skepticism the narrator's claim that the European bedroom is merely a delusion, and he does not ask why the "world of imagination" seems so barren to the narrator at the end of the story.

4. Evidence supporting this premise includes the fact that the narrative is predominantly conducted in the past tense and it contains indications of a distinction between the time of the narrative act (or the moment of remembrance) and the time of the narrated experience: "I think we tried to catch up with the fugitives – I do not recall clearly, but, in any case, we failed" (*RB* 120; *S* 118).

5. The precise date of composition of the work has triggered some disagreement. The date given at the end of the text in *Vesna v Fial'te* is 1929 (*VF* 270); Davydov has argued that the story was written in 1933 ("*Teksty-Matreshki*" 208); Nabokov's introduction to the translation in *A Russian Beauty* indicates that the story had been accepted for publication by 1931 or 1932 (*RB* 46); Field's (93) and Juliar's (240) bibliographies both list the time of writing as December 1931; Brian Boyd's research supports this last date (see *The Russian Years* 373).

6. See Field (*Life in Art* 174–75), Davydov ("*Teksty-Matreshki*" 37–51), and Boyd (*The Russian Years* 374).

7. The editors of *Arion* even provide Tal with his literary identity: they give him the pseudonym under which his work appears in print (*RB* 60; *VF* 266).

8. Davydov notes that the cane in Nabokov's fiction serves as a "mythic instrument of revenge" ("*Teksty-Matreshki*" 22), but he may be in error when he states that Ilya Borisovich is the first to suffer from it. The narrator of *The Eye* is thrashed by his mistress's

husband in chapter 1 of that novel. Soon thereafter, Axel Rex is soundly thrashed by Paul in *Laughter in the Dark*.

9. The term "loophole" is taken from Bakhtin's *Problems of Dostoevsky's Poetics* (see 194–95).

10. Nabokov wrote the novel in 1932; it was published serially in 1934; and it came out as a book in 1936. Nabokov's first English translation appeared in 1937, and his revised translation was published as a book in 1966.

11. Nabokov plants numerous clues about this affair. For a discussion of some of these clues, see Carroll ("The Cartesian Nightmare" 84–85).

12. Geoffrey Green quotes Nabokov's nemesis Freud to elucidate this type of paradox: "The hostile feelings are as much an indication of an emotional tie as the affectionate ones, in the same way as *defiance signifies dependence as much as obedience does*" (*Freud and Nabokov* 78, emphasis added).

13. The narrator of *The Eye* only begins to enjoy self-observation after he has supposedly killed himself and can watch his alter ego Smurov with impunity. At that point, the pleasure he and Hermann experience in self-observation has one distinctive feature – their pleasure is enhanced in proportion to the distance they feel from the self they are observing. Hermann recalls that the ecstasy he felt when watching himself make love to his wife increased with the extent of the interval between his two selves (*D* 38). He later writes that he preferred to hold Felix at a certain distance from himself because he felt that any proximity might have broken the spell of their likeness (*D* 41; *O* 31).

14. At several points Hermann offers hints that he realizes that the professed resemblance is inexact or illusory, but he cannot quite bring himself to confront this fact (see *D* 21, 40, 41, 84, 107; *O* 13, 29, 31, 70, 95).

15. Nabokov increased the comic sexual element in his revised English version, adding details (such as the image of a procession of pencils marching "down an endless tunnel of corruption" *D* 24) which would tease the imagination of the Freudian critics whom he derides in his introduction (*D* 8). Carl Proffer documents the increase in sexual and coprological references in the revised text ("From *Otchaianie*" 260–62). Dabney Stuart comments shrewdly on the inclusion of one such image – the transformation of Felix's sausage and pretzel into the "impersonal trace" left behind by "the unsophisticated wanderer" (*D* 27; *O* 20); he calls it a "marvelous repudiation of the mechanical

input/output procedure of determinist thinking" (*The Dimensions of Parody* 120–21).

16. Substituting the concepts of "literary creator" and "literary character" for the concepts of "immortal self" and "mortal ego," one finds a further observation by Rank illustrative of Hermann's endeavor: "in twin-mythology the typical motif of fratricide turns out to be a symbolic gesture on the part of the immortal self by which it rids itself of the mortal ego" (*Beyond Psychology* 92). (Hermann, of course, characterizes Felix to Lydia as his "younger brother" whose resemblance to Hermann was "perfect" [*D* 147–48; *O* 131–32].) Rank's comment also proves relevant to *Lolita*, where Humbert argues that he had to kill Quilty in order to give immortality to Lolita and to himself (*L* 311). Although Nabokov proclaimed that the *Doppelgänger* theme was a bore (*SO* 83), his fiction charged the subject with new vitality.

17. Hermann does not wish to accept a world made up of unique individuals; perhaps he feels threatened by the lack of personal control such a world implies for him. Thus he embraces Communism and its promise of a world of "identical" fellows (*D* 30; *O* 22). Even better is a world "where all men will resemble one another as Hermann and Felix did; a world of Helixes and Fermanns" (*D* 169; *O* 151). This last declaration suggests that in Hermann's ideal world, all the identical fellows would bear *his* countenance.

18. One can also analyze Hermann's failure from the Bakhtinian perspective discussed in reference to *The Eye*. While Hermann achieves some success in his artistic endeavor by first creating an externalized "hero" and then identifying with that hero (see the beginning of chapter 10 when Hermann speaks in Felix's voice), he fails to follow through with the crucial second stage – the return to his initial position. Indeed, Hermann himself indicates this when he discusses his situation after the murder: "I have grown much too used to an outside view of myself, to being both painter and model ... Try as I may *I do not succeed in getting back into my original envelope*, let alone making myself comfortable *in my old self*" (*D* 29, emphasis added; *O* 21).

19. Once he begins this activity, he becomes as obsessed with the idea of creating verbal art as he had been with creating physical art. Musing on the fact that he writes from noon to dawn, he remarks that even *he* finds peculiar this act of "writing, writing, writing" (*D* 167; *O* 149).

20. Hermann's successor in Nabokov's fiction is Humbert Humbert who goes even further in exposing his dependence on his readers when he exclaims: "Please, reader ... Imagine me; I shall not exist if you do not imagine me" (*L* 131).

21. Davydov cogently discusses the way Sirin/Nabokov disrupts the surface of Hermann's aesthetic mirror ("The Shattered Mirror" 27–29, 32), just as Hermann observes that "a breeze dims the bliss of Narcissus" (*D* 25; *O* 17).

22. It is ironic that Hermann points to detective fiction as the mode of literature against which his work should be measured. As Michael Holquist points out, it is the "supremely rational quality" of detective fiction which accounts for its popularity: "the magic of mind in a world that all too often seems impervious to reason" ("Whodunit" 143). Hermann, of course, falls victim to his own irrational impulses.

23. Hermann's delusion offers an interesting metaliterary twist on Lacan's conceptualization of a basic condition within the human psyche. As Ragland-Sullivan puts it, "the *je* mistakenly thinks that it can represent its own totality by designating itself in a statement" but it is actually oppressed from within by messages of the Other (*Jacques Lacan* 47). In terms of Hermann's discourse, of course, the Other's messages are those of the authentic *auctor* himself.

24. In his study of *Despair* Carroll asserts that "virtually all" of Nabokov's protagonists feel the presence of the "mind behind the mirror" and notes that it is their search for or flight from this mind that "forms a central movement in the novels" (100). Yet although a character such as Luzhin certainly feels the presence of a higher consciousness, Hermann is perhaps the first Nabokov hero who reacts to this sensation by trying to match the higher mind at his own game – the creation of an explicitly *literary* text.

25. Ironically, when Hermann exclaims that "the real author is not I, but my impatient memory" (*D* 47; *O* 37), he is partially correct: he is *not* the "real" author, but that honor belongs not to his impatient memory, but rather to Vladimir Nabokov.

26. Grayson sees a different form of autoreference here, identifying "siren'iu" as a pun on Nabokov's pen-name Sirin (66; see also Carroll 89–90). She does not mention the encoding of the name "Nabokov."

27. Nabokov's manipulation of the flower imagery is even more subtle than first appears. Michaelmas daisies are not the same type of flower as ordinary daisies. They are asters, as the original Russian text indicates. It is a stroke of Nabokovian ingeniousness,

however, to translate *astry* as "Michaelmas daisies" instead of "asters," for the resulting flower imagery evinces a minor reflection of the central doubling theme: the seeming doublet of "Michaelmas daisies" and "a field of daisies" is actually a *false* doublet, like Hermann and Felix. Although on a lexical level the recurrence of the word "daisies" suggests doubling and repetition, the two sets of flowers are not physically identical.

28. Commenting on "Sirin" somewhat later, Nabokov utilized an image of striking relevance to Hermann's state at the end of *Despair*: "His best works are those in which he condemns his people to the *solitary confinement* of their souls" (*CE* 217, emphasis added).

CHAPTER 6 THE STRUGGLE FOR AUTONOMY

1. Chapel Louise Petty explores the interrelationship between character and narrator in her illuminating study of the work ("A Comparison of Hawthorne's 'Wakefield' and Nabokov's 'The Leonardo'"), but she focuses on Romantovski as the central object of the "author-narrator's" projections rather than on the opposition between Romantovski and the brothers as a reflection of the tension within the narrator.

2. At one point in "The Leonardo" Romantovski seems to disappear before the eyes of the drunken brothers: "He, vibrating and diffusing rays, stretched out, thinned, and gradually vanished" (*RB* 18; *VF* 65). This disappearing act both looks forward to Cincinnatus's "criminal exercise" in *Invitation to a Beheading* and recalls Gregson's dissolution in "Terra Incognita."

3. An interesting facet of the narrative discourse in "The Leonardo" and *Invitation to a Beheading* alike is the extent to which it expresses the rage of the surrounding society. The longest passage of free direct discourse in "The Leonardo" occurs just after Romantovski seems to vanish. It begins: "This cannot go on. He poisons the life of honest folks. Why, it can well happen that he will move at the end of the month – intact, whole, never taken to pieces." It concludes: "Hateful is everything that cannot be palpated, measured, counted" (*RB* 18; *VF* 65). This passage anticipates the episode in *Invitation to a Beheading* where the narrator begins describing "the precious quality of Cincinnatus; his fleshy incompleteness" and concludes two pages later: "all this so teased the observer as to make him long to tear apart, cut to shreds, destroy utterly this brazen elusive flesh, and all that it implied and expressed, all that impossible, dazzling freedom" (*IB* 122; *PK*

124). In both works, the narrating consciousness exposes a striking understanding of the urge to dissect the enigma of the individual.

4. The novel was written in 1934, published serially in 1935–36, and it appeared as a separate book in 1938.

5. In the years since its publication the novel has generated a multitude of interpretations – aesthetic, political, and metaphysical. As Davydov and Alexandrov have argued in their explication of Gnostic and other metaphysical motifs, the metaphysical dimension underpins the entire structure of the novel. Nonetheless, the very tale of imprisonment and liberation resonates powerfully in the ethical and aesthetic spheres as well. While I endorse Alexandrov's interpretation of the novel, my discussion primarily focuses on the novel's aesthetic dimension with the understanding that Nabokov's metaphysical vision finds expression through this very dimension.

6. Cincinnatus is also compared to a child who has just learned to walk (*IB* 11; *PK* 25). Nabokov utilizes the child image in much the same way in "The Potato Elf": the novel presents a record of psychological growth and maturation.

7. One can identify an affinity between Cincinnatus's situation and that of Hermann in *Despair*. Both men are surrounded by entities whose true nature they do not comprehend. Yet the process of personal projection works in opposite directions in the two texts. Hermann needs to see those around him as they really are: that is, as beings like himself, and not as his own literary creations. Cincinnatus, in contrast, must suspend his belief that the others are beings like himself, and recognize that they are in fact misshapen models of literary characters.

8. Cincinnatus's penchant for projection is most evident in his relationship to his wife Marthe. Although he wishes to see her as a woman capable of love and understanding, he discovers with a shock that she can be malicious and obstinate. He writes that he was amazed when he discovered that this was her true self (*IB* 63; *PK* 71–72).

9. On the other hand, as D. Barton Johnson has pointed out in correspondence with me, a novel that contains a paragraph which is a page and a half long and in which all the words begin with the letter "p" (*IB* 123; *PK* 125) cannot be considered entirely "naturalistic." Perhaps Nabokov takes on two targets here: works which are excessively naturalistic and works which strive to be ostentatiously avant-garde.

10. See also Johnson (*Worlds* 161), Stuart (78), Davydov (*"Teksty-Matreshki"* 156), and Alexandrov (101).

11. Cincinnatus also uses the word *butafor* (prop man) when chiding his mother for having a wet raincoat and dry shoes: "see, that's careless. Tell the prop man for me" (*IB* 132; *PK* 133).

12. An echo of this initial escape fantasy occurs in chapter 6 when Cincinnatus imagines Marthe leaving her house, followed by a young suitor; after Cincinnatus roams the city in his mind he returns to Marthe, now seeing her on her homeward journey, again followed by a suitor. Then the prison clock finishes striking, "and the jail was back in force" (*IB* 75; *PK* 82). One is reminded of Hermann's comment about the arcs that Felix drew in the dirt with his stick: those drawings reflect "our eternal subjection to the circle in which we are all imprisoned" (*D* 73; *O* 61). Cincinnatus's reveries run in circles, and images of circumscription proliferate throughout the novel. For a discussion of the circle imagery, see Susan Klemtner's essay "To 'Special Space'".

13. The anxiety of a character who senses the watchful presence of an enigmatic other first appeared in Franz's resentment of the foreign couple in *King, Queen, Knave*. Here it assumes more sinister dimensions: ever since childhood Cincinnatus has felt himself to be under the searching gaze of others (see *IB* 24; *PK* 36).

14. For a discussion of the central significance of the pencil in the novel see Barabtarlo's essay on the work ("Within and Without" 391–92).

15. Johnson details just how skillful this formulation is in Nabokov's overall design for the novel (*Worlds* 36).

16. Earlier in the novel, the narrator pointed out that while working in a doll factory Cincinnatus had "artificially developed a fondness for this mythical Nineteenth Century." Cincinnatus, indeed, "was ready to become completely engrossed in the mists of that antiquity and find therein a false shelter" before he met Marthe (*IB* 27; *PK* 39–40). Epithets such as "artificial," "mythical," and "false" indicate the danger of Cincinnatus's predilections. For a discussion of the novel's refutation of the nineteenth-century realist literary tradition, see John Kopper's study "The Prison in Nabokov's *Priglashenie*" (180–81).

17. The dominant mirror image in *Invitation to a Beheading* is not the straightforward reflections produced by everyday mirrors (which may themselves hearken back to the artistic aspirations of nineteenth-century realism), but rather the *nonnon* mirror, a strange glass which transforms seemingly shapeless objects into

beautiful, comprehensible images (see *IB* 135–36; *PK* 136–37). As Hyde notes, Nabokov's novel is itself "the perfect *nonnon* mirror" (139).

18. This shift anticipates the change that occurs within Pnin over the course of the eponymous novel. One can contrast the halting language Pnin uses in his lament at the end of chapter 2 ("I haf nofing left, nofing, nofing!" *Pn* 61) with the assurance with which he writes a letter at the end of chapter 6: "'Dear Hagen,' he wrote in his clear firm hand, 'permit me to recaputilate (crossed out) recapitulate the conversation we had tonight'" (*Pn* 173).

19. One of the poets whose work figures in *Invitation to a Beheading* is Fyodor Tiutchev. Lines from his poem "Last Love" ("Posledniaia liubov'") are recalled by Cincinnatus near the end of the novel (*IB* 193; *PK* 189). A more pertinent Tiutchev text, however, might be the poem "Silentium." The poem declares that "a whole world of mysterious and enchanted thoughts" lies within the soul and that one should not try to articulate them, for an attempt to do so would merely cause distortion. Significantly, Nabokov incorporates a garbled version of the poem's central line (often quoted by the Russian Symbolists) – "A thought uttered is a lie" – into his 1937 story "Oblako, ozero, bashnia" ("Cloud, Castle, Lake"; first published with the title "Ozero, oblako, bashnia"). The line does not appear in the later English version (see *VF* 237; *ND* 115).

20. In the compelling metaphysical exegesis worked out by Davydov ("*Teksty-Matreshki*" 115–16) and Alexandrov (81–87), the two Cincinnatuses represent the dualism of body and spirit.

21. In this regard one should recall that Cincinnatus's mother tells him that she never saw his father's face, but heard "only his voice" (*IB* 133; *PK* 134). She then tells Cincinnatus that his father was also like Cincinnatus (*IB* 133; *PK* 135).

22. The realm toward which Cincinnatus heads undoubtedly possesses the characteristics of that world he envisioned in chapter 8. That world is "suffused with such radiant, tremulous kindness"; "*there* everything strikes one by ... the simplicity of perfect good; *there* everything pleases one's soul, everything is filled with the kind of fun that children know" (*IB* 94; *PK* 99–100). These attributes and images recall Nabokov's own description of "aesthetic bliss" – "a sense of being somehow, somewhere, connected with other states of being where art (curiosity, tenderness, kindness, ecstasy) is the norm" (*L* 316–17).

23. Nabokov spoke about a similar problem in his lecture on Franz Kafka. He commented on the fact that although the absurd

characters in certain of Gogol's and Kafka's works belong to the absurd world around them, they seek to struggle out of those worlds into the human world, and they die in despair (*LL* 254–55). In *Invitation to a Beheading*, though, Nabokov depicts a happier outcome to an analogous struggle.

24. Perhaps the dreamer is "V. Sirin," whom Nabokov called "one of my characters in 'real life'" (*SO* 290). Margaret Boegeman finds in Cincinnatus's dilemma a reflection of Nabokov's anxiety about shifting from the Russian language to English ("Many Shades of Kafka" 115–19). On the other hand, the depiction of Cincinnatus's everyday world as a realm of slumber neatly illustrates the Gnostic view of life in the physical world as a state of sleep (see Alexandrov 94).

25. If this be the case, then *Invitation to a Beheading* manifests a significant development of the situation depicted earlier in Nabokov where a character becomes preoccupied with self-observation (as in the narrator's observation of Smurov in *The Eye*). Here, the extradiegetic dreamer's apprehensive gaze at himself becomes so pervasive that his diegetic representative appears to be the object of scrutiny by an entire world.

26. Nabokov's readers have noted this uncertainty in their discussion of the novel. Laurie Clancy writes of Nabokov: "His narrative voice tends to move almost imperceptibly in and out of the consciousness of different characters, so that one is never quite sure whether the reflections are those of the author or one of his characters" (*The Novels* 72). Clancy conflates here the entities of "narrator" and "author."

27. These characters would reflect the kind of process Nabokov described to an interviewer in which the negative characters in his fiction are displayed outside his inner self like the monsters on a cathedral facade: they are placed there to show that they have been "booted out" (*SO* 19).

28. The émigré critic P. Bitsilli even goes so far as to assert that Cincinnatus and Pierre are "two aspects of 'man in general'" (see his review in Proffer, *A Book of Things About Vladimir Nabokov* 68).

29. Dale Peterson's discussion of Pierre also finds a link between the character and the novelist (although he would presumably exclude Nabokov from the type of writer he has in mind). He writes: "The executioner's pretense of all-knowing intimacy is peculiar to totalitarian regimes – and to the authors of realistic novels" (832). If Gene Barabtarlo is correct when he states that Pierre Delalande is the ostensible author of the text, which is then translated into Russian by Fyodor Godunov-Cherdyntsev, the

hero of *The Gift* ("in order," as Fyodor puts it, "to reach a final dictatorship over words" *G* 376; *Dr* 409, see Barabtarlo, "Within and Without" 396), then Delalande shows a Nabokovian flair for self-ironization when he gives the main villain and clown of his novel his own first name.

30. One must take issue then, with Vladislav Khodasevich's assertion that the end of the novel depicts "the return of the artist from creative work to reality" and that "with the return into the world of 'beings akin to him,' the existence of Cincinnatus the artist is cut off" (98). What is cut off is the nightmarish delirium of Cincinnatus's creator, not Cincinnatus's existence as artist. Only at the conclusion of the novel is the character set free to engage in his artistic pursuits without hindrance.

31. Other comments by Nabokov on sleep also find reflection in *Invitation to a Beheading.* In an interview he spoke of having nightmares which contain "kaleidoscopic arrangements of broken impressions, fragments of day thoughts, and irresponsible mechanical images" (*SO* 29). Cincinnatus expresses something similar when he states that he is surrounded by "wretched specters" who "torment me as can torment only senseless visions, bad dreams, dregs of delirium, the drivel of nightmares" (*IB* 36; *PK* 47).

CHAPTER 7 THE TRANSFORMING RAYS OF CREATIVE CONSCIOUSNESS

1. The incorporation of a mirror image is telling. Mirror imagery in Nabokov often accompanies experiences of dissociation ("Terror," *Despair*) or the activation of artistic impulses (*LL* 377). The mirror image here marks a bifurcation within the narrating entity between his function as a character within the diegetic world and his function as the extradiegetic generator of the narrative discourse itself.

2. This moment echoes that crucial second stage in the process of aesthetic activity in contemplation as outlined by Bakhtin (see the discussion of *The Eye* above). After initially achieving a state of identification with his "hero" (a state marked here by the use of the first-person pronoun in commenting on his location alongside V. I.), the artist must return to his own place and give completed form to his hero (as the narrator does by seeing the man as his external "representative").

3. The image of shade here is suggestive. Nabokov had elsewhere indicated a connection between "the play of light and shadow"

with the workings of the creative imagination (see, for example, "The Fight"), and as Leona Toker points out, the fact that both V. I. and the narrator's representative occupy a place in the shade may indicate their underlying fictional status ("Self-Conscious Paralepsis" 466–67).

4. Just as the narrator projected the identity of "Vasiliy Ivanovich" onto a total stranger, it is also possible that he projects his own identity onto an unknown figure with a Russian newspaper and simply calls this figure his "representative." It is worth noting that a "Vasili Ivanovich" also appears in the story "Cloud, Castle, Lake," which was published just two years after "Recruiting." This second V. I., whom the narrator of that story calls "one of my representatives" (*ND* 113; *VF* 235) displays certain attributes of an authorial agent (see Zimmermann, "The Russian Short Stories" 265–66), and Nabokov himself declared that this figure was his "agent" (Field, *Life in Art* 197). The use of the name "Vasiliy Ivanovich" in "Recruiting," then, may mark the degree to which the text foregrounds issues of creative appropriation.

5. Grisha's sensation of losing the fixed boundaries of his body finds significant expression: "the lane on the other side of the house might be his own arm, while the long skeletal cloud that stretched across the whole sky . . . might be his backbone" (*RB* 29; *VF* 77). This description indicates not so much that Grisha feels himself merging with the larger cosmos (as Fyodor experiences in the Grunewald in *The Gift*: *G* 345–46; *Dr* 373–74), but rather that the surrounding cosmos has become an extension of himself. That is, his own physical features are superimposed onto the features of the external world. This hint of solipsistic projection recalls Hermann Karlovich's attempt to describe the area around the site where he murders Felix: he states that the railway line from Berlin runs along his sleeve and that his wristwatch is the town of Koenigsdorf (*D* 62; *O* 51–52).

6. Similarly, in at least one place, the shift from third to first person occurs within a single sentence, and the immediate context does not involve Grisha's status as a poet (although that status soon resurfaces): "On *his* way out of the dining room *he* noticed *his* father turn his whole torso in his chair to face the wall clock as if it had said something, and then begin turning back – but there the door *I* was closing closed, and *I* did not see that bit to the end" (*RB* 32–33, emphasis added; *VF* 82).

7. Pekka Tammi provides the best description of the variety of narrative perspectives utilized in the novel (*Problems of Nabokov's*

Poetics 80–94), but his discussion also has gaps (for example, he does not analyze the proleptic narrative aside in chapter 1 – "where we dined" *G* 65; *Dr* 62). Iu. Levin also provides an extensive discussion of narrative form (see "Ob osobennostiakh").

8. Some readers state that the entire novel is narrated by Fyodor (see, for example, Bodenstein, "*The Excitement of Verbal Adventure*" 1.249 and Couturier, *Nabokov* 39). Anna Maria Salehar calls the text "a psychogram, perhaps a notebook" of Fyodor's ("Nabokov's *Gift*" 70).

9. Although the situation is too involved for a detailed analysis here, one can find a parallel bifurcation within *each branch* of the general bifurcation. That is, one discerns a kind of duality within the *character* Fyodor ("somebody within *him* ... independently from *him*, had absorbed all this") and also within the first-person *narrative voice* (compare the distinction Tammi draws between CD1 and CD2; 87–88). This structure of nested bifurcations is familiar from *Invitation to a Beheading*.

10. The most poignant illustration of this proclivity occurs when Fyodor envisions himself in Alexander Chernyshevski's place and imagines how the man would see the ghost of his dead son. Later, the narrative again enters Alexander's mind to convey his meditations on impending death. Fyodor's predilection for imagining the inner lives of others reflects a penchant Nabokov recalls from his own childhood (see *SM* 144 and 145).

11. Fyodor's manipulation of the latent ambiguity inherent in the shifter "I" anticipates the identity games Kinbote plays with the third-person pronoun in his Index under the entry "Shade, John" in *Pale Fire*.

12. See Duffield White for a discussion of the varieties of poetic experience explored in *The Gift* ("Radical Aestheticism" 274–84, 289–90).

13. Nabokov wrote of such displacement in his 1937 essay on Pushkin. Asking whether one can imagine and "relive" the reality of another's life in one's mind, and then set it down faithfully on paper without distorting it, he states that this is unlikely. He suggests that thought itself deforms the story even as it shines its light onto that story (P 40). He wrote this essay in the same year that chapter 2 of *The Gift* appeared in print, and he would return to this problem in such novels as *The Real Life of Sebastian Knight*, *Pnin*, and *Pale Fire*.

14. Compare Salehar (77) and Johnson (*Worlds* 98–101). What is striking about the poem is the way it emerges out of the ordinary

flow of the prose narrative. A passage of third-person narrative describing Fyodor's daily routine is suddenly interrupted by the intrusion of a segment with a first-person perspective. It begins: "What shall I call you? Half-Mnemo*syne*? There's a half-shim*mer* in your surname too" and it concludes: "O swear to me that while the heartblood stirs, you will be true to what we shall invent" (*G* 169; *Dr* 176). In contrast to Fyodor's early poetry, in which he saw the "living connection between my divine excitement and my human world" expire in "a fatal gust of words" (*G* 165; *Dr* 172), this poem displays the opposite dynamic: the "pulsating mist" of his prose "suddenly began to speak with a human voice" (*G* 168; *Dr* 175).

15. One should note the inclusion of the number seven here. This is one of several places in the novel where the number seven appears. For example, at the outset Fyodor moves into Seven Tannenberg Street, and from there moves to Zina's apartment. The number three also appears frequently (carrying the most charged association in the image of the "fatal triangle" which dooms poor Yasha). The numbers three and seven appear together in a significant way on the third page of the novel, when the narrator wonders if there is some kind of secret law of composition behind the sequence of shops found on Berlin streets. He speculates that "three" shops on Tannenberg Street may try to establish the proper order, and he describes how one shop moved "so as to be at first seven and then three doors away from the pharmacy" (*G* 17; *Dr* 11), finally seizing the opportunity to form the desired line. Zina mentions Seven Tannenberg Street to Fyodor (*G* 193; *Dr* 203), and later Fyodor describes to her the three attempts Fate made to bring them together, starting just over three years earlier (see *G* 375–76; *Dr* 407–8). Studying the recurrence of these numbers in *The Gift*, one recalls the prominent role they played in Pushkin's "Queen of Spades" where they figure as two of the three cards Hermann needs to play to win a fortune. The third card in Pushkin's story is the Ace, and it is this card that Hermann fails to play in the climactic card game which drives him mad at the end of the story. Curiously, this very card is not only *not* misplayed in *The Gift*, but it appears at a crucial point in the novel – in the midst of Fyodor's pivotal poem about Zina: "upon the *ace* of fancy let us set to win a world of beauty from the night" (*G* 169, emphasis added; *Dr* 176). The gods of fatidic numbers smile more favorably on Fyodor than they did on Hermann.

16. Davydov comes closest to noting these parallels when he observes

that both Fyodor and Chernyshevski "begin with holes in their shoes" and regard ink as their natural element (*"The Gift"* 366).

17. Alexandrov speculates that while Chernyshevski's birth date is in the Old Style, Fyodor's is "probably" in the New Style, thereby making the relationship between them parodic (*Nabokov's Otherworld* 245).

18. Although the two men are different in many substantial ways, the imagery Fyodor employs when writing about them reveals one curious link. In chapter 2 he mentions that his father emanated "something difficult to convey in words, a haze, a mystery" as if he "possessed an aura of something still unknown but which was perhaps the most genuine of all" (*G* 126; *Dr* 130). Of Chernyshevski he writes: "That mysterious 'something' which Steklov talks about in spite of his Marxism ... undoubtedly existed in Chernyshevski and manifested itself with unusual strength just before his banishment to Siberia" (*G* 276; *Dr* 294). Perhaps the very existence of this link serves to underscore the essential difference between the two men, since they channel their special energies in entirely different directions. Godunov-Cherdyntsev's professional knowledge of nature, for example, contrasts sharply with Chernyshevski's ignorance of Siberian flora (see *G* 301; *Dr* 322).

19. A further echo of the theme of ruptured father–son relationships is the relationship between Alexander Chernyshevski and his son Yasha.

20. Hyde notes that Chernyshevski has "the jerky energy of a Gogol character" (*America's Russian Novelist* 31) and points out the comic effects of the automatic or mechanical behavior highlighted in Fyodor's portrait. Toker (*Nabokov* 165) and Davydov (*"The Gift"* 366) note some specific parallels between Chernyshevski and Gogol's Akaky Akakievich (they both look at pictures in the shop windows on Nevsky Prospect and they both have problems with footwear), and Fyodor himself writes at one point, "Nikolay Gavrilovich flew along with the swift gait of a poor Gogolian character" (*G* 236; *Dr* 252). Like Akaky, Chernyshevski is often oblivious to physical reality. When one reads of Chernyshevski burying himself in a book on his way to Petersburg so that "a hole in the road loses its meaning of hole, becoming merely a typographical unevenness, a jump in the line" (*G* 228; *Dr* 243), one recalls how Akaky would be startled to find that "he was not in the middle of a line, but in the middle of the street."

21. The best example of this occurs when the narrator of the biography seems to have difficulty in placing the episode of

Chernyshevski's invention of a machine into his narrative (see *G* 227 and 229; *Dr* 242 and 244). The narrator's confusion is meant to parody Chernyshevski's own style, which Fyodor had defined earlier: "the bogging down of thought in midsentence and the clumsy attempts to extricate it (whereupon it got stuck at once elsewhere, and the author had to start worrying it out all over again)" (*G* 206; *Dr* 219).

22. Fyodor's design was described earlier. He set out to compose his biography in the form of a ring "so that the result would not be the form of a book, which by its finiteness is opposed to the circular nature of everything in existence, but a continuously curving, and thus infinite, sentence" (*G* 216; *Dr* 230). This statement foregrounds the problem of closure in the novel, a problem which Nabokov himself addresses on the last pages of *his* novel. Nabokov's fiction works to "uncoil" the circle, transforming it into a spiral, which Nabokov defined as "a spiritualized circle" (*SM* 275).

23. One problem with the biography is that the verbal frolicking, the reworking of source material, and the introduction of the spurious biographer Strannolyubski (another fictional alter ego), become almost too intrusive and distracting. Fyodor acknowledges as much through his imaginary dialogue with Koncheev (*G* 351–52; *Dr* 380–81), and his creator Nabokov says of the biography that he himself would not have written it that way (Field, *Life In Part* 30).

24. The paradise image hearkens back to the opening pages of chapter 2, where both Fyodor and his father were depicted as stepping out of paradise. The paradise which the elder Godunov-Cherdyntsev left was the base of a rainbow (*G* 89; *Dr* 89); the son steps out of the "hothouse paradise" of memory and onto a Berlin streetcar (*G* 92; *Dr* 92). The son's view of the realm of memory as paradise foreshadows the plane on which he will meet his father again later in chapter 5. Alexandrov surveys the relationship between images of paradise, rainbows, and Fyodor's father under the general heading of what he calls the "footstep motif" (see *Nabokov's Otherworld* 110–12, 122–25).

25. Having stripped, Fyodor states: "I felt myself an athlete, a Tarzan, an Adam" (*G* 345; *Dr* 373). The last figure in this series – Adam – is significant. In two of Nabokov's subsequent works, "Ultima Thule" and *Bend Sinister*, it is a character named Adam who has the experience of coming into contact with "the mind behind the mirror" (*BS* 233) or of discovering the secret of the fictitious nature of the world he inhabits. Fyodor's sense of being

"translated" into the sun in the Grunewald brings him close to a similar intuition.

26. Fyodor's excursion into the natural world of the Grunewald may remind him of the butterfly-filled meadow where he had burst into tears after his father's last departure (*G* 145; *Dr* 151). At one point during his Grunewald excursion, a butterfly settles on his bare chest (*G* 344; *Dr* 372).

27. Brian Boyd argues cogently that when Fyodor wakes up from this dream, he has everything he needs to write the book that will contain all his most cherished things – Zina, his art, and the biography of his father (see *The Russian Years* 470–71).

28. D. Barton Johnson analyzes the multiple significance of keys and key imagery in the novel (*Worlds* 95–106).

29. This metaphysical transformation is what makes Nabokov's design more unusual than the traditional situation in which a mature narrator comments on the actions of his younger self (as in *Great Expectations*, for example). The authorial entity Nabokov creates in *The Gift* is meant to be seen as a different kind of being than the character Fyodor, and this emphasis on difference reflects a distinctly modern (or postmodern) approach to fictional discourse. A comment Patricia Waugh makes in her study of metafiction helps place Nabokov's achievement in perspective: "Metafictional novels which shift from the personal form 'I' of *discourse* to the impersonal 'he' of *story* remind the reader that the narrating 'I' is the subject of the *discourse*, and is a different 'I' from the 'I' who is the subject of the *story*" (*Metafiction* 134–35).

30. This episode highlights the flexible referential properties of the first-person pronoun. While the pronoun 'I' generally refers to the diegetic figure of Fyodor, it can also refer to the authorial consciousness generating the text.

31. Davydov discusses the image of the Möbius strip in relation to the novel's effects (*"Teksty-Matreshki"* 194–99), while Toker delineates the specific features that produce the necessary twist to create the spiral design (*Nabokov* 160–62).

32. Brian Boyd comments on the suggestive traces of the unfinished novel in *The Russian Years* (517–20). A very different work – "The Visit to the Museum" ("Poseshchenie muzeia," published in 1939) – also deals with the haunting legacy of the past through a daring leap of the imagination.

33. See, for example, Fromberg ("The Unwritten Chapters" 434–36), Bader (*Crystal Land* 21–22), and Olcott ("The Author's Special Intention" 110–12).

34. See Rimmon ("Problems of Voice" 506–11) for a discussion of

this issue and of the way various critics have attempted to resolve it.

35. Sebastian's apparent influence on V. is analyzed by Fromberg (438–39), Boyd (*The Russian Years* 498–500), and Alexandrov (148–59). Even if Sebastian's spirit were not directly influencing V., the latter's effort to "find and follow" the undulations of Sebastian's soul is so successful that his quest (and his account of it) takes on the distinctive traits of a work by Sebastian himself. Nicol states that V. *becomes* Sebastian through his attention to Sebastian's novels ("The Mirrors" 93), and Grabes argues that V. seeks to enhance his resemblance to Sebastian to the point of complete identity, thus turning his biography into an autobiography (*Fictitious Biographies* 16). A contrary view to these opinions is expressed by Bruffee, who asserts that V. achieves autonomy and freedom through his narrative ("Form and Meaning" 190).

36. Under this scheme, the jarring confrontation of "real" and fictional characters (for example V. and Siller/Silbermann) dissolves. Since all the figures in the novel – including V., Sebastian Knight, Mr. Siller, and Mr. Silbermann – are fictitious from the point of view of the authorial entity (and the reader), it is not surprising that they can mingle freely. What the reader encounters here is not an opposition of fiction to "reality," but a meeting of different degrees of fictionality.

37. To complicate further the quest to identify this source, one must remember that embedded in the name Botkin is the anagram of the word *nikto* ("no one;" see Field, *Life in Art* 314). In the end, there is simply no way to prove that either Shade, Kinbote, or a third diegetic figure is actually the single author of the text. For a brief survey of the critical debate over the concept of a unitary author, see Tammi, *Problems of Nabokov's Poetics* 201–4.

38. On the other hand, the elaborate set of interconnected themes and motifs inserted into Shade's and Kinbote's respective texts (see Tammi, *Problems of Nabokov's Poetics* 204–18 and Alexandrov, *Nabokov's Otherworld* 200–12) underscores the unitary vision of their joint creator, Vladimir Nabokov (see also Edelstein, *"Pale Fire"* 214–15 and de Jonge, "Nabokov's Uses of Pattern" 66–67). Priscilla Meyer's work on the novel indicates that the synthesis Nabokov achieves in *Pale Fire* is more complex than the casual reader might realize (see *Find What The Sailor Has Hidden*).

39. Barabtarlo provides the most detailed description of the peculiarities in the narrator's relationship to Pnin in *Phantom of Fact* (26–38).

40. For the pivotal impact of Victor's presence in Pnin's life, see

Connolly, "*Pnin*: The Wonder of Recurrence and Transformation." It is worth noting that the first part of *Mira Bel*ochkin's name is suggestively close to the Latin *mirabilis* ("wonderful, marvelous") and connects her to that realm of potential "miracle" to which Pnin is headed at the conclusion of the novel. W. W. Rowe attempts to identify Mira's influence in Pnin's life (62–66), but his discussion may overstate the case somewhat.

41. Those critics who conflate the fictive narrator with the author Nabokov run the risk of obscuring the design (see, for example, Grams, "The Biographer as Meddler").

42. D. Barton Johnson presents a concise treatment of the dual identity theme in *Look at the Harlequins!* in *Worlds in Regression* (140–45).

43. A further distinction must of course be made between the narrator "Humbert Humbert" and the entity which I have been calling the authentic *auctor*. Tamir-Ghez offers an excellent analysis of the way this distinction operates in *Lolita* (see "The Art of Persuasion").

44. The critical literature devoted to Humbert, his rhetorical strategies, and the extent of his repentance, is extensive. Nearly every commentator on the novel devotes some remarks to the subject. Tammi provides a short summary of representative opinions (*Problems of Nabokov's Poetics* 277–79).

45. Martin Green outlines this concept in its extreme form when he writes that the novel invites us to believe that "Humbert first invented Quilty ... and then killed him, to purge himself symbolically" ("Tolstoy and Nabokov" 17). Toker (*Nabokov* 209–11) and Tekiner (see "Time in *Lolita*") explore a more restricted version of this concept when they point out that the chronology Humbert himself provides suggests that his murder of Quilty (and his last meeting with Dolly Schiller) may be merely his fictive invention, created during the time he writes his memoir.

46. Appel perceives Quilty as both a "projection of Humbert's guilt and a parody of the psychological Double" (*L* lxiii). This parodic aspect of Quilty's relationship to Humbert (and Nabokov's own suspicion of the tradition Doppelgänger theme) in part accounts for the failure of Humbert's murder to have the cathartic effect he might have anticipated (see *L* 306). One cannot purge oneself of one's negative traits so easily. Yet there is a second reason for this failure as well. The intentional murder of another, even if it takes place in a fantasy, involves some of those same negative emotions that one might wish to expunge from oneself. Thus, even after

killing his rival (an aficionado of executions), Humbert feels "all covered with Quilty" (*L* 308).

47. Although the full measure of Humbert's crime toward Dolores Haze can never be absolved, his apparent remorse and his determination to record the experience in all its dimensions achieve at least partial success, as Nabokov indicates when discussing the respective fates of Humbert and Hermann Karlovich in his Foreword to *Despair*. Both characters are "neurotic scoundrels," but Humbert's attempts at atonement through art earn him one evening's respite in Paradise each year (*D* 9).

Bibliography

For works by Nabokov see the list of abbreviations (xii–xiii).

Afanas'ev, A. N. *Narodnye russkie skazki*, ed. A. L. Barag and N. V. Novikov, 3 vols., Moscow: Nauka, 1985
   Russian Fairy Tales, trans. Norbert Guterman, New York: Pantheon Books, 1975
   Russkie narodnye skazki, ed. A. E. Gruzinskii, 4th edn., 5 vols., Moscow, 1913–14
Aikhenval'd, Iu. "Literaturnye zametki," *Rul'* 31 Mar. 1926 2–3
Albright, Daniel. *Representation and the Imagination: Beckett, Kafka, Nabokov, and Schoenberg*, Chicago: University of Chicago Press, 1981
Alexandrov, Vladimir E. *Nabokov's Otherworld*, Princeton: Princeton University Press, 1991
Alter, Robert. "*Invitation to a Beheading*: Nabokov and the Art of Politics," Appel, Jr. and Newman 41–59
Appel, Alfred, Jr. Introduction, *The Annotated Lolita*, by Vladimir Nabokov, ed. Alfred Appel, Jr., New York: McGraw-Hill, 1970 xv–lxxi
   Nabokov's Dark Cinema, New York: Oxford University Press, 1974
Appel, Alfred, Jr. and Charles Newman, eds. *Nabokov: Criticism, Reminiscences, Translations and Tributes*, Evanston: Northwestern University Press, 1971
Bader, Julia. *Crystal Land: Artifice in Nabokov's English Novels*, Berkeley: University of California Press, 1972
Bakhtin, Mikhail. "Avtor i geroi v èstetiticheskoi deiatel'nosti" [Author and Hero in Aesthetic Activity], *Èstetika slovesnogo tvorchestva*, Moscow: Iskusstvo, 1979
   Problems of Dostoevsky's Poetics, trans. R. W. Rotsel, Ann Arbor: Ardis, 1973
Barabtarlo, Gennadi. *Phantom of Fact: A Guide to Nabokov's Pnin*, Ann Arbor: Ardis, 1989

"Within and Without Cincinnatus's Cell: Reference Gauges in Nabokov's *Invitation to a Beheading*," *Slavic Review* 49 (1990) 390–97

Barnstead, John A. "Nabokov, Kuzmin, Chekhov and Gogol': Systems of Reference in 'Lips to Lips'," Connolly and Ketchian 50–60

Berman, Jeffrey. *The Talking Cure: Literary Representations of Psychoanalysis*, New York: New York University Press, 1985

Bitsilli, P. M. Rev. of *Invitation to a Beheading* and *The Eye*, trans. D. Barton Johnson, Proffer, *A Book of Things About Vladimir Nabokov* 65–69

Bodenstein, Jürgen. *"The Excitement of Verbal Adventure": A Study of Nabokov's English Prose*, 2 vols., diss. Ruprecht-Karl-Universität, 1977. Heidelberg, 1977

Boegeman, Margaret Byrd. *"Invitation to a Beheading* and the Many Shades of Kafka," Rivers and Nicol 105–21

Booth, Wayne C. *The Rhetoric of Fiction*, Chicago: University of Chicago Press, 1961

Boyd, Brian. *Nabokov's "Ada": The Place of Consciousness*, Ann Arbor: Ardis, 1985

"The Problem of Pattern: Nabokov's *Defense*," *Modern Fiction Studies* 33 (1987) 575–604

Vladimir Nabokov: The Russian Years, Princeton: Princeton University Press, 1990

Boyd, Michael. *The Reflexive Novel*, Lewisburg: Bucknell University Press, 1983

Bruffee, K. A. "Form and Meaning in Nabokov's *The Real Life of Sebastian Knight*: An Example of Elegiac Romance," *Modern Language Quarterly* 34 (1973) 180–90

Carroll, William C. "The Cartesian Nightmare of *Despair*," Rivers and Nicol 82–104

Clancy, Laurie. *The Novels of Vladimir Nabokov*, New York: St. Martin's Press, 1984

Clifton, Gladys M. "Humbert Humbert and the Limits of Artistic License," Rivers and Nicol 153–70

Cohn, Dorrit. *Transparent Minds: Narrative Modes for Presenting Consciousness in Fiction*, Princeton: Princeton University Press, 1983

Connolly, Julian W. "Delusions or Clairvoyance? A Second Look at Madness in V. Nabokov's Fiction," *Aspects of Modern Russian and Czech Literature*, ed. Arnold McMillin, Columbus, Ohio: Slavica, 1989 110–17

"The Function of Literary Allusion in Nabokov's *Despair*," *Slavic and East European Journal* 26 (1982) 302–13

"Madness and Doubling: From Dostoevsky's *The Double* to Nabokov's *The Eye*," *Russian Literature Triquarterly*, 24 (1990) 129–39

"Nabokov's 'Terra Incognita' and 'Invitation to a Beheading': The Struggle for Imaginative Freedom," *Wiener Slawistischer Almanach* 12 (1983) 55–65

"*Pnin*: The Wonders of Recurrence and Transformation," Rivers and Nicol 195–210

"Vladimir Nabokov and Valerij Brjusov: An Examination of a Literary Heritage," *Die Welt der Slaven* 33 (1988) 69–86

"Vladimir Nabokov's *Defense* and the Legacy of Nikolai Gogol," *Studies in Modern and Classical Languages and Literatures II*, ed. Ruth M. Mésavage, Madrid: Orígenes, 1989 131–38

Connolly, Julian W. and Sonia I. Ketchian, eds. *Studies in Russian Literature in Honor of Vsevolod Setchkarev*, Columbus: Slavica, 1986

Couturier, Maurice. *Nabokov*, CISTRE Essai 7, Lausanne: L'Age d'Homme, 1979

Davydov, Sergei. "*The Gift*: Nabokov's Aesthetic Exorcism of Chernyshevskii," *Canadian-American Slavic Studies* 19 (1985) 357–74

"The Shattered Mirror: A Study of Nabokov's Destructive Method in *Despair*," *Structuralist Review* 2.2 (1981) 25–38

"*Teksty-Matreshki*" *Vladimira Nabokova*, Munich: Otto Sagner, 1982

de Jonge, Alex. "Nabokov's Uses of Pattern," Quennell 59–72

Dembo, L. S., ed. *Nabokov: The Man and His Work*, Madison: University of Wisconsin Press, 1967

Devlin, Kimberley. "'See ourselves as others see us': Joyce's Look at the Eye of the Other," *PMLA* 104 (1989) 882–93

Dostoevsky, Fyodor. *Notes from Underground. White Nights. The Dream of a Ridiculous Man*, trans. Andrew R. MacAndrew, New York: Signet, 1961

Polnoe sobranie sochinenii v tridtsati tomakh, vol. 1, Leningrad: Nauka, 1972

Edelstein, Marilyn. "*Pale Fire*: The Art of Consciousness," Rivers and Nicol 213–23

Evans, Walter. "The Conjurer in 'The Potato Elf'," Rivers and Nicol 75–81

Field, Andrew. *Nabokov: A Bibliography*, New York: McGraw-Hill, 1973
Nabokov: His Life in Art, Boston: Little, Brown and Co., 1967
Nabokov: His Life in Part, New York: Viking Press, 1977

Freiwald, Bina. "A Pliable Reality: Towards a Construction of a Nabokovian Narrative Model," *The Canadian Journal of Research in Semiotics* 8 (1980–81) 111–22

Fromberg, Susan. "The Unwritten Chapters in *The Real Life of Sebastian Knight*," *Modern Fiction Studies* 13 (1967) 427–42

Genette, Gérard. *Narrative Discourse: An Essay in Method*, trans. Jane E. Lewin, Ithaca: Cornell University Press, 1985

Gogol, Nikolai. *The Complete Tales of Nikolai Gogol*, ed. Leonard J. Kent, 2 vols., Chicago: The University of Chicago Press, 1985

Grabes, H. *Fictitious Biographies: Vladimir Nabokov's English Novels*, The Hague: Mouton, 1977

Grams, Paul. "*Pnin*: The Biographer as Meddler," Proffer, *A Book of Things about Vladimir Nabokov* 193–202

Grayson, Jane. *Nabokov Translated: A Comparison of Nabokov's Russian and English Prose*, Oxford: Oxford University Press, 1977

Green, Geoffrey. *Freud and Nabokov*, Lincoln: University of Nebraska Press, 1988

Green, Martin. "Tolstoy and Nabokov: The Morality of *Lolita*," *Vladimir Nabokov's Lolita*, ed. Harold Bloom, Modern Critical Interpretations, New York: Chelsea House, 1987 13–33

Heidegger, Martin. "The Origin of the Work of Art," *Poetry, Language, Thought*, trans. Albert Hofstadter, New York: Harper and Row, 1971

Holquist, Michael. "Whodunit and Other Questions: Metaphysical Detective Stories in Post-War Fiction," *New Literary History* 3 (1971) 135–56

Houk, Guy. "The Spider and the Moth: Nabokov's *Priglashenie na kazn'* as Epistemological Exhortation," *Russian Literature* 18 (1985) 31–41

Hutcheon, Linda. *Narcissistic Narrative: The Metafictional Paradox*, New York: Methuen, 1985

Hyde, G. M. *Vladimir Nabokov: America's Russian Novelist*, London: Marion Boyars, 1977

Jakobson, Roman. "Shifters, Verbal Categories, and the Russian Verb," *Selected Writings*, vol. II, The Hague: Mouton, 1971 130–47, 8 vols. 1971–88

Johnson, D. Barton. "The Books Reflected in Nabokov's *The Eye*," *Slavic and East European Journal* 29 (1985) 393–404

"Eyeing Nabokov's *Eye*," *Canadian-American Slavic Studies* 19 (1985) 328–50

"A Guide to Nabokov's 'A Guide to Berlin'," *Slavic and East European Journal* 23 (1979) 353–61

"Nabokov's 'Terror': Pre-texts and Post-texts," forthcoming in *A Small Alpine Form: Studies in Nabokov's Short Fiction*, ed. Gennadi Barabtarlo and Charles Nicol, New York: Garland Publishing, Inc.

Worlds in Regression: Some Novels of Vladimir Nabokov, Ann Arbor: Ardis, 1985

Juliar, Michael. *Vladimir Nabokov: A Descriptive Bibliography*, Garland Reference Library of the Humanities 656, New York: Garland Publishing, Inc., 1986

Karlinsky, Simon. "Vladimir Nabokov's Novel *Dar* as a Work of Literary Criticism: A Structural Analysis," *Slavic and East European Journal* 7 (1963) 184–90

Kayser, Wolfgang. *The Grotesque in Art and Literature*, trans. Ulrich Weisstein, New York: Columbia University Press, 1981

Kellman, Steven G. "The Fiction of Self-Begetting," *MLN* 91 (1976) 1243–56

Kermode, Frank. *The Sense of an Ending: Studies in the Theory of Fiction*, New York: Oxford University Press, 1968

Khodasevich, Vladislav. "On Sirin," Appel and Newman 96–101

Klemtner, Susan Strehle. "To 'Special Space': Transformotion in *Invitation to a Beheading*," *Modern Fiction Studies* 25 (1979) 427–38

Kopper, John M. "Nabokov's Art of Translation in *Solus Rex*," *Slavic and East European Journal* 33 (1989) 255–74

"The Prison in Nabokov's *Priglashenie*: A Place to Have the Time of One's Life," *Russian Language Journal* 41 (1987) 175–84

Kristeva, Julia. *Tales of Love*, trans. Leon S. Roudiez, New York: Columbia University Press, 1987

Lacan, Jacques. *Écrits: A Selection*, trans. Alan Sheridan, New York: W. W. Norton, 1977

The Four Fundamental Concepts of Psycho-Analysis, ed. Jacques-Alain Miller, trans. Alan Sheridan, New York: W. W. Norton, 1978

Layton, Lynne, and Barbara Ann Schapiro, eds. *Narcissism and the Text: Studies in Literature and the Psychology of the Self*, New York: New York University Press, 1986

Lee, L. L. *Vladimir Nabokov*, Boston: Twayne, 1976

Levin, Iu. I. "Ob osobennostiakh povestvovatel'noi struktury i obraznogo stroia romana V. Nabokova *Dar*," *Russian Literature* 9 (1981) 191–229

Maddox, Lucy. *Nabokov's Novels in English*, Athens, Georgia: University of Georgia Press, 1983

Meyer, Priscilla. *Find What the Sailor Has Hidden: Vladimir Nabokov's "Pale Fire"*, Middletown: Wesleyan University Press, 1988

Naumann, Marina Turkevich. *Blue Evenings in Berlin: Nabokov's Short Stories of the 1920s*, New York: New York University Press, 1978

Nicol, Charles. "The Mirrors of Sebastian Knight," Dembo 85–94

Olcott, Anthony. "The Author's Special Intention: A Study of *The Real Life of Sebastian Knight*," Proffer, *A Book of Things about Vladimir Nabokov* 104–21

Parker, Stephen Jan. *Understanding Vladimir Nabokov*, Columbia: University of South Carolina, 1987

Pasternak, Boris. "Okhrannaia gramota," *Vozdushnye puti*, Moscow: Sovetskii pisatel', 1983 191–284

Patterson, David. *Literature and Spirit: Essays on Bakhtin and His Contemporaries*, Lexington: University Press of Kentucky, 1988

Peterson, Dale. "Nabokov's *Invitation*: Literature as Execution," *PMLA* 96 (1981) 824–36

Petty, Chapel Louise. "A Comparison of Hawthorne's 'Wakefield' and Nabokov's 'The Leonardo': Narrative Commentary and the Struggle of the Literary Artist," *Modern Fiction Studies* 25 (1979) 499–507

Pifer, Ellen. *Nabokov and the Novel*, Cambridge, Massachusetts: Harvard University Press, 1980

"On Human Freedom and Inhuman Art: Nabokov," *Slavic and East European Journal* 22 (1978) 52–63

Proffer, Carl. "From *Otchaianie* to *Despair*," *Slavic Review* 27 (1968) 258–67

"A new deck for Nabokov's Knaves," Appel and Newman 293–309

Proffer, Carl, ed. *A Book of Things About Vladimir Nabokov*, Ann Arbor: Ardis, 1974

Purdy, Strother B. "Solus Rex: Nabokov and the Chess Novel," *Modern Fiction Studies* 14 (1968–69) 379–95

Quennell, Peter, ed. *Vladimir Nabokov: A Tribute*, New York: William Morrow, 1980

Ragland-Sullivan, Ellie. *Jacques Lacan and the Philosophy of Psychoanalysis*, Urbana: University of Illinois Press, 1987

Rampton, David. *Vladimir Nabokov: A Critical Study of the Novels*, Cambridge: Cambridge University Press, 1984

Rank, Otto. *Beyond Psychology*, New York: Dover, 1958

Richter, David H. "Narrative Entrapment in *Pnin* and 'Signs and Symbols'," *Papers on Language and Literature* 20 (1984) 418–30

Rimmon, Shlomith. "Problems of Voice in Nabokov's *The Real Life of Sebastian Knight*," *PTL: A Journal for Descriptive Poetics and Theory of Literature* 1 (1976) 489–512

Rimmon-Kenan, Shlomith. *Narrative Fiction: Contemporary Poetics*, New York: Methuen, 1987

Rivers, J. E. and Charles Nicol, eds. *Nabokov's Fifth Arc: Nabokov and Others on His Life's Work*, Austin: University of Texas Press, 1982

Rorty, Richard. *Contingency, irony, and solidarity*, Cambridge: Cambridge University Press, 1989

Rosenfield, Claire. "*Despair* and the Lust for Immortality," Dembo 66–84

Roth, Phyllis. "Toward the Man behind the Mystification," Rivers and Nicol 43–59

Rowe, William Woodin. *Nabokov's Spectral Dimension*, Ann Arbor: Ardis, 1981

Salehar, Anna Maria. "Nabokov's *Gift*: An Apprenticeship in Creativity," Proffer, *A Book of Things About Vladimir Nabokov* 70–83

Schaeffer, Susan Fromberg. "The Editing Blinks of Vladimir Nabokov's *The Eye*," *The University of Windsor Review* 8 (1972) 5–30

Schroeter, J. "Detective Stories and Aesthetic Bliss in Nabokov," *Delta* 17 (1983) 23–32

Shapiro, Gavriel. "Russkie literaturnye alliuzii v romane Nabokova *Priglashenie na kazn'*," *Russian Literature* 9 (1981) 369–78

Stegner, Page. *Escape into Aesthetics: The Art of Vladimir Nabokov*, New York: The Dial Press, 1966

Struve, Gleb. "Notes on Nabokov as a Russian Writer," Dembo 45–56

Stuart, Dabney. *Nabokov: The Dimensions of Parody*, Baton Rouge: Louisiana State University Press, 1978

Tamir-Ghez, Nomi. "The Art of Persuasion in Nabokov's *Lolita*," *Poetics Today* 1 (1979) 65–83

Tammi, Pekka. *Problems of Nabokov's Poetics: A Narratological Analysis*, Suomalaisen Tiedeakatemian Toimituksia Annales Academiae Scientiarum Fennicae B 231, Helsinki: Suomalainen Tiedeakatemia, 1985

Tekiner, Christina. "Time in *Lolita*," *Modern Fiction Studies* 25 (1979) 463–69

Toker, Leona. *Nabokov: The Mystery of Literary Structures*, Ithaca: Cornell University Press, 1989

"Self-Conscious Paralepsis in Vladimir Nabokov's *Pnin* and 'Recruiting'," *Poetics Today* 7 (1986) 459–69

Tolstoy, Leo. *Great Short Works of Leo Tolstoy*, trans. Louise and Aylmer Maude, New York: Harper and Row, 1967

Tsetlin, M. Rev. of *Korol'. Dama. Valet*, *Sovremennye zapiski* 37 (1928) 536–38

Updike, John. "Grandmaster Nabokov," *Assorted Prose*, London: Andre Deutsch, 1965

Waugh, Patricia. *Metafiction: The Theory and Practice of Self-Conscious Fiction*, New York: Methuen, 1985

Weidle, Vladimir. rev. of *Sovremennye zapiski* 44, *Vozrozhdenie* 30 Oct. 1930 2–3

"Vladimir Weidle on Sirin," *Critical Essays on Vladimir Nabokov*, ed. Phyllis Roth. Boston: G. K. Hall, 1984 53–55

White, Duffield. "Radical Aestheticism and Metaphysical Realism in

Nabokov's *The Gift*," *Russian Literature and American Critics*, ed. Kenneth N. Brostrom, Papers in Slavic Philology 4, Ann Arbor: Department of Slavic Languages and Literatures, University of Michigan, 1984 273–91

Yokoyama, Olga. "Studies in Russian Functional Syntax," *Harvard Studies in Syntax and Semantics* 3, ed. Susumu Kuno, Cambridge: Harvard University Dept. of Linguistics, 1980 451–774

Zimmermann, Linda Saputelli. "The Russian Short Stories of Vladimir Nabokov: A Thematic and Structural Analysis," diss. Harvard University, 1978

Index

Velimir Khlebnikov
RAYMOND COOKE

Dostoyevsky and the process of literary creation
JACQUES CATTEAU
translated by Audrey Littlewood

The poetic imagination of Vyacheslav Ivanov
PAMELA DAVIDSON

Joseph Brodsky
VALENTINA POLUKHINA

Petrushka – the Russian carnival puppet theatre
CATRIONA KELLY

Turgenev
FRANK FRIEDEBERG SEELEY

From the idyll to the novel
GITTA HAMMARBERG

The Brothers Karamazov *and the poetics of memory*
DIANE OENNING THOMPSON

Andrei Platonov
THOMAS SEIFRID